CREATIVE RESEARCH METHODS
IN EDUCATION
Principles and Pract

Helen Kara, Narelle Lemon, Daw
and Megan McPherson

P

First published in Great Britain in 2021 by

Policy Press, an imprint of
Bristol University Press
University of Bristol
1–9 Old Park Hill
Bristol BS2 8BB
UK
t: +44 (0)117 954 5940
e: bup-info@bristol.ac.uk

Details of international sales and distribution partners are available at
policy.bristoluniversitypress.co.uk

© Bristol University Press 2021

British Library Cataloguing in Publication Data
A catalogue record for this book is available from the British Library.

ISBN 978-1-4473-5706-3 hardcover
ISBN 978-1-4473-5707-0 paperback
ISBN 978-1-4473-5708-7 ePub
ISBN 978-1-4473-5709-4 ePdf

Cover design by Qube Design Associates, Bristol
Front cover: image kindly supplied by istock.com
Printed and bound in Great Britain by CMP, Poole
Bristol University Press and Policy Press use environmentally
responsible print partners.

We dedicate this book in loving memory of

Helen's mother, Julie Miller.

Contents

List of case studies

List of figures, photos and tables

Figures

Photos

Tables

Preface

Introducing the authors

All researchers have stories to tell about why they chose to work with particular topics and approaches; and *Creative Research Methods in Education: Principles and Practices* is very much a reflection of the authors' journeys. Creative approaches often involve techniques that invite participants to engage differently from more conventional methods employed in education research, and in our own practice and teaching we have frequently wanted to refer to or recommend a book that brings together creative methods and the field of education studies. This book has emerged from a collaborative venture between four authors, Helen Kara, Narelle Lemon, Dawn Mannay and Megan McPherson, and we offer brief introductions to provide some insights about our relationships with creative ways of working in educational spaces.

· **Helen Kara** is an independent researcher based in England with interests in the areas of social care, health and the voluntary sector. She teaches research methods to practitioners and students through training and through speaking at conferences nationally and internationally. Helen wrote the key texts *Creative Research Methods: A Practical Guide* (Policy Press, 2nd edn 2020) and *Research Ethics in the Real World: Euro-Western and Indigenous Perspectives* (Policy Press, 2018). She has become a well-known figure on social media through her blog at https:// helenkara.com/blog/ and her creative research methods chat on Twitter. Helen uses the hashtag #CRMethods for general discussions on creative methods and #CRMethodsChat for a monthly discussion on a key topic – and everyone is welcome to contribute.

Narelle Lemon is an education researcher and Associate Professor based at the Department of Education, Faculty of Health, Arts and Design in Swinburne University of Technology in Melbourne, Australia. Narelle has a wealth of experience in educational practice, having been a primary and secondary school teacher, and now works with undergraduate and postgraduate students in the university sector. Narelle has produced numerous research outputs focusing on arts education, creative pedagogies, digital technologies and well-being, including her edited book *Revolutionizing Arts Education in K-12 Classrooms through Technological Integration* (Hershey, 2015) and the co-authored book *Representations of Working in the Arts: Deepening the Conversations* (Intellect, 2014).

Dawn Mannay is a Reader (Associate Professor) in the School of Social Sciences at Cardiff University in Wales, with interests in education, inequalities, children and young people and identities. Dawn teaches creative methods in the UK and internationally, and authored the book *Visual, Narrative and Creative Research Methods: Application, Reflection and Ethics* (Routledge, 2016a), based on her lectures with undergraduate and postgraduate students. Dawn also co-edited the second edition of *The Sage Handbook of Visual Research Methods* (Sage, 2020) with Luc Pauwels. Dawn is committed to working creatively with communities to produce data and disseminate the messages from research findings in innovative ways that move beyond the standard academic report or journal article, thereby increasing impact and the potential for social and educational change.

Megan McPherson is a practising artist, educator and Tutor in Art and Intercultural Research at The University of Melbourne, Australia. As an artist, Megan has exhibited professionally since 1989 and her artwork has featured in significant printmaking and installation works in the state of Victoria and regional art galleries. Megan has published widely on the topics of creative practice, social media and arts education (McPherson, 2018, 2015).

Having offered brief introductions, it is important to explain why we came together to write this book. We were primarily motivated to work together because of the conversations we had with students and practitioners, face-to-face and online, in our working lives. Although there are a range of useful books on visual and creative methods (see Pink, 2001; Reavey, 2011b; Harper, 2012; Banks and Zeitlyn, 2015; Rose, 2016), these do not have a specific focus on education research or practice. Consequently, students and practitioners often ask us about where they can find a text about how to work creatively in the field of education, preferably one with a range of concrete examples, case studies and practical advice. This book is an attempt to attend to these requests and is the result of a collaborative journey of bringing together best-practice examples and reflecting on creative research in education in all its stages – design, data gathering, analysis and dissemination. We invite you to join us on the journey that this book represents and engage with familiar and unfamiliar materials, ideas, concepts, frameworks and reflections across the pages of *Creative Research Methods in Education: Principles and Practices*.

Who this book is for

You do not have to be an artist, designer or engineer to use creative research methods. Everyone is creative, and engaging with creative research methods offers many opportunities to support learning, whether your own or that of others. Singing, dance, theatre, movement, crafting, sculptures, drawing, crochet, cartoons, poetry, writing, blogging, journaling, photography or visual representations (to name a few) within the space of education offer powerful ways to ignite and illuminate voice, participation and engagement. This book will be of interest to anyone wanting to find out more about creative research methods and research projects across the field of education. However, primarily the book was developed for undergraduate education students, educational practitioners and postgraduates in the field of education who have had little access to teaching on creative research methods. This audience has influenced the design of the book, and each of the chapters offers a background to contextualise the set topic, a range of best-practice case studies and reflective questions to support the reader.

How to use the book

We have written this book to illustrate how creative methods can be accessible and connect theoretical positions with practical solutions. The book brings together concrete applications of creative research methods in education research, with a range of case studies and reflective and discussion questions to support learning. We have aimed to inform and inspire education researchers and practitioners to conduct more creative research.

The following chapters unpack case studies through the format of 'Who and where', 'What', 'Why', 'How', 'Tips' and 'Traps' and a series of 'Reflective questions'. Given the central importance of ethical practice, each chapter also features a section dedicated to ethics in education research. The book is intended to support students who want to draw on creative approaches in their undergraduate projects and dissertation studies; postgraduate researchers in the field of education; and practitioners, researchers or students interested in implementing education-focused forms of inquiry. As such, all phases of the research process are explored so that the reader can be supported with designing and implementing a study and analysing, writing up and sharing research findings.

The book offers:

• insights into the potential of creative methods in education research;
• case studies providing concrete real-life examples;
• practical advice and tips on how to use creative methods in education research;
• reflective and discussion questions to support learning.

Importantly, you can engage with this book in any way that suits your needs and preferences. You may want to read from front to back, dip in and out of different chapters and case studies, or read in line with particular topics and assessments linked with your taught modules or practice-based experience. It is your book. However, we have written it to reflect the specific detail that students, researchers and practitioners would require in order to consider and reconsider how to engage with and implement creative research methods in education. Consequently, the ordering of the book offers some contextualisation for the reader before reflecting on the stages of the research process.

We welcome you to the book and hope that here you will find answers to questions about the thinking, planning, doing and disseminating of creative research in education. We very much enjoyed researching for and writing *Creative Research Methods in Education: Principles and Practices*. We hope that you too will enjoy the journey – and that the case studies and examples presented will be a source of support and inspiration in trying new approaches and working more creatively.

Acknowledgements

In bringing together *Creative Research Methods in Education: Principles and Practices*, there are many people who should be thanked and acknowledged.

It is important to thank all of the researchers, participants, practitioners and students that we have worked with, who have inspired us to write this book, offered ideas and engaged with us in informal conversations that have been central in bringing this project to fruition.

Katy Vigurs was instrumental in the early stages of helping to shape the book, and we are grateful for her guidance and input. Additionally, we are thankful to everyone who gave us permission to use images in our case studies, namely Stacy Bias, Clare Danek, Constantino Dumangane, EJ Renold, Jon Rainford, Pat Thomson, Katy Vigurs, Kate Wall and Jo Earp on behalf of the Australian Council for Educational Research.

We would like to acknowledge the reviewers for their comments and suggestions, which were invaluable in developing this book. We are also grateful to the commissioning, editorial, production and marketing team at Policy Press for their guidance throughout the process of bringing the book to completion. We could not have produced this book without the support of our ever-helpful editors at Policy Press, first Catherine Gray and then Philippa Grand, and their colleagues, whose input has been essential in preparing the manuscript for publication.

Lastly, we would like to thank all our great colleagues, friends and family, and in particular those that are most involved in our everyday lives for their loving presence and enduring support.

On this basis, Helen would like to thank Zoë Clarke, Su Connan, Leigh Forbes, Radhika Holmström, Sharon Inglis, Lucy Pickering, Jon Rainford, Janet Salmons and Katy Vigurs; Mark Miller, Rosalind Round and Jamie Round; and her beloved partner, Nik Holmes.

Narelle would like to thank Katy and Helen for saying yes to her original idea when she pitched this book on a hot sunny day in Derby, and Megan and Dawn, who later joined the team. She would also like to acknowledge Michelle Stockley, Gina Panebianco, Janet Salmons, Siobhan O'Brien, Susie Garvis, Catherine Hoyser, Marni Binder and Sharon McDonough, who have explored various creative ways of working with her over the years.

Dawn would like to thank David, Jamie, Jordon, Sherelle, Tahlia, Taya, Tilleah, Tim, Toyah, Travis and Travis Jay.

Megan would like to thank her family and all the critters, and all her colleagues over the years who have supported her creative research practices. Special thanks to Narelle for her reading and feedback, plotting and friendship over many years.

Introduction

Chapter summary

In this introductory chapter we invite you to consider the place of creative methods and methodologies in your approach to education research. You may be a teacher, pre-service teacher, teacher-researcher, artist-researcher, artist-teacher or someone who is looking to engage with research to support your role in formal or informal education and learning contexts. No matter what your background, everyone is creative and can engage with creative ways of doing research. Our focus is to introduce key ideas and concepts and to begin to connect with creative research methods that are influenced by arts-based research, digitally mediated research, mobile methods, place-based research and transformative research frameworks.

This chapter is a good place to begin if you want to gain an insight into and an overview of creative approaches in education. We then invite you to dig deeper into examples with our case studies and reflective questions to find out more as you progress through the book.

Introduction

This chapter introduces multiple approaches to creative research methods and their use in education research. Creativity and creative thinking will be explored in creative research as ways to help make new knowledge and to challenge assumptions and expectations of what creative research methods can do (Ellsworth, 2005; Gauntlett, 2007; Thomson and Hall, 2008; Barone and Eisner, 2012; Harris, 2014; Pauwels and Mannay, 2020). Creative methodologies in education research will be introduced. We invite you to read the chapters in order, or to jump in and out, reading back and forth, or to use a chapter as a touch point while working on your research project. The case studies are examples to help you think through key questions and responses in the developing and doing of research. The last chapter has four activities to help you develop, generate and reflect on your way of doing creative research. In each chapter we offer case studies that show how creative methods can work in practice; however, this does not mean all research projects have to work in these ways.

Within education research, different disciplinary approaches influence the ways in which creative research is practised (Cahnmann-Taylor and Siegesmund, 2008;

Smith and Dean, 2009; Barrett and Bolt, 2010; O'Toole and Beckett, 2010; Thomson and Sefton-Green, 2011; Nelson, 2013; Naughton et al, 2018). This book includes arts-based research, digitally mediated research, mobile methods, place-based research and transformative research frameworks such as participatory, feminist and activist research. As evaluation research is a key topic in contemporary education disciplines, we discuss what creative research methods can do to help question assumptions and expectations. Creative research methodologies challenge what education research may look like: inquiry as emergent, as not having answers, as posing questions, as situated in place, spaces and time and as relational – with others, ourselves and the world and its matter and matterings. This research may pose more questions than it answers, but in doing so gives opportunities to activate actions and doings that may not have been given space in other types of research. In this way, the unexpected becomes a possibility and an opportunity.

In each of the chapters contained in this book, through the use of case studies we aim to introduce creative research methods for those who are unfamiliar with the topic. The field of creative research methods is continually developing and expanding, and is relevant for quantitative, qualitative and mixed-methods researchers in education and across disciplines. There are various different ways we can work as researchers – for example, through song, dance, theatre, movement, craft, sculpture, sketch, crochet, cartoon, poetry, writing, blogging, journalling or photography. These offer powerful ways to ignite and illuminate voice, participation and engagement across the various different stages of research design and dissemination.

This book does not cover all creative research methods and methodologies but, rather, highlights key research projects that illustrate the diversity of practices undertaken in this area. We do not revisit the basics of qualitative research methods, as there are many books on research methods in education and the social sciences. (If you are not aware of these we would suggest starting with *Research Methods in Education* by Cohen, Manion and Morrison, currently in its eighth edition.) Rather, we focus on research projects that use creative methodologies and methods, and explore these projects with innovation and creativity in mind. These projects may use creative methods in any or all of their design, context-setting, data-gathering, analysis, reporting, presentation, dissemination and implementation processes.

Creative research methodologies bring complexities to the surface with different questions and methods of analysing data, generating inquiries into the layers of context, ways of knowing, doing and being, feelings and expression of lived experiences, reflexivity and ethics. In each of the chapters we discuss the ethical implications, the roles of others and the researcher, within a framework of reflexivity. We offer case study examples of research in the extended field of education, from formal to informal educational settings and situated in communities and other places of learning. Our aim is to guide and facilitate you if you are accessing creative research methods for the first time and want an introduction to what might be possible in working creatively in education research. We also aim to offer education-focused information and support for more experienced users of creative research methods.

Where research begins

In Margaret Somerville's creative research publication, *Water in a Dry Land* (2013), she describes a moment in her drought-stricken garden looking for a suitable place to position a bore. The water dowser can feel underground water, and when Margaret holds the dowsing rods she too feels 'a different image grows in my body of deep water flowing inside the earth's surface' (Somerville, 2013, p xviii). It is at that moment and place that she realises the beginnings of the idea for a creative research project about water in particular places and its Indigenous and non-Indigenous creative and cultural affordances in Australia. *Water in a Dry Land* is an example of cross-cultural creative research with Indigenous and non-Indigenous artists and researchers investigating and activating knowledge about water in Australia. In creative research, learning and teaching takes on different shapes than those found in schools and formal places of education; creativity prompts questions and allows a diversity of responses that encompass informal learning – for example, learning in gardens about water and your environment.

Education researchers can start with their physical context – within centres, schools or higher education, or informal learning environments such as museums, open spaces, art galleries, in the water, after-school dance and music classes – actually, anywhere where someone is learning or teaching. Observing and questioning particular habits and behaviours, considering how a practice is undertaken and what is happening is a way to start thinking about research and education (see, for example, Sinek, 2014). For some researchers, their inquiry is about exploration of a place, ideas, a practice or activity (Somerville, 2013; Mannay et al, 2017; Purcell, 2018; McPherson, 2019). Other researchers identify a gap in knowledge about a practice and describe this practice and its affordances and constraints (Cancienne and Snowber, 2003; Lemon, 2019) in order to understand the practice and its use. To explain a particular way of doing an activity can be a research aim (Morriss, 2016). For some researchers it is about making change in their communities (Smith, 2017; Levy et al, 2018) and activism (Perez, 2007; Ringrose and Renold, 2011); for others it is about evaluating practices (Thomson, 2012, 2017), or Indigenous ways of doing, knowing and being (Martin, 2003; Smith, 2017). Patricia Leavy (2017, p 54) states: 'researchers initially come to a topic because of their personal interests, experiences and values, previous research experience, and/or opportunities in the form of funding or collaborations'.

Creativity, creative thinking and the researcher

Creativity, creative thinking and the researcher is an area of contested dialogues. The study of creativity is a large area that overflows into many disciplines. In this book we use case studies to highlight research projects that have wide-ranging notions of what creativity is and how the projects investigate creativity. We focus on creative methods that invite researchers and their participant collaborators to engage differently in research activities rather than in creativity as such. The following list is a starting point to think about what the notion of creativity is to you.

In education research, among other options, creativity may be considered:

- as possibility thinking (Craft, 2001);
- about art being unteachable (Elkins, 2001);
- a risk (Craft and Jeffrey, 2008);
- about making things (Gauntlett, 2011);
- about the role arts can play in education, questioning practices and reinventing pedagogies (Naughton and Cole, 2018).

We invite you to consider, in each of the case studies, how the researchers position creativity in their research.

Harris (2014) argues that discussion about creativity is ever present in education and encourages a move toward celebrating creativity for its generative value in schools. Biesta (2018) suggests that encountering the doing of art is about being in the world as dialogue, that we are always having a discussion, if you like, about what it means to be in education. Each of these views is epistemology – a way of knowing – that influences how research is thought about, enacted and contextualised. For further discussion of creativity and creative thinking see Chapter 5 of Kara (2020).

Methodology, theory and method

Creative research methodologies (sometimes called 'paradigms') offer us different approaches to methods. Our decisions about which methodologies to work with are informed by our epistemology, or theory about how we know things, and our ontology, or worldview. And although we mention these here, we suggest that they are areas for you to explore further, and to consider your position(s) around, as you think about your research design while working through the chapters in this book.

Creative research methodologies are about knowledge inquiries that are firmly situated in the social world. These methodologies use methods that recall and respond to creative practices in, for example, poetry, artmaking, performances of music, drama or dance; computer programming and writing algorithms; the use of social media; and combinations of such practices. These practices are embedded in the researcher's epistemology and ontology as ways of knowing the world and being/doing in the world.

Any research we conduct represents and enacts our theoretical positioning of ourselves. A theoretical perspective is important for research design and enactment, as it serves to organise our thoughts and ideas. And a part of this is making those thoughts and ideas clear to others. A theoretical framework, as Collins and Stockton (2018, p 2) remind us, is at the intersection of:

1. existing knowledge and previously formed ideas about complex phenomena,
2. the researcher's epistemological dispositions, and
3. a lens and a methodically analytic approach.

Methodology encompasses both theory and methods in the ways we think through the research problem at hand and do the methods of the research. In research, methodologies and theories are used to describe the positioning of the research. Methodologies such as positivism arose in the early 1800s with the French philosopher Auguste Comte's study of the phenomena of society (Babbie, 2015, p 34). In contemporary research, Leavy suggests six methodologies that are influenced by the researcher's ontology and epistemology (Leavy, 2017, p 12). These include postpositivism, constructivist or interpretative, critical, transformative, pragmatic and arts–based/aesthetic intersubjective methodologies (Leavy, 2017).

Postpositivism, with its school of thought based in empiricism, suggests that knowledge is based in the lived experience. This worldview is based in rationalism and privileges a scientific method of testing, with an objective researcher at the centre of the research and with findings that are able to be replicated (Leavy, 2017; Babbie, 2015).

In education research, constructivist methodologies highlight ways in which people learn and construct their own knowledge and understanding of their world through and with their reflection on their experiences. As we interpret the world, we construct and reconstruct our understandings and make meaning with how we experience interactions with others, events and situations (Meltzoff and Cooper, 2018). In contrast, arts–based or aesthetic intersubjective methodologies value relational and embodied knowledge such as 'sensory, emotional, perceptual, kinaesthetic, and imaginal knowledge' (Leavy, 2017, p 14). Critical methodologies in education research cover theories to do with critique: postmodernisms, poststructuralisms, feminisms, critical race and queerness (Leavy, 2017). These methodologies of critique sometimes overlap with transformative concepts of critical theory, critical pedagogy and critical race theory. Whereas a pragmatism-based methodology can use whatever tools are needed in different contexts, it is action – what takes place – which is the focus (Leavy, 2017).

Indigenous research encompasses a diverse range of approaches and frameworks and pre-dates Euro–Western research by tens of thousands of years (Cram et al, 2013, p 11). It is a highly politicised and contentious issue in many regions with a colonial settler or invasion history, such as Australia, New Zealand, Africa, Asia, the Americas and the Arctic. Many Indigenous methods and methodologies are holistic, community focused and relationship based and can be highly ethical. They are intimately linked with Indigenous ways of life, and – unlike Euro–Western methods – cannot be separated from their context (Kara, 2018, p 23). Therefore Indigenous knowledges should be sought and drawn on in any education research where Indigenous people or peoples are involved, ideally by including relevant Indigenous people as co-researchers or research advisors.

Thomson (2013a, para 9) positions 'methodology to be theory' and highlights the choices a researcher makes. Choices such as what, who and where to study; which research tradition to work within; what knowledges to draw on; what to include and exclude, foreground and background and the consequences of these decisions; what counts as data and why; relational and ethical concerns; how to represent the findings; and how to disseminate the research (Thomson, 2013a). O'Toole and Beckett (2010, p 81) remind us that there is a strong relationship between methodologies and methods, and when 'mixing and matching' research methods to consider 'purpose, character and emphasis'. Working through these questions brings into focus how creative research methods and methodologies can be used in your project.

Methodology is a complex topic which we will unpack further in Chapter 2. As a brief summary for now: creative research methodologies can encompass particular ways of thinking about research and going about research in education. For all sorts of people – artists, teachers, researchers, artists working in education, teachers thinking through creative ways of working, educators exploring creative methods, or as someone new to creative methods bringing their lived experiences, background and discipline – creative methodologies offer different ways to explore the world. Further to arts education approaches, art as research (Nelson, 2013), or practice-led research and research-led practice (Cahnmann-Taylor and Siegesmund, 2008; Smith and Dean, 2009; Barrett and Bolt, 2010) may come from practitioner- or academic-led research. This research may be made from creative practice – in tangible and intangible forms – and reported using approaches varying from academic to artful.

Imagination in research

Imagination is key in all research when we ask the question 'What is possible?'. This is not a new idea. Imagination has been described as a central plank of the craft of research (Mills, 1959, pp 211–12) and as a 'primary tool' for research (Rapport, 2004, p 102). When we imagine what approaches can be used in research, we examine our contexts, our interests and our passions in different ways and from different perspectives (Lapum et al, 2012, p 103). When we ask the question 'What can this methodology do?' we are thinking through the ways we are 'in' the world and about what different approaches, understandings and tools offer to us as researchers. When we consider our research ideas, we reflect on how our way of thinking through the research tradition is influencing the 'what, how, why, when and why now?' of our work.

Research in education is usually a social endeavour. Researchers work with others, as research participants, as collaborators and as research partners. Each of these terms denotes an approach that is influenced by a methodology and one or more theories. In the case studies in this book, different approaches are taken. For example, in Coleman's case study in Chapter 4 there are artist co-participants: artists who are named and identified in the research with links to their artist websites (Coleman, 2018). In the case studies of LEGO® and sandboxing featured in Chapter 5, the researchers work with participants, but participants' data is anonymised and they are not identified in research outputs. And in Chapter 3, Hall (2019) and her work with poetry invites participants to respond to others' texts through written and spoken words, igniting a bouncing-off of narrative layers that enacts an embodied response to creating and responding to data. In each of these research processes the terms and actions used signal different approaches to relations, relationships and connections between researcher and who and what is being researched.

Others in the research may include research managers and leaders, funders of research and research supervisors. Each of these specialised roles can add to the contextual complexity of the research in hand. Research managers and leaders may have particular agendas to uphold around the kinds of research undertaken; control of the funds available to researchers; and institutional values of research behaviours. Funders of research similarly may have agendas relating to the fit of the research with their needs and values. Academic supervisors may work with particular research conventions. Researchers negotiate these relationships as part of their research work and those connections will shape their approach to creative research methodologies and methods.

Reflexivity and reflection in creative research methodologies may take on different approaches. Reflection as an autoethnographic approach can be questioned and criticised, as it centres the researcher. In this approach, it is difficult for the researcher alone to take the in-between space of the self and other, and to figure out and explain how subjectivities are constituted. In *Water in a Dry Land*, Somerville writes of her approach to reflexivity,

> acknowledging, interrogating, and disrupting the presence of the researcher 'I'. Enduring questions for researcher reflexivity are: Where am I in this research and how do my actions as a researcher shape the knowledge made possible through this research and its representations? (Somerville, 2013, p 11)

Somerville further states her context to clarify her background and interests in doing this research. This suggests that the use of reflexivity has pushed her to examine new possibilities for developing research that stretches how we think about place and country, through visual and spatial means. Some suggest that reflexivity has as much use for quantitative as for qualitative researchers (Shimp, 2007, p 150), and, by extension, this also applies to mixed-methods researchers.

Evaluation research in education

In the education context, evaluation research is usually thought of as assessment of the effectiveness of an intervention or programme. However, evaluation in research can include both effect as a measurement and affect as emotion. Evaluation can be scientific, with findings showing particular results leading to ideas about improvements or strengths or lack. Evaluation can also be approached as thoughtful and detailed representations of what the data has shown. Understanding what your data can do in evaluation is an important part of planning your research.

As such, the research can share voice, represent and be a creative outcome as part of process and/or output. Evaluation could also be a product from the evaluative process through, for example, the production of an evaluative artwork which is then used as data and presented in an evaluation report. This kind of approach can be very different from an interview transcript with coded themes or a bar graph showing a particular response to a question. Evaluative research in education invites you to think about your role as a researcher, and to consider the aim, audience and the appropriateness of what you plan to generate.

This book includes a range of research approaches that can be used in evaluation research in education. In Pat Thomson's research of professional learning for teachers, gallery educators and artists at the Tate Gallery in London, England, the regular professional development programme by gallery educators is consistently evaluated using conventional methods (Thomson, 2014a). However, for the Tate's Summer School, the researchers offered an alternative approach to evaluation using artistic processes. This approach focused on the possibilities of the available opportunities:

- to work with practising contemporary artists;
- to investigate performance art approaches and historical background;
- to experience the Tate as both an exhibition and performance space;
- to participate in artists' practice and work; and
- to experiment with artists' practice and work. (Thomson, 2014a)

The researchers comment: 'This was however a first step towards building an alternative inquiry-based approach to the more usual evaluation "types". We were convinced by this trial that a focus on "what's going on here" via the notion of affordances – what was on offer, what was taken up, by whom, how and when and in what context – was worth pursuing further' (Thomson, 2014a, para 73).

Ethical researching

A university ethics form can seem daunting: pages and pages of questions to answer.

We like to consider 'doing ethics' as a creative action to affirm and reaffirm your research designs, aims and purpose. Formal research ethics processes can confirm and strengthen the design of the research, so that it makes sense and proceeds in a way that is considered ethical by your ethics committee. Each of the questions asked makes you consider how your research project will work, what will happen and what people will do in your project. It will ask what kind of data you will gather. How will you generate data and how will you store it safely? Data in creative methods can be visual, sound, text, conversations (which may be online), songs, dances, meditations, to name just a few types. Data can be developed from an encounter or intervention, a material or process. How will you inform others of what you will be doing? Whose permission will you need in order to contact participants or collaborators? How will you release the findings? And so on – the list is extensive. The ethics application gives order to this list and can aid your thinking through an institutional ethics frame.

However, ethics applications often ask quite a limited set of questions. They do not always ask about how you will analyse data, or how you will disseminate your findings, or how you will safeguard your own well-being. In this book we will encourage you to go further, to think and act ethically throughout your education research work. Acting and thinking ethically is about considering who, how and what your research project will affect – you included. It is about considering beneficence – who benefits from your research. It is about honouring the project, participants, process and yourself in the making of research. It is thinking about power, and how power is used and taken through the research process. It is about what voices are heard and amplified, and what and who gets ignored, unseen or unconsidered. It is thinking about a research question or a response with an embodied wholeness as the research project consumes your time and efforts.

Different communities may have different views and beliefs about the value of ethics. Your job as a researcher is to mediate the space between your project and its fit within an ethical framework. This fit includes your ethics, and the stakeholders in the project, the institutions you are connected with, the researched institutions, peoples, problem, situations, behaviours and attitudes you are investigating.

In Australia, when working with First Nations people and cultures, researchers adhere to a number of ethical guidelines. These include government guidelines developed for research with Aboriginal and Torres Strait Islander individuals, communities and cultures; the Australia Council for the Arts guidelines for working with Indigenous art; and the National Association for the Visual Arts ethical pay rates for artists. The research guidelines highlight six core values: spirit and integrity, cultural continuity, equity, reciprocity, respect and responsibility (National Health and Medical Research Council, 2018). These extend the National Statement on Ethical Conduct of Research (2018), which applies research merit and integrity, justice, beneficence and respect as a set of deliberations in context, with judgement and considerable thoughtfulness to values and principles of the individual researcher towards others, communities and institutions. There are also guidelines for research work with First Nations and Indigenous peoples in some other countries such as Canada and New Zealand. And some Indigenous peoples around the world have begun to produce their own guidelines which any researcher will have to follow if they want to work with people from that community (Patterson et al, 2006, pp 53–4; Gray et al, 2017, pp 24–5; Nordling, 2017).

In Margaret Somerville's project mentioned at the start of this chapter, she writes of talking to Ngemba custodian Brad Steadman about the ancient fish traps on the river at Brewarrina near Narran Lake, the largest freshwater lake in New South Wales, Australia. He talks with Somerville at length about the Ngemba fish traps, but when Somerville moves to talk about Narran Lake, Steadman states,

> he cannot speak for the Narran Lake, there are old people in Walgett who can take me [Somerville] out there and know its stories. They speak a different language and they know different stories. They also know stories of the fish traps but cannot speak for the fish traps. (Somerville, 2013, p 42)

Ethics involves listening and learning about what stories are tellable, who is responsible for speaking these stories and who is telling them. In each of the chapters in this book we invite you to read and learn from each case study and from the sections on ethics. We further invite you to acknowledge that ethics and ethical practice need to be considered, reconsidered and negotiated at all stages of the research, from design to data gathering to analysis, reporting, dissemination and implementation.

Synopsis of each chapter

Each chapter of this book investigates particular research actions through a close study of a variety of case studies so that you can follow the references for more details. The book has been organised to take you through the stages of a research project, and we encourage this way of engaging with the text. As you become more comfortable, or if you are experienced in some areas, you are also encouraged to read lightly and move on to the next area, or jump to where you need to go to in order to progress your research project.

Chapter 2 is concerned with research design. It offers advice about how to design creative education research, how to think about developing a research study to meet its aims and objectives and how to generate research questions. This chapter will be an effective resource for designing good-quality research.

Chapter 3 focuses on context setting. It approaches the context of research and looks at different ways in which the researcher works with creative methods and positions self and others. The chapter shares ways to approach working in and establishing the context in educational spaces, and it is essential reading to prepare for data gathering.

Chapters 4 and 5 are both concerned with creative methods of data gathering. Chapter 4 focuses on studies involving children and young people, while Chapter 5 focuses on research with adult participants. Both chapters discuss the opportunities and limitations of a wide range of creative data-generation techniques and the associated ethical considerations. These two chapters provide an accessible but comprehensive overview of the field that can support readers to introduce creative approaches to gathering data for their own work, and to be more confident in this part of the 'doing' of creative education research.

Chapter 6 outlines good practice in data analysis and introduces a range of creative methods of analysing data. It offers an effective foundation for readers thinking through how to work with and analyse research data creatively, effectively and ethically.

Chapter 7 directs your attention to positioning research reporting as creative communication with your research audience. The chapter covers issues such as using plain language, editing your report and seeking reviewers' feedback to help you to articulate your research. It showcases examples using poetic forms, graphic novels and technology such as blogging, video, podcasts and animation.

Chapter 8 covers the presentation of research in ways that diverge from the conventional conference or meeting presentation. This chapter includes case studies with data from participants using expanded notions of texts, such as screenplays and using video, digital storytelling and whiteboard animation techniques.

Chapter 9 is about what happens next in terms of creative ways of disseminating the messages from research to diverse audiences using multimodal techniques. Chapters 7, 8 and 9 combined provide the reader with a wide range of innovative practices to record, share and communicate research findings. These techniques can help to increase audience engagement and therefore increase the potential to achieve impact and positive change.

The concluding chapter reflects on lessons learned and further opportunities for, and challenges to, working with creative techniques in the field of education, both as a research tool and as a pedagogic approach to learning and development. There are prompts to generatively activate your thinking about your research focus and passion. The specific focus is on activities to support you in making progress with your thinking and research design skills, and to explore the ideas that have resonated with you.

Conclusion

As this book takes you through a cycle of research processes, it connects the thinking and doing of methods and theory. Thinking and doing are two of the main reflective and reflexive actions you need to do as a researcher. How do you position yourself and your project in its design and context? How do you gather data and analyse all of your work and processes? These thinkings and doings ultimately affect how you present and report on your work. Making research and developing viable connections are creative acts. Making visible your processes in your research projects develops your – and others' – understanding of how research operates and matters. Taking responsibility for your project and how it progresses is a part of developing and maintaining your skills as a creative researcher. This book is a starting point – dive into the case studies, follow and extend others' research tracks and make new ways of seeing, feeling and experiencing research.

CHAPTER DISCUSSION QUESTIONS

1. How do you identify where you will position yourself in your research?

2. What, for you, is the 'why' of working with creative methods?

3. How could creative methods support you in connecting with your research topic or question?

4. How can working with creative methods assist you in working with your research project?

5. How could working with creative methods help you to communicate outcomes of the research?

2

Research design

Chapter summary

In reading this chapter on research design you are invited to consider the overall approach that you select to integrate the different components of your study. This needs to be done in a coherent and logical way that addresses your research question, situates the topic you are investigating and considers carefully the participants, context and contribution to the field. The design of your study can become a blueprint for others to follow, a map setting out how they may contribute to the field by building on and extending your work. When working with creative methods we consider how we can work in ways that honour the context, participants and researcher. In this chapter we invite you to consider different ways to design creative research that can connect with the topic you are investigating and your research questions in education contexts, whether formal or informal. We highlight that designing research is an enactment of both creative and critical thinking. This chapter connects with cases to extend your thinking about research design through:

- design thinking in the informal learning space of an art gallery between teachers and artists and the researcher;
- activism with children and art making with an artist-researcher;
- art exhibition installation and performance research;
- creative and cultural practice and education research as a way to investigate wellness; and
- questions of identity and positionality.

Introduction

This chapter attends to the ways creative research design can diverge from the Euro-Western conventions of designing research and how researchers position themselves in and with the research. The process of design directly influences each of the processes of the research and its outcomes. Creative research may be co-designed with research collaborators and participants, other artist-researchers, industry, funders, teachers, artist-students and/or others. Facilitation, collaboration and negotiation are key. This is how different perspectives, ideas and privileges all come into play with varying effects and affects that become a part of the methodological approach. How much of the research design is tied down in the beginning becomes a matter of methodology and the context. It is important to understand your context before you begin designing your research, so this chapter should be read in conjunction with Chapter 3, which covers context setting in detail.

Research design may become influenced by emergent forces through facilitation, collaboration and negotiation, and the gathering and analysis of data, which can be developed if allowance is made for the affordances and constraints that may occur. The chapter demonstrates how research design has a key relevance to the research to be carried out. We invite you to consider:

- how to design creative research for use in formal and informal educational settings;
- generating and working with research questions;
- engaging with partners and collaborators;
- developing over time: installations and participant engagement;
- creative cultural practices: weaving knowledge;
- designing good-quality research; and
- ethical considerations.

Designing creative research in education

Designing research has as much to do with the research topic or question as with the process and outcome of the research. The 'why' of your research design has to do with what you want to problematise, question, respond to and what you want to document, continue, appraise, evaluate or improve. Designing research is concerned with being prepared for the unexpected, thinking through what might and might not happen. It involves thinking about research questions and experiences and attending to how things may happen. Design involves thinking and doing in complex situations. The potentials and pitfalls of what your research experience could be, and that of participants and other stakeholders, are first and foremost about its design. Key leads may emerge from each research activity and it is up to you and your research design to consider whether – and, if so, how – to follow each lead.

Designing research involves acting with creative and critical thinking. It requires critically thinking about the possibilities and constraints of the process and action of doing research. Thinking comes to the fore in methodology, where it becomes a way to see (Eisner, 2002; Cahnmann-Taylor, 2008), feel, experience and theorise what you include in, and what you exclude from, the research. Thinking creatively attends to both slow and fast thinking (Kahneman, 2011, pp 12–13). Kahneman describes thinking fast as automatic, with intuition, sensations and affects, and thinking slow as effortful – in the detail and with processes (Kahneman, 2011). Thinking fast and slow encompasses thinking in the moment, in practice, while making, in reflection and with reflexivity and theories, among other research-related examples. Thinking about research design involves both slow and fast thinking as you create the shapes and forms of your research project.

Research design is about facilitation, collaboration and negotiation and keeping in mind your research question (see below for more on research questions). Facilitation includes facilitating the possibilities of your research, and facilitating people and actions to move towards an answer to your research question. Collaboration is key, and how you want to work with others, individuals and communities is a guide to how to conduct the research. Negotiation of research needs to be enacted in conventional and creative research methods, but understanding where research can be positioned is central to working with others and in communities. The research design may be developed and negotiated with collaborators, other researchers, participants, stakeholders and research partners.

Questions to consider in designing research include the following.

- What is your role in the research? (For example, are you a creative practice researcher working with others and canvassing their opinions, such as a choreographer–researcher teaching a troupe a new dance and gathering feedback data from the troupe?)
- What kinds of relationships do you want your research to foster?
- What kind of data do you want to generate?
- What do you want to do with the data?
- How do you want to analyse the data?
- What are the ethical issues in your research?
- Is a formal research ethics process necessary to your project?
- How are you considering your well-being and the well-being of others in the research design?
- What strategies will you employ to disseminate your research findings and who are your intended audiences?

Generating and working with research questions

Once you have decided on your research topic, you need to define your research question or questions. Leavy (2017) suggests a process of narrowing focus from a broad topic to one that incorporates elements like specificity in cohorts or experiences, location and relationships between participants. One example Leavy gives is from a broad focus of bullying, which can be then narrowed by location, and then by cohort or relationship. We build on Leavy's work to unpack this in Table 2.1 by general theme, location and relationship to demonstrate the potential for this kind of thinking. Remember as you read this example that this is one way to approach the research design. Table 2.1 demonstrates how you can narrow down your focus as you design your research, and each line presents a different way of thinking.

Table 2.1: Thinking about research design

General theme	Location	Relationship
Bullying	Bullying in the playground	Playground bullying between young primary school-aged children
Bullying	Bullying behaviours in multicultural schools	Bullying behaviours among pupils in multicultural high schools
Bullying	Bullying in the staff room	Bullying between colleagues in the staff room

Source: Developed from Leavy (2017, pp 55–7)

Each of these focused topics would result in very different research projects, participants and contexts. The topic's viability should be checked by sampling the published literature. At the time of writing, when we checked the literature on 'bullying in schools' in Google Scholar, there were about 350,000 results. When we added 'arts education' to bullying in schools, we got over 88,000 results. When we added 'playgrounds' to 'bullying in schools' there were about 24,300 results; then, adding arts education, we had about 18,500 results. However, when we searched for 'creative methods' with 'bullying in schools' we got 40 results with varying relevance to the focused topic. A quick look at some of the literature's results, abstracts and key words will enable you to gauge the viability of researching your topic.

When you design research one of the things you need to consider is the research question or questions. Thinking about design and questions is contextualised by a methodological framework and/or by a theoretical position. As you create your research questions you also need to be aware of your own position, where you are coming from – your lens for seeing the world, if you like. We ask the question: how are you privileged as a researcher and how does that frame your research?

As you develop your research design you need to consider the influences of your philosophical assumptions and consequently determine how these are significant to decisions relating to the research, including research questions, goals and outcomes. The assumptions that have implications for research have been defined as:

- ontology – the nature of reality, or claims researchers make regarding knowledge;
- epistemology – how individuals arrive at that knowledge and how researchers justify those claims;
- axiology – the role of values and how the researcher acknowledges values in research; and
- methodology – the process of research. (Creswell and Poth, 2017, p 20)

Methodology also includes how the research is framed by the researcher, and how the method and theory are enacted. You as the researcher are the one that links the methodology, methods and approach with the research question, together with your beliefs, views and values (Kara, 2017; Mason, 2018, pp 237–8). Methodology is how your beliefs, views and values interact with your positionality, your context and your research project.

Five commonly used methodologies include positivist, realist, constructionist, interpretivist and transformative. There are diverse approaches to each of these methodologies which enable different perspectives of ontology, epistemology and axiology to develop, and what types of methods are used. Kara (2017, p 48, table 2.1) lays out some of the methods and approaches undertaken. This is not exhaustive but can be used as a guide for further work in developing your methodology.

As you develop your research design, your research question(s) can focus the methods and methodology you use, and your emerging design will influence the way you respond to your research question(s). Some researchers will generate a research question that considers 'what, why and how'. Other questions will be constructed in different ways, perhaps by starting with a creative practice such as dance or painting and allowing the question to emerge from the 'material thinking' in practice (Bolt, 2010, p 29). At the heart of your research design, you will need to consider how the research question affects the type of research you want to conduct. It may be research that describes or investigates a problem

Table 2.2: Methodologies, ontologies, epistemologies and methods

Methodology type	Positivist	Realist	Constructionist	Interpretivist	Transformative
Sub-divisions include:	Post-positivist	Critical realist	Postmodernist Grounded theory	Phenomenologist Symbolic interactionist Hermeneutic	Participatory Feminist Emancipatory/ activist User led Decolonising
Ontology (how the world is known)	Facts and phenomena exist independently of people	Facts and phenomena are entwined in complex contexts	People construct facts and phenomena	People interpret facts and phenomena	People, facts and phenomena can combine to create change
Epistemology (how that knowledge of the world is learned)	Through observation and measurement	Through assessment of complexity in context	By creating meaning from experience	By identifying and interpreting multiple realities	Through relationships with people and the environment
Methods likely to be used	Randomised controlled trials, surveys, technology-based methods	Mixed methods	Interviews, arts-based methods, discourse analysis	Interviews, focus groups, participant observation	Arts-based methods, interviews, community-based research

Source: Kara (2017, p 48)

or issue. It may be a project that wants to explain how something happens. It may be a project intended to activate or change a situation, or to evaluate an intervention. Leavy suggests that research can also 'evoke, provoke or unsettle' (Leavy, 2017, p 7). This is a particular strength of creative research in developing embodied, creative and action-based responses and generating new ways of thinking and doing.

In the next section of this chapter we offer a number of case studies for you to consider various ways of formulating a research design. The following case studies provide inspiration for approaching, working in and establishing the context in educational spaces:

- design thinking in the informal learning space of an art gallery between teachers and artists, where the researcher blogged the research activities each day;
- activism with children and art making with an artist-researcher;
- art exhibition installation, performance research and focus group interviews; and
- creative and cultural practice and education research as a way to investigate wellness and identity.

Each of the case studies focuses on research designed in different ways. Each project involves collaboration: collaboration and action with pre-service teachers and artists in a museum environment and blogging the research process (Thomson, 2012); with children in a classroom community (Liversedge, 2014); and with a community (Cole and McIntyre, 2004b; Smith, 2017). Each case study features creative making processes, including song writing, traditional Māori cloak weaving (Smith, 2017), theatre, installation practice and focus group interviews (Cole and McIntyre, 2006) and workshops facilitated through diverse art-making forms (Thomson, 2012). The research projects use these creative and mixed, interdisciplinary methods to conceptualise and theorise their pedagogical inquiries.

Despite their similarities, these case studies have very different approaches, from the design of the research questions that reflect on their intent and contexts to how they generate responses to the research questions. In choosing case studies focusing on collaboration, we are focusing on research design that includes creative outputs and experiences of making, and the non-textual, which could include video, performance, song, dance, activism, art exhibitions and installations, festivals and events. Each case study shows different perspectives, privileges and ideas on doing and thinking about research. We share these to scaffold and inspire your thinking.

Designing research projects for an embodied experience

An embodied response is one that takes into account, and considers what can be learned from, the person's sensory experience. In designing research to generate an embodied experience, the following case study uses facets of the design thinking process in developing research with collaborators and users. Design thinking is a cyclic process of five stages:

- empathy as developing understanding of the problem to be tackled;
- defining the problem with the people you are working with;
- ideation (that is, generating ideas) to challenge the assumptions of the issue at hand and to develop multiple innovative potential solutions;
- prototype as experimenting with ideas, materials, tools and techniques; and
- testing out the approaches.

This process can also be iterative. Ideation is a key stage in the case study and its iterations. There is a constant use of visual ideation with post-it notes, drawings and diagrams in the documentation. Affinity mapping used in user–experience design is a way of thinking about how to clump, cluster or group ideas. In conventional research it may be thought of as analysis. However, in this research design it is used collaboratively for data gathering within the embodied experience of the research immersion.

CASE STUDY 2.1: DESIGN THINKING, IDEATION AND AFFINITY MAPPING

Who and where: Pat Thomson, the Tate Summer School Professional Development team and artist-facilitators in London, UK (Thomson, 2012–19).

What: The researcher Pat Thomson and the Tate Schools and Teachers team worked with artist-facilitators to deliver an intensive workshop summer school for teachers over a number of years.

Why: The researchers and artist-facilitators aimed to understand how education happens in museums and to develop new ways of teacher development in this context.

How: Over five days, the artist-facilitators devised a series of active learning and reflection experiences for the participants responding to prompts from the gallery's collection and the artist-facilitators themselves. Each day's activities were themed with events or offerings to prompt thinking and doing facilitated by artists in a 'pedagogy of encouragement' (Thomson, 2014b). The activities were proposed by the invited artist-facilitators working in collaboration with a schedule of reflective activities, making, performing, ideation and looking at artworks in the collection and special exhibits.

There were reflective activities to develop ideas of what it means to teach art and what it meant to the participant to be both a learner and a teacher. Pat Thomson documented the programme on her blog and took field notes; videos, photographs, artworks and artefacts were made; there were a participant diary room, debriefing notes and 'reflection grid' (Thomson, 2013b); insight into diverse artists' worlds; sensory experiences (Thomson, 2019); and zine and gif-making workshops (Thomson, 2017), among other making and reflecting experiences. The 2017 summer school used timelines and affinity mapping (Thomson, 2017) and theming to document learning activities about gender and the possibilities of drag to play with gender. Drag – dressing in another gender's clothing, sometimes with 'larger-than-life' personas (McIntyre, 2018) – was one of the many gender identities used to inquire 'how making and being with art can support young people to explore and express their gender identity, thinking through teaching and learning practices' (Thomson, 2017).

Photos 2.1 and 2.2: Ideas about gender and representation in the 2017 summer school

Source: Thomson (2017)

Tips

- Understanding the dual position as both researcher and participant in the experience is key in this research design. This position allows and attends to affordances – what the research activity attends to is pivotal to the design.
- Consider working up from the ground as in this case study, rather than imposing a research idea. However, don't forget the importance of planning.
- Continuous blogging can support data analysis by theming. Thomson's daily blogging documented how she started to theme her analysis, during and after the experience.

Traps

- The amount of data produced in one iteration of the summer school was substantial, and this can cause problems later in a project, without careful planning of time and resources.
- Confidentiality and anonymity can be impossible to achieve in group research. It is vital to provide initial information about this, or consent to take part will not be fully informed.
- Data may be difficult to remove from the pool of data if a participant wants to remove their contribution from the project.

Reflective questions

1. How does this research approach to learning experiences allow for affordances (how the context or environment complements the research approach)?
2. What do you imagine are some of the constraints of this research approach?
3. How do you think this generative approach could be used in other contexts?
4. What does this way of working inspire for you in your research design?

Engaging with partners and collaborators

Case study 2.2 features how socially engaged art-making practices can lead to different kinds of research outcomes that extend the definition of what research can achieve. Engaging in partnerships with children can focus research on how and what they are interested in and what they want to amplify. The different kinds of data featured in this case study – writing protest songs, banner making, singing and protesting – contextualise children's activism, which features and amplifies children's voice and agency (Thomson, 2008; Lemon, 2007, 2008, 2019). There is some pushback against the idea that researchers can 'give' voice to participants or 'share' participants' voices, because those voices are not the researchers' to share (Jackson and Mazzei, 2008).

CASE STUDY 2.2: ACTIVISM WITH CHILDREN

Who and where: In 2014 the British artist Peter Liversidge worked with Year 3 children from a London school over four months. The aim was to develop an exhibition at the Whitechapel Gallery of the children's song writing, with choral protest songs as the exhibited video and 'sign paintings' and banners.

What: The artist prepared a written proposal for the project and investigation and collaborated with others to implement the project. He worked with the children to develop songs such as 'Less trucks and cars / More chocolate bars!' and 'No more dog dirt' (Liversidge, 2014). These protest songs were performed and exhibited on video in a gallery setting.

Why: 'Notes on protesting' investigated children's activism and what they wanted to protest about. It explored what and how you can change, and the rules of particular spaces and how to break those rules, moving from inside the school to the wider community.

How: Liversidge first worked with the children to create and put together brain maps of things that they liked and did not like. The banners were then developed so that people could see what the children were singing about and know that they were protesting (Liversidge, 2014). The outcomes, the exhibition and videos of the project show development of an approach of working with children to amplify voice, to show powerful activism from children and to pinpoint concerns the children have in their lives and local areas. The outcomes are very different from those that a survey of children's opinions would generate, and powerfully illuminate children's concerns to audiences.

Tips

- However complex your project may be, develop a concise proposal, summarising the project, to use as the project design artefact. Liversidge develops a very short one-page proposal for all of the artworks he facilitates. Other projects may need more comprehensive information, depending on the artist's positionality and intent.
- Working with children in a classroom is very different from working with them in a museum context. Introducing children as artists in the art gallery is a powerful way to make connections with art-making processes, contexts and audiences.
- The video recordings of the development of the project, its performances and the artist working with children become integral to the research project. In the research design, consider how your project can be documented.

Traps

- Artist-researchers need to consider how their intention to develop artworks as research may intersect with children, the school and the art gallery. Failing to acknowledge the contributions of others could cause upset, conflict and reputational damage.
- There is a pervasive danger of being prescriptive, and so amplifying the researcher's voice rather than the voices of participants. In this example, children were not involved in the initial proposal or design; however, the collective actions of the group show how children's interests and views can be highlighted.

Reflective questions

1. In what ways does the research design allow children's voices to be amplified?
2. What are the affordances of the art installation/project?
3. What do you imagine are some of the constraints of this research approach?
4. How do you think this generative approach may be used in other contexts?

Developing over time: installations and participant engagement

In case study 2.3, 'The Alzheimer's Project', the researchers designed interventions where caregivers have the opportunity to contribute their views to an exhibition installation. The research design is a considered response to the issue of asking for the participants' contributions. The researchers use an engagement approach, identifying carers, asking for contributions, thoughts and feelings to be jotted down and displayed in a public exhibition. The exhibition developed over the period of its display.

CASE STUDY 2.3: THE ALZHEIMER'S PROJECT

Who and where: Canadian researchers Ardra Cole and Maura McIntyre developed 'The Alzheimer's Project', a multiple art exhibition installation and performance research project, from their lived experience of caring for their mothers with Alzheimer's disease. This project was one of the first installation art projects (Leavy, 2019), developed and positioned as installation art where the audience engagement moves from passively consuming art to actively embodying responses to the artwork (Cole and McIntyre, 2004c; Bishop, 2012; Leavy, 2019; Tate, nd). Cole and McIntyre state that their research contributes to and invokes an ethic of caregiving, developing knowledge that communicates the complexities of caregiving (Cole and McIntyre, 2004b).

What: Over a series of three installation exhibitions in high-profile public spaces across Canada, Cole and McIntyre developed a mixed-methods research project that addressed 'how relational roles may shift through wellness and illness' (Cole and McIntyre, 2004a website, para 7). The installation incorporated a clothesline of collected clothing from patients, photographs of clotheslines and the fronts of carers' fridges with the ephemera of everyday lives, responses from carers, spoken-word performances and gathered artefacts from carers' lives. Participating community carers were invited to contribute to one-to-one and group conversations, and the audience contributed written responses and artefacts related to their experiences (Cole and McIntyre, 2004b). Carers added clothing and text contributions during the exhibition of the installation, with focus group and text additions and artwork.

Why: Cole and McIntyre wanted to highlight the plight of carers in this situation, to enable learning. As an early example of an art installation and socially engaged practice in research, the project focused on carers' agency and voice, contributing an 'aesthetic contemplation' (McIntyre and Cole, 2007, p 2) of the lives of carers. The researchers considered how images from the installation were interpreted, with the premise that there 'is no such thing as a one to one correspondence between message intended and message received' (McIntyre and Cole, 2007, p 2). The researchers also focused on the audience's role as engaging with and reading the research (McIntyre and Cole, 2007).

How: The 'aesthetic contemplation' is a reflective process that arises from experiencing the installation. Affective experience, of perception and emotion, contributes to meaning making over time.

Tips
- The consideration of where exhibitions are to take place should be central to the research design.
- Take advantage of the diversity of installation practices. Multiple art-making processes can be exhibited together for an experience in which audiences can develop their own meaning-making through making connections.

Trap
- Audience and carer participation and engagement is difficult to plan and manage – what happens to your research when no one turns up or consent is not given?

Reflective questions
1. How could art installations be a way to enhance your research design?
2. What is possible when an ethic of caregiving, developing knowledge that communicates the complexities of caregiving, is enacted?
3. How can art-making processes exhibited together form an experience for the audience to develop their own meaning-making through making connections? How can this be incorporated into a research design?
4. How can engaging with art installations and exhibitions honour participant and audience voices? How can this be incorporated into a research design?
5. How else could researchers include scope for divergent response(s) to research questions?

Creative cultural practices: weaving knowledge

Creative and cultural practice and education research is a way to investigate wellness, identity and making techniques. In Hinekura Smith's PhD thesis, she developed and responded to her topic of what it means to live as Māori. She used a Māori Indigenous research methodology that is relational in its approach rather than a Euro–Western approach which centres on problematising an issue. Developing the research in this way allowed the research question to emerge from a narrative and lived experience of being raised as Māori in a colonised land. It also allowed Smith to respond to the question of 'How do Māori women reclaim "living as Māori" through the creation of storied whatu kākahu?' (Smith, 2017, p 30).

This is a decolonising approach to research. Decolonisation is 'a shift of imagination' (Patel, 2016, p 7) with the aim to 'unsettle the very settler colonial logics that should be dismantled' (Patel, 2016, pp 87–8). Decolonising approaches are perhaps particularly important in education research because Euro–Western education was historically, and is today, an instrument of colonisation (Patel, 2016, p 15). Today we all, colonisers and colonised, and those who may regard themselves as both or neither, have a role to play in decolonisation. In educational research, that role involves moving away from concepts of ownership, territoriality and 'fixedness', and towards concepts of sharing, relationality and mutability. This is not a simple or straightforward process (Patel, 2016, p 48), but neither is it doomed to failure, particularly as others have gone before to show us the way.

If you want to know more about decolonisation, we would recommend these readings:

Moreton-Robinson, A. (2020) *Talkin' Up to the White Woman: Aboriginal Women and Feminism*, University of Queensland Press.
Tuck, E. and Yang, K.W. (2012) 'Decolonization is not a metaphor', *Decolonization: Indigeneity, Education & Society*, 1(1).
Smith, L.T. (2012) *Decolonizing Methodologies: Research and Indigenous Peoples* (2nd edn), Zed Books Ltd.

CASE STUDY 2.4: KAHU AND RECLAMATION OF INDIGENOUS KNOWLEDGES

Who and where: Hinekura Smith's PhD thesis develops a creative methodology of Indigenous knowledge and customs and a pedagogy of making kahu, a traditionally woven cloak of feathers and twine (Smith, 2017). Smith is based in urban Aotearoa New Zealand but closely connected to her Māori Marae, a place and house of gathering and connections on land of her Māori community.

What: Over a year, Smith and her participants met eight times to learn to make traditional Māori cloaks and to converse. They also wrote journals of their experience of living as Māori women, an experience which Smith (2017, p 47) described as having 'variable' opportunities available, as colonisation has disrupted Māori cultural life and customs. Smith prompted the journal writing by e-mailing her participant group a series of questions or statements to encourage the writing of the journals over the research period. The researcher, Smith, and her mother participated in the 'data' gathering, and this involvement and relationship are described in her thesis.

Why: Deeply influenced by the transformative praxis (Freire, 1972, 1993) of decolonising theories of education, and using a Kaupapa Māori model, Smith situated her research in the reclamation of Indigenous knowledge and practices of making cloaks using the process of weaving to conceptualise her theorisations (Smith, 2017).

Smith's experience as a Māori educator, of growing up and then teaching in western education systems, influenced her theoretical conceptualisation of the research as Indigenous, focused on Māori Indigeneity, reclamation, self-determination and relationships with materials, creative practices and customs.

How: Smith theorised the weaving, the tools and materials used in her workshops as an embodied practice of reclamation of Indigenous knowledge. She situated her research positionality through relationships with people, place, materials and cultural traditions and her practice as an educator. In the workshops, Smith taught her participants to weave traditional feather cloaks and audio-recorded these meetings. She analysed data from the journals and audio. Smith's theoretical framing of her research as Māori informs her research design through its engagement over time, pedagogical focus and reclamation of Māori traditional skills and cultural material practices.

Tips
- Early consultation with community and developing relationships is pivotal in developing research projects such as Smith's cloak-making project, and this influenced her research design.
- Positioning the researcher and the research in community, in praxis and in relationships adds complexity. Smith's project was deeply grounded in her indigeneity, community and pedagogical and creative practice.

Traps
- What happens if you can't reach the 'right' people? How can research happen if you are not given permission to go ahead from community leaders? Working with complexities of place, community and relationships can add risks to research design.

Reflective questions
1. How does your positioning as a researcher in the project affect your research design?
2. How can theoretical frameworks influence a research design?
3. How do you think creative practice could be useful in the reclamation of cultural knowledge?

Designing good-quality research

At the research design stage, it is important to think through and be able to argue the quality of research you are using to inform your work (Hammersley, 2009, p 26). Conventionally, reliability, replicability and validity (Bryman, 2016, p 41) are held to be the markers of quality research. Reliability refers to the measures you are using in your research, for scales, behaviours and attributes and experiences. For example, a large urban-population school of 1,000 may give very different findings about an intervention compared to a very small, remote school with a population of 50. This example of school population is also related to replicability – how an intervention can be repeated, in different places, by different practitioners and with different participants. How valid is the research in intersecting and questioning the findings and what they appear to show? Validity has different forms, including:

- internal validity – whether there is a demonstrable relationship between cause and effect within the research context;
- external validity – the extent to which the results of a study can be generalised beyond the research context;
- measurement validity, also known as construct validity – whether a scale or test really measures what it sets out to measure;
- ecological validity – the extent to which research findings have relevance to real life; and
- testimonial validity – validity confirmed by checking with participants (Kara, 2020, p 90).

In contrast, creative research projects may seek more creative responses to the issues of reliability, replicability and validity. Sarah Tracy argues for eight criteria of quality (Tracy, 2010, p 838) that encapsulate the research elements:

- a worthy topic (relevant, topical, interesting);
- rigorous (suitably critical and rigorous methodology, enough data);
- sincere (reflexive and transparent);
- credible (detail and explanation, different perspectives and trustworthy findings);
- resonant (affective impact on audience, transferable findings);
- significant (making a contribution to different forms of knowledge, such as practical, theoretical, methodological and/or ethical);
- ethical (holistic); and
- coherent (doing what it claims to do, with its methods and methodology, and making meaningful connections throughout).

Other academic researchers look for different ways to express and affirm their research purpose. One example is the Interfaith Childhood Project, which explores connections and relationships in faith communities by art making and dialogue with children and their parents, schools and communities (Hickey-Moody, 2018; n.d.). This project gathered narratives of communities of migrants and what matters to them and how this mattering sustains connections (Hickey-Moody, n.d.). The project used concepts from Rosi Braidotti's posthuman research theory to make sense of our flexible and multiple identities (2013) in a world of digital 'second life', robotics, genetically modified food and the ethics of affirmation. This positioning (Hickey-Moody, 2018) is informed by intra-active and diffractive methods and theories (Haraway, 1991; Barad, 2007) which are useful in working with complexity.

Ethics of creative research design in education

In each of the case studies discussed in this chapter the ethical positioning of the researcher is evident in the way the research is conducted. All of the researchers in this chapter are academics, based in education, and use creative practice as a part of their research process and output. An ethical approach is inherent in each of the projects. Smith's thesis contains a participant information sheet informing participants of the project and detailing what the researcher wants to do, how data will be generated and managed and what the participant will be doing. Based on this information, and sometimes further conversation, consent is gathered from participants. In Smith's case this process was approved by a university ethics committee, which constitutes a Euro-Western approach to research ethics. Indigenous research ethics operate very differently, emphasising principles such as relational accountability, communality of knowledge, reciprocity and benefit sharing (Chilisa, 2012, p 22; Wilson and Wilson, 2013, p 343). This means that Indigenous researchers who work in Euro-Western contexts can have considerable difficulty in reconciling the two different approaches to research ethics (Absolon in Kovach, 2009, p 153; Chilisa, 2012, p 76).

In other projects with practice-based researchers, community-based researchers and others who don't have access to formal ethical review processes, other means of getting agreement, consent processes and permission to use data materials need to be established. Each project will have its own ethical process to follow, due to its context. However, as creative methods are relatively new in education research and in creative practice fields, there may be some confusion or reticence to engage with ethical processes in universities (Bolt et al, 2017). Advice needs to be sought from a number of people: research supervisors, ethics committee chairs and ethics administrators are useful to consult. In projects that research Indigeneity issues and Indigenous communities, an advisory panel of community members and academics can be developed as a part of the research design. This panel is placed to consult on issues that crop up. Doing ethics applications in the university for research projects in education is a very common occurrence, as it entails working with others, finding out about their experiences and attending to contexts. As we saw in Chapter 1, in some parts of the world Indigenous peoples now operate their own ethical processes for research, so some research projects need to seek both Euro-Western and Indigenous ethical approval.

Research projects in all formal and informal educational contexts can highlight complex issues of dependencies, power relationships and consent when working with others. The research design is an act of ethical positioning of you as a researcher and as leader or facilitator of the research project and process.

Conclusion

In this chapter we have discussed four different case studies to expand the idea of what research design can do when incorporating creative methods. A common theme in the case studies is collaborating with communities to make creative outcomes as a part of the research design. In Thomson's research, the creative experience intervention and artist-facilitators changed over the project; however, there were stages of consultation with research partners, attention to ethical aspects, collaboration with artist-facilitators, the creative practice experience as a week-long intervention, and pre- and post-intervention data gathering. Then there were more stages: reflection, analysis of the gathered data, and report writing, publication (blog, creative, fictional, scholarly and academic) and presentation.

Designing research involves both creative and critical thinking. It encompasses what you will be doing and how you as a researcher prompt and respond to experiences, situations, contexts, people and materials. It can be daunting to design a research project, but equally it can be exciting to think through the possibilities of your research. This is a starting point to consider – the what and how of the ways we intend to work that honour the context, participants and researcher. Thinking about what you are doing and what you are asking others to do is what you are designing – will these 'doings' generate the data you are expecting? And perhaps some that you are not expecting?

Another starting point to reflect on your design is understanding and acknowledging the privilege it is to enact research. Discussing your research design with colleagues is a great way to check its coherence and your sense-making. In the following chapters of this book, each of the case studies has a research design that you can explore further by examining the sources cited.

CHAPTER DISCUSSION QUESTIONS

1. What creative approaches resonate with you as you design your research?

2. What lenses of thinking or privilege influence how you construct your research design? Consider your ontology, epistemology and axiology lenses.

3. How will you construct an argument that demonstrates the quality of your research design?

4. What are some different ways you can design research that honour participant voice in creative ways?

3

Context setting

Chapter summary

Context setting is vital in research. In this chapter we explore different ways in which the researcher can locate the immediate and wider contexts for their research. We introduce you to the use of literature to contextualise research in its field, identify gaps and establish what you are going to build on. We then reflect on ways to position your research context as researcher, teacher-researcher or participant. We use case studies that demonstrate how you can consider and reconsider crafting the context when working with creative methods. These case studies cover walking interviews, drawing, dance, poetry through *lectio divina*, and hip hop to provide inspiration for approaching, identifying and working with the context in educational spaces. In presenting these case studies we invite you to consider different ways in which a context can be constructed about, for and with participants in education. We conclude the chapter by highlighting some ethical considerations that you need to think through with respect to context setting and identification.

Introduction

This chapter approaches the context of research and looks at different ways in which the researcher can work with creative methods to position self and others. In each case study the positionality of participants and/or researcher is unpacked to consider different ways of working in education research contexts. There is a focus on how educators work with different creative methods to illuminate lived experience, and specifically how this contributes to identifying the context. The chapter demonstrates how context has a key relevance to any research. We invite you to consider:

- why context is important in research;
- how to identify the context;
- the place of the literature review in establishing the context;
- different creative methods that support context setting;
- creative ways to position self and others; and
- ethical considerations that honour the context.

Locating and communicating context

When we are researching, context is crucial. Context can be considered in multiple ways, such as the field you are researching in, the location of the research environment, your own context or positionality and the contexts of your participants and other actors within your research. The concept of context is a complex one. This chapter is designed to help you understand the importance of context(s) in research and gain insight into why and how you can work with context in your own research.

Your research needs to be positioned within the context of the field you are researching in. We often do this through a literature review. However, you need to be aware that not all research includes a literature review. For example, evaluation research often does not, though it may use a document analysis instead. Also, practitioner research may not use a literature review to set context, depending on the purpose of and audience for that research; instead, the researcher may simply write a description of the context.

If you are using a literature review, this will be an important part of your research process, whether or not you are working with creative methods. Reviewing literature is itself a creative process that can be conducted in many established and innovative ways (Kara, 2020, pp 82–3). It is beyond the scope of this book to give details of those approaches, but we can say that the role of the literature review is both a process and a product. It is a process that sets the context of your research by:

- your searching for and engaging with existing research and other information relevant to your research topic and questions;
- enabling you to familiarise yourself with the relevant research; and
- enabling you to locate your research within the field.

This process also helps you to:

- find key authors and arguments that are relevant to your topic;
- locate significant findings that you can build on in your research;
- identify issues in the existing research and gaps that you can address in your own research;
- critically analyse the work that has and has not been done; and
- demonstrate how you are going to take this forward in your research.

You also need to identify the location(s) of the research context itself, the environment or environments you are to research in. This consideration of context connects the researcher with the participants, their environment and the readers. It is important to know the location of the context before you begin designing your research.

In qualitative research the context takes into account the natural environments where we work. These include face-to-face or virtual learning environments; places and locations where learning and teaching may occur, including schools, classrooms, galleries, museums, libraries, community or online platforms; learning management systems; and social media.

In selecting settings and communicating the location of contexts it is important to note that 'the "reality" we perceive is constructed by our social, cultural, historical and individual contexts' (Korstjens and Moser, 2017, p 274). Thus, as educators, researchers, teacher-researchers or student-researchers we look for ways to describe, explore or explain phenomena in real-world contexts. In this consideration, we are required to think about how we position self and others. It is inevitable that there will be influence from you as the researcher; however, it is advisable to consider how you can 'minimalize your interfering with people's natural settings, [so that] you can get a "behind the scenes" picture of how people feel or what other forces are at work' (Korstjens and Moser, 2017, p 275). We consider questions such as the following.

- What is the context for this research?
- How can we best capture the natural context?
- What is my own context, or positionality?
- What are the contexts of my participants?
- How do I, as a researcher, engage with participants in the natural context?
- How can I glean the best data to position self and others in relation to the context?
- How am I, as the researcher, a part of the research context?
- In what ways can we communicate these contexts to our audience/reader?
- What is the relevance and significance of these contexts?
- How can participants support the communication of these contexts?

When we share and describe the contexts of our participants, we aim to provide a rich and in-depth picture. This allows us to consider how we communicate the experiences, perceptions, behaviours, actions and idiosyncrasies that connect participants with readers, while also honouring participants and allowing for others to think about how they could transfer the research to their own contexts (Liamputtong, 2012; Korstjens and Moser, 2017). Contexts help us to understand the research that was carried out within a particular framework. Researchers are required to accurately describe the research context and to locate themselves and their role within that context.

Each of the case studies in this chapter connects to different ways in which a researcher can work with participants while working with creative methods. We can approach this in a number of ways, with thinking about it from the perspective of telling a narrative being one beneficial way (McAlpin, 2016). From this perspective we can make connections between time, events and situations to show the influence of the contexts on a research design that leads to recounting personal meanings of experience (Coulter and Smith, 2009; McAlpin, 2016). James Hayton (2019, para 1) has blogged some strategies for thinking about how we can communicate the context in our research reporting to provide a starting point for crafting a context narrative. We have paraphrased these as follows.

1. Open with the big picture, describe a situation.
2. Then describe a problem or question that arises from that big-picture situation, narrowing down to your specific focus for the research while connecting to the context you are working in.
3. Connect to how others have explored or approached that problem or question in your literature review (or equivalent).
4. Connect to this previous work by explaining a need to approach it in an alternative way, or describe how you will expand upon what currently exists.
5. Articulate what you aim to do by describing who, when, where, how and why.

Another way that we can craft the context when working with creative methods is to reflect on previous studies. The following case studies provide inspiration for approaching, working in and establishing the context in educational spaces:

• walking interviews where the researcher positions the participant at the heart of the natural context by walking alongside while being guided by the participant during an interview and physical location tour;
• drawing weekly lived experiences on a postcard to highlight how pen and paper can be used to engage with line symbols, colour, texture and materials to communicate context as part of a self-study;
• dance as a way of knowing where the researcher is embodied in the context and process;
• *lectio divina*, where the researcher positions the participant response, and creation of text that communicates context; and
• hip hop that integrates context through the research process.

Walking interviews

Walking interviews, sometimes referred to as 'intraviews' (Kuntz and Presnall, 2012), enable researcher and participant to work together and be in the context of the research setting in unique ways. This is particularly useful when the field or site is relevant to both the research (aims and questions) and the participants. During this process the interview is recorded and photographs of the context may also be generated (Cox, 2017; Kinney, 2017). Walking interviews are usually carried out with the researcher walking alongside the participant in a given location or space (Kinney, 2017). As a creative method this way of working is emerging in qualitative research to place the participant at the centre of the research (Sheller and Urry, 2006). In studies using a participatory methodology, the participant selects the location and the route for the interview (Evans and Jones, 2011). Walking together helps to reduce the impact of any power imbalances and encourages spontaneous conversation or non-rehearsed responses (Moles, 2008; Saunders and Moles, 2016; Cox, 2017; Kinney, 2017; Springgay and Truman, 2019). The process enables the focus on sharing and an opening up or freedom to connect as it is viewed that 'talking becomes easier with walking' (Kinney, 2017, p 1). The participant becomes the expert, who guides or escorts the researcher around, to and between specific areas in their lives or context that are significant to them. Thus, there is a combination of interview questions and participant observation with the aim 'to provide insight into the sense of attachment a participant has with their neighbourhood' (Kinney, 2017, p 2).

CASE STUDY 3.1: WALKING INTERVIEW IN A LIBRARY AS AN INFORMAL LEARNING SPACE

Who and where: In 2015 the University of Sheffield, UK library team investigated the student experience of their learning spaces and/or facilities. This investigation included a space of 19 labs, speciality teaching facilities and a 24/7 library. The research was led by Andrew Cox.

What: Cox (2017) aimed to investigate student experience of the informal learning spaces in a higher education library to draw out how 11 students from a number of social science departments perceived the library.

Why: Walking interviews offered the researchers an opportunity to gain insights into their participants' connections to place and glean how they engaged with the environment. In this case, the walking interview method enabled the researchers to describe the context within the research, unpack the physical space, associations and engagement and provide a rich, in-depth narrative of the participants' experiences.

How: The researcher initially met with each of the participants individually in a warm-up interview. At this face-to-face meeting the researcher worked with the participant to focus on route planning and rapport building. Following this conversation, the walking interview began where the participant guided the researcher around the library, leading them to specific locations and talking through their experiences. There was also an invitation to take photos to record what was seen and discussed. At the conclusion of the walking interview, photos were used to support further discussion.

Tips
- The participant needs to know the brief of the research to be able to contribute meaningfully.
- As a researcher, have some prepared questions to guide the conversation as required.

- Talking about a space and engagement with it can become easier when walking to support the recall of memories and/or experiences. This allows for the context to be expressed in more detail and in connection to associations, versus undertaking a sedentary face-to-face interview.
- Allow the participant to make all the decisions, including the route to be followed, the length of time the walking interview will take and what they would like to show. The participant is in control of the interview; they are the 'tour guide' (Hughes et al, 2014); regard them as experts in their context.
- An alternative can be just walking and talking where the location is not as important to the outcome; rather, it is the process of walking and talking that is important, where the participant can recount experiences that are important to them in relation to the research topic. This has been called bimbling (Kinney, 2017).

Traps

- A hazard for a walking interview is when it is carried out in a public space, opening up the need for awareness of the location. For example, think about traffic, other people, natural hurdles – such as weather – as well as the time of the day the walk is done when considering possible interference.
- Incorrect selection of appropriate recording equipment can cause problems. To mitigate this, be careful to select equipment you are familiar with and that can record accurately and clearly, while not obstructing the process, when you are on the move.
- Confidentiality cannot be assured if the walking interview is in a public place (Emmel and Clark, 2009). Before undertaking a walking interview in a public space discuss with the participant some protocols that would support how they would like to handle a situation where they meet someone they know while on the walking interview.

Reflective questions

1. How could walking interviews enable you to communicate your research context?
2. How can walking interviews support the communication of the participant voice and lived experience?
3. How can walking interviews work in partnership with other methods to capture the context?
4. What benefits exist for you as a researcher to engage with a walking interview, versus engaging with a conventional, sedentary interview? What impact could this have on communicating the context of your research?

Drawing data

Drawing data can offer a participatory experience in research, though we acknowledge that sometimes drawing is used in researcher-directed and quantitative studies which do not take a participatory approach (see, for example, the work of Kate Coleman as referred to in Chapter 4 or discussion of this in the work of Philippa Lyon, 2019). In this section we focus on drawing as a participatory experience. From this perspective, it is a data-gathering method that offers great flexibility. It could stand alone as a way to share insights connected to the research question(s), it could be used to communicate the context or it could be data that can sit alongside data from other methods such as interviews or focus groups.

In self-study, researchers draw on a wide range of methods to produce, collect and interpret data (Pithouse et al, 2009) that focus on understanding self that is a resource for both professional and personal development (Margolis, 2018). These methods are often qualitative and offer much opportunity for creative approaches to be explored, including other methods such as poetry, dance, drama, movement, art making or journaling. Pen-to-paper drawing is a method for recollecting, representing and examining context and lived experiences (Derry, 2005; Pithouse, 2011). Giorgina Lupi and Stefanie Posavec (2016) have worked with drawing in self-study as an everyday act that is tangible for the creation of data. We unpack this in the following case study.

CASE STUDY 3.2: DRAWING WEEKLY LIVED EXPERIENCES ON A POSTCARD

Who and where: For a year, Giorgina Lupi (UK) and Stefanie Posavec (US) communicated with each other via postcards as both researchers and participants.

What: Postcards were hand-drawn, communicating engagement, participation and experience of lived experiences and the context of daily life. The researcher-participants started with creative exploration through drawing to communicate and work with context as data. The exploration of line, shape, texture, colour and materials enabled a slowing down and noticing of how they engaged with self and others.

Why: Through this hand-drawn visualisation a 'personal documentary' is created whereby we can 'see data as a creative material like paint or paper, an outcome of a new way of seeing and engaging with our world' (Lupi and Posavec, 2016, p xi). The act of this noticing and documenting is in itself a way to communicate context, as it invites one to 'slow down and appreciate the small details of life, and to make connections with other people' (Lupi and Posavec, 2016, p xi). The researcher-participants also found that paying attention to these behaviours through drawing caused expansion of such behaviours, and argued that therefore they could 'use the data to become more humane and to connect with ourselves and others at a deeper level' (Lupi and Posavec, 2016, p xi).

How: The process involves:

- beginning with a question – what do you want to explore?
- thinking about what you are noticing (themes and timeframe);
- collecting and drawing with data – raw initial capturing, then final representation;
- spending time with the data before visually representing it;
- noticing, based on a theme, then visually representing it (connecting back to the question);
- organising and categorising (finding the main story);
- developing a code to decipher the visual icons and overall picture to help decode how to read them;
- sketching a first idea of visualisation; and
- drawing a final visual iteration.

Tips

- Hand-written is the key, and is celebrated through drawing, even if generated digitally through a tablet and e-pen.
- Explore different symbols and materials to depict themes.
- Consider how context and time are communicated.
- Be careful to be accurate, but simplify.
- In order to facilitate audience engagement, remember to develop a key to support the interpretation of drawings.

Traps

- Too much detail can distract attention from the context and data.
- Drawings can be difficult to interpret.

Reflective questions

1. How can drawing inform the communication of context(s)?
2. How could you use drawing as a form of data?
3. How can a participant be part of the data-collection phase when using drawing?
4. What ways of drawing might you consider? Individual? Group? Random? As a part of an interview process? Standalone? Other?
5. How could the process of drawing support your connection to the research question and the participants involved?

Text, poetry and creative expression

Creative writing expressed through text such as poetry has long been used in education as a form of reflection, expression and/or contemplative practice. In this way it can be a representation of participants and/or context (Fernández-Giménez et al, 2018; McDonough, 2018). Poetic representation as a creative research method provides a vehicle to connect participants with an audience through representations of lived experience, thus providing a deeper connection to the research area being communicated (Pickering and Kara, 2017). This is especially important when thinking about and communicating the context.

For educators, poetry can provide opportunities to highlight how voice and lived experiences can be expressed in authentic ways that humanise practice, theory and education (Fernández-Giménez et al, 2018; Hall, 2019). For example, Sharon McDonough (2018) used poetry to represent interviews with mentors – those working in schools as teachers taking on mentoring roles with pre-service teachers during work experience (there is more information about this in case study 6.3). Similarly, Clarrie Smith (2019, p 78) illustrated career stories lived by early-childhood professionals, giving agency to 'how stories become tools through which individuals attempt to navigate their intensions [sic], desires or wishes amongst the structural forces that shape their lives'. Maureen Hall (2019) enacted poetry as a contemplative practice integrated into the curriculum as a pedagogical process to illuminate the whole person and voices of the K–10 classroom. In this way poetry was a process and outcome.

Each of these three examples showcases how poetry can transform experience and enable an empathy for self and others while exploring self in relation to the larger world. In case study 3.3 we focus on Hall's work using the method of *lectio divina* as a contemplative practice that is located within transformative learning theory. This is a 'process by which individuals can craft a new or revised interpretation of meaning of their experience', thus enabling 'deeper, more personal, and perhaps more insightful ways of constructing knowledge' (Dalton et al, 2019, p 7). Opportunities are provided for communal engagement and meaning making, enhancing connections to the context of research and positioning self and others in creative ways.

CASE STUDY 3.3: *LECTIO DIVINA* AS A WAY TO CREATE MEANING OF LIVED EXPERIENCES

Who and where: Maureen Hall, a teacher/educator at the University of Massachusetts, Dartmouth, US, integrates *lectio divina* as a way to experience language and meaning in a secondary classroom.

What: *Lectio divina* as a pedagogical intervention humanises the educational process, where people read texts and respond through poetry or prose as a contemplative practice that supports participants in feeling empathy for self and others within their community.

Why: To provide an opportunity to be present with learning and to highlight connectivity, insight, relationality. This approach also helps to build meaningful relationships between and with one's own experiences and those of others in context. Opportunity is afforded to embody learning offering a 'deep reading' where attention is experienced to the moment right now. At the heart of working this way is listening to lived experiences with heart, soul and ears, offering a holistic way to engage with meaning-making.

How: *Lectio divina* involves four phases.

1. *Lectio* phase. A short poem or piece of writing is chosen by the facilitator. The first phase of reading occurs. Participants are invited to silently read, consider and ponder on the text as a whole and sections of it while noting words and phrases individually. After reading, there is a period of silence to consider and reflect upon the text. Following this silence, participants are asked to identify a word or phrase that captures their attention, and this is shared with the group.
2. *Meditatio phase.* The selected short poem or piece of writing is read aloud. The facilitator invites participants to make connections to the text and share insights as to meaning. As this phase progresses participants are invited to share their reaction to the process in relation to the text. Participants are then invited to analyse, make connections through clustering words, phrases, meanings, and also to consider their own relationship with the text. Following this discussion, a period of silence follows to process readers' personal relationship with a specific phrase within the text; then this is shared with the group.
3. *Oratio phase.* This involves responding to the specific phrase identified in the meditatio phase. This may be in the form of poetry, a letter or a written expression of gratitude to the author. An invitation to share is offered.
4. *Contemplatio phase.* This phase sees a resting in the contemplation of the text to spark wisdom and insight. Participants are invited to let go of the words and embrace an embodiment that sees them share what they have learned. Further response is sought – what has changed you? What have you noticed in yourself? What insights have been sparked?

Tips
*   Select an appropriate text to support engagement in this way of processing knowledge and meaning making.
*   In an alternative approach, *Visio divina*, a text is replaced with a visual item such as an artwork.
*   The facilitator needs to be involved in the process of learning with the participants.
*   Each participant's responses will be unique, and an openness to embracing this is encouraged.
*   Invite participants to share their own text so as to be a part of the process.

Traps

- This process takes time, and without enough time engagement may not be meaningful.
- Without mutual respect, participants will not be open to different perspectives.
- Care is needed in choosing the text to represent the purpose of your research, identifying the nature of embodiment and lived experiences being shared.

Reflective questions

1. How could a *lectio divina* contribute to setting up the context, relevance and significance of a research project?
2. How can different texts prompt a specific topic or theme focus that is connected to your research questions and context?
3. How would you document the process and end product as part of the research process in a way that acknowledges the context?
4. Where do you locate the participant voice so that this approach to data generation is indicative of the context?

Dance

Dance in education research enables movement, exploration, capacity to respond and a presence that facilitates negotiation of moving the body with others and in space (Rank, 2011). It is:

> interactive, holistic and it's specific. When people dance, they're aware of past experience. They're also actively engaged in the present: considering the quality, size, speed, direction, orientation and intent of their movement while simultaneously negotiating their moving bodies with other dancers in the space. (Rank, 2011, p 2)

Dance brings to the fore the embodiment of research – a process that some have argued can never truly be 'disembodied' (Ellingson, 2017; Thanem and Knights, 2019). Dance as a creative research method foregrounds an 'alternative narrative inquiry that allows for the exploration of one's own lived experiences evoking the communication of multi-cultural knowledge, self-understanding, and representation of being' (Bochner and Ellis, 2003, p 506). From an arts-based inquiry perspective, dance is one example of a creative expression that utilises artistic process; that is, the action of making and doing as a means of understanding experience. In this perspective, dance may be used to understand specific aspects of dance, or to understand the way choreography communicates meaning and/or context (Savin-Baden and Wimpenny, 2014).

Dance can be used as an evaluative process and also for dissemination (Cancienne and Snowber, 2003). This illuminates how creative processes can be positioned as central to both presenting the whole person and facilitating the understanding of an issue. Thus, dance 'is not only an expression of our research but a form of inquiry into the research process' (Cancienne and Snowber, 2003, p 237). It is an essential part of discovery and curiosity that places the context of the participant, audience and reader at the heart. Dance becomes a way of knowing (Snowber, 2012), and thus dance is being positioned as one context where research takes place, as well as a potential element within that or other research.

CASE STUDY 3.4: DANCE AS A WAY OF KNOWING

Who and where: Mary Beth Cancienne and Celeste Snowber, located in the US and Canada, call themselves 'moving researchers' (Cancienne and Snowber, 2003, p 237). They use choreography, dance and writing as integral parts of their work as arts-based researchers.

What: Cancienne and Snowber use choreography to explore dance as a place of inquiry and the body as a site for knowledge. They do this to examine how this awareness influences their interpretation of education research, including contexts. They view dance as 'a form of inquiry into the research process' (Cancienne and Snowber, 2003, p 237) that draws on 'phenomenological curriculum research as well as autobiographical and narrative inquiry as models for integrating dance within the research process' (Cancienne and Snowber, 2003, p 238).

Why: The body is viewed as a site of knowledge. Dance is seen as fundamental to this as expression and as part of the research process with 'each person's movement schema express[ing] social and cultural meanings' (Cancienne and Snowber, 2003, p 239) that are communicated 'through voice, gesture, and movement' (Cancienne and Snowber, 2003, pp 243–4).

How: The process involves:

1. exploring a theme or topic positioned in context;
2. writing the performance, reflecting on aspects of the research process where the body is not just the tool to express but is also the locus for discovery (self as a place of discovery) (Cancienne and Snowber, 2003);
3. while writing, selecting music, space and place to express context and cultural connections while also exploring how the body can communicate – how hands, legs, torso, face, limbs, gestures are understood;
4. rehearsing;
5. performing;
6. participating in a post-performance dialogue with the audience; and
7. reflecting and connecting to knowledge and meaning-making.

Tips

- Remember that dance and choreographic process involves sorting, sifting, editing, forming, making and remaking in connection to context, participants, research process and audience.
- Connect with the audience about how the performance can inform their own educational journey and discoveries.
- Notice and embrace the difference in inquiry, paying attention to the present.
- Writing of the performance and any subsequent performance becomes a part of the discovery and research process.

Trap

- Body and movement can often be silenced in education and education research. For this approach to work, the body should be seen as a way to release, connect and understand without restriction.

Reflective questions

1. How can dance communicate knowledge?
2. How can dance be a form of creative method that communicates context?
3. How would you document the process and end product of dance as part of the research process while including the context?
4. What is the place of the participant voice in this approach to data generation that is indicative of the context?

Song, hip hop and spoken-word poetry

Popular culture expressed through music, song and spoken-word poetry enables participants to use their voices (Emdin and Adjapong, 2018). Educators and researchers have been exploring how the context of marginalised voices, especially young people's voices, can be expressed through these techniques (Emdin and Adjapong, 2018; Levy et al, 2018). Embodiment and leadership can be expressed through song and the spoken word in ways not able to be achieved through other methods (Avolio et al, 2009; Ashkanasy and Dasborough, 2010; Ladkin and Taylor, 2010; Winther, 2012, 2013). Embracing this way of working highlights how sound and music can support the communication of context and lived experiences. This can support the communication of an educational process that can be difficult to document through non-verbal language alone (Winther, 2018).

CASE STUDY 3.5: HIP HOP AND YOUTH VOICE

Who and where: Researchers, educators and counsellors in the US have been working with youth of colour to highlight a 'shift in pedagogical and counselling frameworks to highlight youth voice and culture' (Levy et al, 2018, p 8). These people illuminated the 'importance of hip-hop culture as a community-driven movement that has enabled marginalized communities to share untold stories and navigate the stressors they faced in daily lives' (Levy et al, 2018, p 2).

What: A two-fold process was developed. First, youth participatory action research (YPAR) is a research process conducted between youth and school counsellors who engage in shared discussion to investigate a topic of direct interest to young people's personal lives and their communities. This is amalgamated with a second step called Hip Hop and Spoken Word Therapy (HHSWT), where youth engage with music to share the context of their lived experience specifically focusing on those from a background of colour where mental health and inequalities, ethnic, racial and socioeconomic issues are experienced as a result of racism. In this second step, sharing of knowledge through mix tapes occurs. Mix tapes are compilations of music that people curate themselves. This is underpinned by a counselling framework designed to take the young people through a process of discussing and analysing difficult emotional experiences. The aim is to convert thoughts and feelings into hip-hop songs.

Why: YPAR and HHSWT involves a shared decision-making process where the youth and counsellors work collaboratively. Hip hop is seen as one way to harness conversation and is used 'as a tool to effectively communicate and teach new skills and strategies and to challenge thoughts, ideas, and actions that are largely negative and destructive to minority youth groups' (Levy et al, 2018, p 2). In this way the integration of YPAR and HHSWT processes allows the youth to 'use hip-hop lyric writing, recording, and performing to critically analyse, research, and report on issues of personal importance to them' (Levy et al, 2018, p 5). This positions youth culture at the forefront of the process and context.

How

1. Students in the setting are recognised as experts.
2. Students brainstorm shared objectives with a counsellor, collaborating to scaffold an action-oriented research process.
3. A YPAR group is formed.
4. Students and counsellor collaborate to identify a research topic that is of interest. Encouragement is given to the students to select a topic that captures unique racial, social class, religious and gender-based experiences.
5. Students lead data collection and analyse the topic. The counsellor supports the process by scaffolding and guiding the process of finding data while also supporting the processing of reactions to the data findings.

6. A shared action plan is developed based on the findings, with ongoing reflection occurring and development of awareness skills.
7. Findings are disseminated by the students with support from the school context and the counsellor.
8. The YPAR process and outcomes are reflected on.
9. The findings are then amalgamated in the HHSWT process where hip hop culture is embraced as a way to communicate knowledge, context and experiences. Mix tapes are created, and this becomes a therapeutic process anchored in the creation of an emotionally themed collection of songs.
10. A six-stage cyclical process is used: identify area of interest for the mix tape; research mix tape content; discuss and process findings; develop a track list; plan and record for a release of a mix tape; evaluate mix tape process and response.

Tips
- Embrace the student voice and the context of their lived experience.
- The process should be fluid and student centred.
- Be aware of the context of the youth you are working with and have support systems in place to scaffold reflection and processing of data and findings.
- Respect the themes addressed by the youth as they inquire into the issues that are important to them right now.
- Be mindful of ethical protocols to protect the youth when writing up and disseminating this work.

Trap
- A hazard in working this way can be to become teacher or researcher centred. Remember that this is a student-centred experience. For you as a researcher, setting up protocols to support this way of working is recommended.

Reflective questions
1. What ethical considerations need to be taken into account in setting the context for marginalised voices?
2. How could YPAR and HHSWT be applied in your context to support the sharing of marginalised voices?
3. How can the processes of YPAR and HHSWT support the research context?
4. How can you ensure confidentiality?

Ethical considerations for context setting

Setting the context in education research and considering how participants align to it is important for a number of reasons. Sellers suggests that we need to outline the context for research in a way that illuminates integrity and ethical practice. He states: 'context can be the difference between research and insights' (Sellers, 2014, para 1). It is important to understand the context before we begin our research, and to allow for others to be able to connect and to look at how the research can be both relevant and transferable.

For educators engaging in research within education contexts there are different ways to communicate those contexts and engage with the context that can help to position the research while considering research ethics. To write 'we conducted this research in a classroom' would simply not be enough information. What classroom? When? Where? For how long? What age group? What was the demographic? Was a teacher-researcher or someone else collecting or generating the data? How were the participants engaged in communicating the context? How were they a part of the research collection? What was the classroom like? How was it set up? How did it fit within the wider context of a school, sector or community? And the questions could keep flowing. However, it is also important to remember that sometimes we do not have many words to describe the context (for example, in journal articles or an executive summary in a research report); thus we need to be concise but detailed and accurate at the same time. Likewise, in sharing the details of the context we must be responsible in regard to the safety of those we are working with, while also being responsible for accurate reporting (Gravetter and Forzano, 2018). This is a reminder as to who we identify and how we do this work.

Ethically, when communicating the context in your writing – and indeed when we are in the research context itself – we need to be aware of how we honour the space and participants. We also need to honour past research through accurate citation practices that respect the scholars' work on which we are building. The creative methods shared in this chapter highlight how the participant is vital to the context. No matter what the method – walking interview, dance, poetry, song or drawing – we need to be respectful of the participant(s) in how they engage in the context themselves and how they wish to share their lived experiences. For the researcher, honouring a participant's voice is important, and we also need to carefully consider how the participant is a part of the context and what their role is in communicating this to us. In regard to the context setting, it is vital to consider what you can, cannot and should not reveal as a researcher in regard to self and working with young people and others in educational contexts. This is important for maintaining confidentiality and researcher well-being. It is especially important to consider this as part of ethical processes, and also to include the participants in this process, where possible, when negotiating and communicating our research contexts.

Conclusion

As you work with creative methods there are different ways in which the contexts can be communicated. The role of the researcher is to decide how to do this while both respecting participants and revealing accurate information about the field, site, space and time. In this chapter we have offered a broad overview with case studies that are focused on how the participant and researcher are located.

We have also offered a suggestion for approaching how you can position the contexts within the broader field or area on which your research is focused. In the next two chapters, we delve into examples of two- and three-dimensional and performative data-gathering approaches in education research with young people and adults as ways to support the development of creative research practice in action. As you explore further, we encourage you to consider your research design and how the contexts are revealed.

CHAPTER DISCUSSION QUESTIONS

1. How do you position your research within the context of others' work and the field?

2. How do you position yourself as a researcher within the context you are working in?

3. How do you position the context within the broader scheme of ethical research?

4. What ideas have emerged for you as to how you could approach involving participants in establishing the context of your research?

5. What creative methods could you explore that would connect your audience with the context?

4

Data gathering: research with children and young people

Chapter summary

We begin this chapter by introducing data gathering and discussing good practice in connecting with creative ways to generate data. This includes working to meet the needs of your audience or audiences and engaging with two- or three-dimensional creative methods. We introduce you to some of the different approaches you can take in education research. Then we look specifically at two-dimensional creative methods, keeping in mind this chapter is to be read together with Chapter 5, which covers three-dimensional creative methods.

As we unpack some examples of two-dimensional creative methods we also introduce you to working with children and young people. We frame this as a way to acknowledge that, as educators, much of our research will involve these participants. We invite you to consider ways you can work with young people and children that are inclusive of them as a part of the research process, extending conventional notions of research being done about them. Much of what we discuss in this chapter can be transferred to working with adults in the educational context. Key to this is the place of voice in creative data gathering.

Throughout the chapter we invite you to consider how to work across different sites to collect data; and some ethical considerations for data gathering are raised. This chapter also draws your attention to how hand-held and/or accessible technology can support creative data gathering.

Introduction

When we think about data gathering we are considering a process that may require us to collect, produce and/or measure information on one or more variables of interest. Some data is produced, collected or observational, for example. How we approach and work with data can be influenced by our context, research questions and methodology. In this chapter we focus on data gathering, especially with children and young people.

Data is often gathered in a systematic way, or through a process, with the aim of enabling you to answer research questions, explore a hypothesis or evaluate outcomes. With a creative research methods approach this is no different. When considering data gathering through creative methods the ability to be creative in approach and mindset supports the very act of creativity: engaging with ideas while recognising and supporting the use of imagination, intuition, ingenuity, insight and inspiration. Really, this is an overt acknowledgement of how researchers have always worked.

Data gathering through creative methods is exciting. But we do note that gathering data in creative ways can be so much fun that at times we can forget to stop, and so end up with too much data and a headache at the analysis stage. In the case studies we acknowledge this through the inclusion of subheadings on tips and traps. These are designed to help you recognise some of the thinking required behind creative data-gathering processes.

This chapter presents some examples of creative research data gathering in educational settings as a way to inspire possibilities for how you might work when gathering data. Case studies are provided to stimulate this process, and also to scaffold your plans for research design. We invite you to consider:

- different creative data sources;
- different uses of familiar ways to work in education;
- ways to collaborate in generating data;
- participants as co-researchers for generating data;
- how to work across different sites to collect data;
- how hand-held and accessible technology can support creative data gathering;
- the place of voice in creative data gathering; and
- ethical issues in data gathering.

Creative ways to gather data for education research with children and young people

Gathering and organising data can be fun and creative. When there is openness to exploring, more options for how and what is possible in relation to the communication of information become evident. With the creative process, the progress and effort are in some ways boundaryless. There is a constant moving between infant, developing and mature ways of working that is underpinned by delays, setbacks, curve balls, tangents and inspiring creative steps. This is what makes it exhilarating – though sometimes also frustrating – to work in creative ways. However, when we are working on a research project it can be necessary for some guiding principles to be put in place. This can be approached in a variety of ways, such as through systems that support the data-gathering phase.

Data can be produced in four main ways:

- by a researcher, for research purposes;
- by research participants, for research purposes;

- by researcher and participants together, for research purposes; or
- by anyone for any non-research purpose, then later used for research.

Data from the first three, where it is generated specifically for research, is known as primary data. Data from the fourth is known as secondary data.

If you are coming to creative methods for the first time or are familiar with them but wish to extend possibilities, it can be helpful to have ideas for stimulation. In Table 4.1, we offer some starting points. It is not an extensive list of creative methods but, rather, a beginning point, as the act of creative thinking supports the generation of ideas that might not exist now but can be possible. This is one reason why working this way can be so exciting.

As approaches to doing research are explored, the use of creative research methods lends itself to working with participants and data in different ways. As a result, opportunities arise for new ways of working as part of the engagement with social aspects and the lived experience within the education context. Thus, this extends what data may be able to be, beyond the outputs of more conventional methods such as the quantitative survey, focus groups or interviews.

When working with creative methods and considering the place of data gathering or generation, working collaboratively with participants often becomes possible. It is common practice for participants to have greater editorial control over their material when working with some types of creative data, as they can erase or modify their artefacts and thereby portray aspects important to them. Also for consideration is how the ability to share voice in different ways can be an empowering experience within the education environment. The place of the

Table 4.1: Ideas for creative data gathering

Two-dimensional	Three-dimensional	Performative	Technological
Drawing	Modelling – clay, pipe-cleaners, wire, cardboard, wood, found objects and so on	Dance	Video
Painting	Textile art – knitting, crochet, quilting, embroidery, appliqué and so on	Drama	Social media
Photography	Construction – LEGO®, bricks, boxes and so on	Music	Apps, such as Procreate, Garage band, Adobe suite
Cartoons, comics, graphic novels, zines	Artefacts – constructed, foraged, repurposed	Mobile methods	Smartphones
Maps	Carving, sculpture	Enhanced interviews	Digital portfolios
Graphic organisers	Laser cutting, book art	Poetry reading	Online surveys

researcher needs to be considered in terms of the position of authority and how this is interpreted by the participants. For example, when working with young people, what is the researcher: a teacher, a visitor such as an artist or someone viewed as an authority figure? How does this appear to the participants? What strategies and support systems are put in place to support the construction of a community that is underpinned by mutual respect, trust and openness? How does this impact on the flow connected to creativity and the methods selected?

In this chapter we connect with some of the ideas presented in Table 4.1. We consider some examples of how and what is possible when we collect data in and through creative ways. We share data possibilities in educational spaces with digital portfolios (technological), photography (two-dimensional and technological), graphic organisers as learning and teaching artefacts (two-dimensional) and cartoon storyboards (two-dimensional). The case studies presented in this chapter emphasise data gathering with children and young people in the compulsory education sector. In Chapter 5 we focus on data gathering with adults.

Digital portfolios for reflection and learning in art education

A digital portfolio is a space where one can curate and design personal and professional identity through artefacts that are generated over time and space (Coleman, 2018). In a portfolio there is opportunity to share reflections that link to learning. Sometimes these are aligned to specific criteria, formally or informally; however, they are underpinned by a documentation process that showcases or makes visible skills or expertise. A portfolio is also a space of memory and invites critical thinking and critique. A digital portfolio can be a form of critical autoethnography (Marx et al, 2017) that involves taking a gaze inwardly – that is, reflecting upon oneself and sharing the journey of becoming through a personal story narrative. Coleman (2018, p 95) notes that a digital portfolio is a 'curated site of exhibition, a digital cabinet of wonder, a *wunderkammer* created and systemised for the audience through a process of self-reflection in open digital spaces'. As such, the digital element of a portfolio enables an enactment where both self and an audience, those viewing, can connect. Making, thinking, doing and curating are enacted in a digital portfolio with new knowledge about practice and creativity presented and performed, and this can be through a variety of forms such as digital journal entries, narratives, poetry, personal writing, visual narratives or blogs.

CASE STUDY 4.1: A LIVING INQUIRY OF DIGITAL PORTFOLIOS FOR REFLECTION AND LEARNING IN ART EDUCATION

Who and where: This case study outlines research on digital portfolios for reflection and learning in art education by Kate Coleman, a teacher/educator in art and creativity studies in Melbourne, Australia.

What: Coleman's focus was on how digital portfolios support identity development and the formation of self as an artist. She used a combination of autoethnographic writing, action research practices, practice-based art research and arts-based education research in her study to attend to contemporary professional visual artist portfolios.

Why: The proposition was that learning through the ways that we design and curate our digital portfolios enables reflection over time. Portfolios and the artwork they contain become part of the process of making and reflection whereby stories are told and retold as the portfolio develops a narrative structure of research participation.

How: Coleman interviewed ten artists, who were also secondary school teachers, about their arts practices and how they used their digital artist portfolio to support learning. The interviews were video-recorded and edited into films to support the written thesis. Coleman also developed her own portfolio through her arts practice, with her artworks informing critical reflection on her analysis of the data and findings and her own formation as an artist. Coleman's artwork of collage, paper weavings, photographs, paintings and drawings was exhibited as part of the research process.

Tips
- Identify artists and artistic communities that may be interested in your research. Your research contribution to the community may become an important aspect of your study.
- Be aware that there are many different art worlds in play; artists who show in commercial galleries may approach their work in different ways to artists who show artworks in artist-run spaces or have a social, community or academic research practice.

Trap
- The main principles of this study were giving voice to the way artists make artwork and the development of their portfolios to enable a reflective learning approach. This is a risky proposition for artists, as the usually private act of developing new skills and capacities is made public. However, if they are part of a supportive community of artists, this risk can be mitigated.

Reflective questions

1. What are some examples of art making and portfolio development which could enhance data generation?
2. How might the researcher's own art-making and portfolio practices affect learning?
3. What do you think is the role of reflection in data generation when the researcher has access to and is participating in an artistic community?
4. How could art making be a part of data gathering for your project?
5. How can art making and portfolio practices activate reflection as part of the data-gathering process?
6. How could students be co-researchers in the classroom using digital portfolios?

Students as co-researchers, technology and being a digital image maker

In gathering data in educational spaces, young people can be viewed as capable co-researchers. An approach as researcher(s) builds on the notion that 'children have a voice, but it is a voice that is seldom heard' (Egg et al, 2004, p 3). In viewing children as co-researchers who can *do* research *with* the teacher-researcher, this approach challenges what we understand about children and childhood. In taking this stance, education is seen as critical practice and young people are seen as active learners (MacNaughton, 2005) who are able to articulate their ideas. Therefore, it is the task of adults to understand the ways in which children choose to express themselves (Egg et al, 2004; Lemon, 2019). When a researcher or research team takes this approach these methods have the potential to give voice to the voiceless and centre young people who are the intended beneficiaries of curriculum policies and reform.

There are many creative approaches to investigating education spaces in this way. One approach can be to invite children as co-researchers to be digital image makers (Lemon, 2017, 2019) and to utilise technology as a data-gathering tool. A strength of working visually in education is that digital technology makes it possible to slow down and repeat observations (Prosser, 1998) of learning environments. Digital cameras are a resource for teaching in the classroom and in other educational spaces (Eber, 2002; Lemon, 2007, 2019). While the digital camera is in use in the classroom as part of the curriculum, as a tool for reflection, the learning space is being promoted as one where real-life and practical experiences are supported and provided (authentic and inclusive learning) (Thelning and Lawes, 2001; Lemon and Finger, 2013; Lemon, 2019). Other technology with camera capacity, such as tablets and smartphones, can also be used (Clark and Moss, 2001; Tinker and Krakcik, 2001; Swan et al, 2005; Lemon, 2019). The technology allows the user to take a photo, see immediately if it needs to be retaken, delete if necessary, print to a printer or save directly to a computer, all at the touch of a couple of buttons. These digital resources offer children and young people ways to explore, interact with and influence their environments and solve problems while also being creative by representing their ideas in words, sounds and images. Learning activities with and for digital technologies can be open ended, relevant, supportive and purposeful, and they provide immediate feedback.

Photo self-elicitation uses photographs taken by the participants, rather than provided by the researcher, as data to inform the research interview (Harper, 2002).[1] In this method, the use of photographs evokes feelings and additional information that are connected to memories, and supports the telling of a story. It should be noted that multiple readings can come from a reading and rereading and, as such, the narrative can evolve.

CASE STUDY 4.2: CHILDREN AS DIGITAL IMAGE MAKERS – PHOTO SELF-ELICITATION

Who and where: The case study is set in an early childhood classroom in Melbourne, Australia where one of the authors (Lemon) was the teacher and researcher.

What: To explore the perspectives of teaching and learning of 17 children aged between five and seven years. The students, as co-researchers, actively contributed as digital image-makers (Lemon, 2007, 2019) by photographing their lived classroom experiences.

Why: In this study, the digital photographs generated by the children provided multiple perspectives on teaching and learning. From a constructivist position, these photographs allowed audiences – be they parents, teachers, academics, adults, community, youth or children – to discuss teaching and learning from a perspective other than the teacher's or a researcher's.

Photos 4.1 to 4.5: Ben's visual narratives after 30 minutes of using the digital camera in the classroom

Photo 4.1

Ben: They were working really good. No one was looking at me they just knew I was taking a picture.
Narelle: How did you take the photo?
Ben: I crouched down like a ball was going to hit me, so when they were working I just took the photo.
Narelle: What is this photo of?
Ben: It is when they were working really quiet.

Narelle: What were they doing?

Ben: They are working really quiet on bingo, and they have to listen to what number you are saying.

Narelle: What did you learn from taking the photo?

Ben: Like how quiet they can work.

Photo 4.2

Ben: That one's about like you are telling like saying bingo. Celia is coming up to show you bingo. You are telling him to stay down while she is coming through.

Photo 4.3

Ben: It about ... it is another crouch back one. They are working quiet playing bingo.

Narelle: Do you mean that they are concentrating?

Ben: Yep and that they are not looking at other people's stuff, they are looking at their own, so they can say bingo.

Photo 4.4

Ben: I wanted to see what Stan was thinking.

Photo 4.5

Narelle: Tell me about this one?

Ben: Well this one, they are all helping each other, to see each other if they have the number, to help them if they didn't see the number. And also, they were working quietly.

Narelle: How did you take the photo?

Ben: I looked down at them, I stood on my tippee toes and that is how I took it.

Narelle: Did you like using the camera?

Ben: Yes, it was pretty fun taking the photos.

Narelle: Why?

Ben: Well it was like also fun looking at the picture bit after I took it, it was like I was looking through binoculars but it remembers what I was seeing.

How: In this study, the children were asked to participate in classroom activities as usual, and were invited to use a digital camera as another way for them to reflect on their learning and to share their voice.

In setting up the use of a digital camera in the classroom for students to be digital image makers some guidelines need to be established. Think about:

- establishing a schedule co-designed with the children;
- setting guidelines about not posing for the camera when it is in use. Rather, data is being collected visually to support an understanding of learning in a naturalist environment;
- choice and agency for each child if they want to use the digital camera in their scheduled time;
- the time allocated for use of the camera by each child;
- safety for the children and technology; and
- how the children will share their narrative associated to the photograph(s). The following are examples of how you could invite reflection from the children.
  - Use a part of a photograph, draw what is missing and then reflect about what is happening.
  - Take a 'photograph in your head' of something that happened to you at school today. Draw and write about that.
  - As a class, create a graffiti wall about a series of photos or a photo.
  - Talk about your photos one-to-one with your teacher.
  - Present your photos to the class. Create a mind map about a photo you have taken.
  - Take a self-portrait and write about yourself. Look at a photo of the class participating in an activity and write about that.

    —   Take a series of photos or one photo and write or talk about them.

    —   Take five photos that are important to you anywhere in the school.

    —   Write a story about what your photographs mean to you.

Tips

- Plan and develop guidelines with the students so that they will feel valued for contributing their voice (see below for ideas).
- Be open to different learning and teaching moments that enable you to use the student-generated photographs to create visual narratives.
- The digital camera should be a part of the classroom, not an extra element on the side but an integral part of the teaching and learning for all 'learners' in the classroom. The children become collaborators in the process of documenting, gathering data and curating their lived experiences in the classroom.

Trap

- It is important that all the voices of the classroom are heard. This challenges traditional power notions of a classroom where the teacher directs the learning, and opens the perspective that we are all learners, acknowledging that the role of 'teacher' could be transferred to anyone. This can be a challenging proposition for some educators.

Reflective questions

1. How might digital technologies be a part of data generation?
2. What are some examples of new and emerging digital technologies which you believe could enhance data generation?
3. What do you think is parents'/caregivers' role in helping young children to participate in the use of digital technologies for data generation?
4. What are the potential and possibilities for the use of digital cameras to support and enhance data gathering in education research?
5. How can students be co-researchers in the classroom?
6. How could photo self-elicitation be a part of data gathering for your project?
7. How can photographs empower participants as part of the data-gathering process?

Visual ways to show thinking: learning and teaching artefacts

In different educational settings graphic organisers, or visual organisers as they are sometimes called, are used to visually develop and represent people's thinking to themselves and others. Graphic organisers facilitate understanding through visual representations (Kim et al, 2004) and can take the form of a knowledge map, concept map, mind map, web map, story map, cognitive organiser, advance organiser or concept diagram. In education, graphic organisers are used as a pedagogical tool where visual symbols are used to express relationships between knowledge and concepts.

Graphic organisers are commonly used as a type of advance organiser that represents thinking. They are presented before, during or at the conclusion of learning so that the learner can organise and interpret new, incoming information. They are also a tool used to reflect and to show development of understanding. Wilson and Murdoch (2009) note that one of the benefits of graphic organisers is that they are an innovative and creative way to communicate thinking that requires few words. There are many opportunities to use these planning tools as research data.

Various different types of graphic organiser can support the key ideas in a specific task (Novak and Gowin, 1984), providing the flexibility to:

- show planning;
- communicate thinking;
- provide a visual road map, with pathways to connect meanings or ideas; or
- support a schematic summary of what has been learned or questions that are posed.

Nettelbeck (2005) contends that there is nothing difficult about using graphic organisers in learning and teaching, though it does require a supportive, cooperative, risk-taking culture within schools or educational settings. Utilising graphic organisers provides the option to diversify learning tasks and make learning more creative, open-ended and exciting, thus supporting creativity and ingenuity among those creating the visual. For educators looking to investigate creative research methods, graphic organisers afford the opportunity to explore how pedagogical tools can also produce data.

In the next part of this chapter we share two case studies that apply the use of visual representations of thinking in two different ways. The first is graphic organisers, and this is followed by cartoon storyboards.

CASE STUDY 4.3: GRAPHIC ORGANISERS AS PART OF THE CURRICULUM AND A DATA SOURCE

Who and where: 'What is public art?' was an overarching question posed as part of a two-year project carried out with primary school art teachers. The project involved a partnership in Australia across a number of organisations: the Department of Education and Early Childhood Development (Victoria); the New South Wales Department of Education; Kaldor Public Art Projects; Teamboard Australian; and the teaching professional support body Art Education Victoria.

What: A total of ten teachers and 964 students from Grades 1 to 6 (aged 6 to 12 years) participated in the project to showcase the place public art can have in and across the primary school curriculum.

Why: The project aimed to motivate primary school art teachers to extend their professional knowledge of contemporary artists, the visual arts curriculum and how their students learn in and through art.

Figure 4.1: Venn diagram as used in uncovering types of public art work

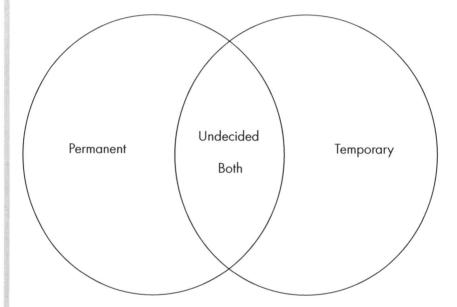

How: Different sets of data were collected to support the understanding of student learning over time through the inquiry stages of engage, explore, explain, elaborate and evaluate. These sets of data were gathered using graphic organisers such as:

- Y charts;
- Venn diagrams;
- T charts;
- storyboards;
- SWOT data capturing strengths, weaknesses, observations (rather than opportunities) and threats;
- reflection placements;
- mind maps; and
- web maps.

These were also supported by other creative research methods, including:

- wonder walls, where inquiry questions were posed;
- the generation of artwork;
- student-led interviews that investigated the overarching inquiry question with the community;
- exhibition;
- walking reflections;
- online journals capturing reflections and understanding over time;
- performances through drama and dance;
- photographs; and
- video.

Photos 4.6 and 4.7 show one example of an interactive learning activity utilising a Venn diagram model to help students decide which artworks were permanent or temporary or a bit of both. The teacher placed hoops on the carpet to form a Venn diagram, and each child was given a photo of a type of public art work that they had to classify by placing it in the relevant section of the Venn diagram. This engaging inquiry activity generated data which was analysed to influence the curriculum design.

Photo 4.6: Georgia, Shae, Sarah, James and Cody (Grade 1) are discussing their decisions about where they placed their examples of public art in the Venn diagram.

Photo 4.7: Josh (Grade 1) is placing his example of public art in the permanent section.

Tips

- It is possible to adapt various organisers to suit a range of purposes, but it is important that the intended purpose is clear and the organiser chosen is appropriate and suitable for the kind of thinking involved.
- Discuss with students the background to the graphic organiser selected and how it can communicate the processing of thinking. Also discuss why it is relevant for the learning process, and indeed the research process.
- Plan ahead for the use of creative method in the classroom and how this can be documented in a meaningful way.
- Move beyond a paper version of a graphic organiser.
- Support students' thinking and ask them to explain their ideas as they draft and complete a final version of a graphic organiser.

Trap

- This cannot be done quickly. Students need time to draft how they might present their thinking before completing the final product. If insufficient time is allocated or available, this method will not be useful.

Reflective questions

1. How could a graphic organiser support data gathering for your project?
2. What other ways of working with graphic organisers could be used, rather than paper recording?
3. How would you document the process and end product as part of the research process?
4. What is the place of the participant in this approach to data generation?

Pedagogical approaches for data generation

Creative research methods and the act of data generation can allow participants to play a meaningful part in the research process (Lemon, 2013a). In Kaye Johnson's (2008) work with young children photographing and drawing their everyday experiences of school, she highlights a pedagogical approach that enables children to become competent co-researchers in representing, interpreting and responding to their everyday school experiences. In so doing she illuminates the need to be able to develop young people's specific skills and expertise in engaging with creative research methods. Johnson recommends explicitly teaching the 'research skills and processes that children would need to become active, confident co-researchers' (Johnson, 2008, p 79).

The pedagogical approach developed recommends:

- finding out what children understand about research and how it connects with their knowledge and experiences;
- exploring the use of creative research methods with the children; and

- giving information about the research you are interested in as an educator, the purposes of the research you propose to carry out and the associated ethical considerations.

This illuminates how children need to be taught how to be co-researchers and how they are to work in collecting the data (Fielding, 2001). Case study 4.4 is an example of such a pedagogical approach in practice.

CASE STUDY 4.4: CARTOON STORYBOARDS

Who and where: Kate Wall and her colleagues in the UK worked with students aged 4–16 in over 50 schools, including primary, secondary and special schools, in four regions of England in 2003–10.

What: An investigation of students' understandings of how they learn and why they learn in those ways, using blank cartoon storyboard templates of six boxes in two rows of three for students to tell the story of when they learned something new. This was in a wider context of practitioner inquiry through action research (Wall et al, 2017, p 211).

Why: To provide a task that was both understandable and enjoyable, within a supportive environment. Also, to facilitate communication in a way that did not rely exclusively on literacy, with the aim of making participation more accessible and inclusive for younger children and those with special needs; and to facilitate more detailed and authentic reflections on students' experiences by moving away from the standard question-and-answer approach. Visual methods were previously shown to work well for this purpose (Wall, Higgins and Packard, 2007). The use of speech and thought bubbles can help even very young children to discuss learning and demonstrate metacognitive awareness (Wall, 2008; Wall et al, 2013). Sequential storytelling allows exploration beyond a single learning moment to a series over time.

How: Usually in small groups of five or six students working with a member of the research team; sometimes with the whole class when necessary. The prompt given was: 'Tell me the story of when you learned something new.' It was made clear that this did not have to be at school, and could be any kind of learning – a skill, some information or something about the pupil themselves – in any environment. This proved to be a very successful way of gathering data. The researchers collected 212 completed storyboards from pupils aged 4–16 which formed a rich and complex dataset (Wall et al, 2017, p 215).

Tip
- When working with creative methods, always have a plan B for participants who don't want to join in with plan A. In this research, pupils who didn't want to participate were allowed to do other fun things such as use a computer.

Traps

- The medium can influence the nature of the response (Wall et al, 2017, p 222). In this case, for example, younger children were more likely to draw pictures in the top three boxes with text in the bottom row, which suggests that the task was more challenging for younger children. It is essential to pilot creative methods effectively so to avoid these kinds of problems.
- The way the task is structured can also influence the nature of the response. The approach taken here led to most storyboards not focusing on school learning. The researchers suggest that for more specific responses you should structure the task accordingly.
- With large visual datasets, analysis can be very challenging. The researchers developed an innovative mixed-methods approach to analysing their data which is outlined in case study 6.8.

Reflective questions

1. Can you think of non-school educational settings where cartoon storyboards might be useful for data gathering?
2. If you used cartoon storyboards for data gathering, would you always use six boxes in two rows of three, or might you sometimes use a different format? If so, what and why?
3. What might be some disadvantages of using cartoon storyboards for data gathering other than those given in the case study?
4. Could cartoon storyboards be useful for your project? If so, how?
5. What ethical issues might you encounter when using cartoon storyboards for data gathering? How would you address them?

Ethical considerations for data gathering with children and young people

Data gathering is the stage of research that receives most attention during formal ethical review. The aspect of data gathering that receives most attention is the well-being of participants. Of course, it is essential that researchers respect participants; tell them enough about the research so that they can make a fully informed decision about whether or not to take part; and maintain their anonymity and confidentiality (where that is appropriate). However, there are other ethical considerations at the data–gathering stage, such as: working with gatekeepers; seeking consent from parents or carers; gathering data in communities; and researcher safety.

Gatekeepers are people who can put you in touch with participants – or refuse to do so. You should treat gatekeepers with respect and politeness, even if they are saying 'no' when you want them to say 'yes'. This can be frustrating, but remember that they may have reasons that they are not free to share with you. Working through gatekeepers can be particularly complex in research with children and young people, where you may need to go through several different gatekeepers before you can speak to a potential participant. For example, if you want to do research in a school you may need agreement first from the principal or head teacher, then from a departmental head or class teacher, and you may even have to deal with 'peer gatekeepers', who can influence their friends' decisions about whether or not to take part in your research (Agbebiyi, 2013, p 537). You would also need permission from the board which oversees the school governance, and then permission from the parents or carers of children under the age of majority. And in many situations, it is good practice to also seek permission from the young people themselves.

It is worth remembering that some parents or carers may experience difficulties that can impair their ability to give consent. These difficulties may stem from alcohol or drug addiction, poor mental health or adverse side-effects from prescribed medication. In such cases the children may be more able to give consent than their parents or carers (Bray, 2014, p 32). The only way to resolve this is through continuing engagement with the family (Bray, 2014, p 34).

Gathering education research data in communities presents a range of ethical problems. Bekisizwe Ndimande conducted research in South Africa, exploring the preferences of Black parents for their children's education in formerly segregated schools. Ndimande worked in Gauteng province, which is one of the most racially and ethnically diverse areas of South Africa. A variety of Indigenous languages are spoken in Gauteng province, such as IsiZulu, Sesotho, IsiXhosa and IsiNdebele. English is also widely spoken, but it is most people's second or third language. Ndimande argues that in this setting it is unethical to force participants to use English, which is the language of colonial dominance (Ndimande, 2012, p 218). Also, allowing participants to switch between languages in their responses, as they would do in everyday life, generates richer data (Ndimande, 2012, p 217).

The safety of researchers is also important. If you are conducting education research in an institution, such as a school, prison or hospital, the institution should have policies and procedures covering the health and safety of visiting professionals. Make sure that you read and understand these before you start work. If you are visiting participants in their homes or community centres you will need to be aware of potential dangers such as aggressive dogs, loose wires or toys on the floor that you could trip over (Bahn and Weatherill, 2013, p 26). Take care to think through any hazards you might encounter while you are gathering data. Research is important, but not important enough to put yourself at risk.

Conclusion

There are a huge variety of creative methods for gathering data in education research. In this chapter we have offered a broad overview with a few examples that are focused on technological and two-dimensional techniques such as digital portfolios, photography, graphic organisers and cartoon storyboards. In the following chapter we delve into examples of data-gathering approaches in education research with adults, focusing on three-dimensional techniques such as LEGO®, sandboxing and work with objects and artefacts. As you explore further, we encourage you to use the bibliography to follow up on methods of interest.

CHAPTER DISCUSSION QUESTIONS

1. What ideas have emerged for you about how you could approach creative research data gathering with children?

2. What data-gathering methods could you explore through two-dimensional or technological approaches that would connect to your research questions?

3. What ethical considerations do you need to bear in mind when gathering data, apart from participant well-being?

Note

[1] Photo self-elicitation has parallels with photovoice; however, the latter method involves one difference. Although researchers invite participants to use cameras, the focus is on individuals to capture representations of everyday life in relation to the often-silenced political sphere within their community. The photos are narrated using their own voices (Foster-Fishman et al, 2005), to become catalysts for social change (Sutton-Brown, 2014).

5

Data gathering: research with adults

Chapter summary

This chapter focuses on creative forms of data gathering with adults. The chapter first sets out a key advantage of applying creative methods in terms of countering familiarity. This is followed by a closer examination of the techniques of LEGO®, sandboxing and work with objects and artefacts. Each of these techniques is outlined and then case studies are introduced to demonstrate how researchers have applied these creative methods in their work. Case studies from England and Wales reflect on research with adult participants – both students and practitioners – using LEGO, sandboxing and object-based approaches. A case study from South Africa provides an insight to how university educators used artefacts to gain an understanding of their own professional practice. Each case study is followed by tips, traps and reflective questions that examine the strengths, limitations and opportunities of creative methods of data gathering. The chapter then offers an account of ethics and ethical practice. The chapter builds on and extends the range of creative methods of data gathering introduced in Chapter 4 and invites you to consider how you could draw on creative ways of working with adults in your own research projects.

Introduction

As we saw in Chapter 4, creative approaches often involve techniques that invite participants to engage differently from conventional methods employed in education research such as interviews and focus groups. The over-reliance on interview techniques has been widely critiqued (see Delamont, 2012), and many researchers have turned to more creative forms of data production to address the limitations of this question–and–answer approach to fieldwork (Mannay, 2016; Kara, 2020). Creative methods of data gathering can provide an opportunity to move beyond standard talk–and–text–based techniques to explore our multidimensional experiences (Bagnoli, 2009). However, as you will see in the case studies presented in this chapter, participants often discuss the creative data they produce with the researcher. This discussion is referred to as an elicitation interview. In this way, creative methods can be combined with talk-based approaches to better understand the meanings that participants assign to the creative materials they produce.

In Chapter 4 we explored creative approaches to data gathering with children and young people, focusing on the techniques of digital portfolios; photography; graphic organisers as learning and teaching artefacts; and cartoon storyboards. However, education also involves adults as students and practitioners, and creative approaches have been used effectively to generate data in a wide range of studies with adult participants. Considering creative techniques as something 'just for children' or 'just for adults' overlooks the opportunities that these hold for all participants to reflect on and represent their educational experiences. This is why we have chosen to offer examples of data gathering with children, young people and adults in this book.

This chapter explores the potentialities and limitations of innovative and creative techniques for engaging adult learners and practitioners. It considers a range of ways in which creative techniques of data gathering have been applied, with the aim of gaining a more nuanced understanding of higher education settings. One advantageous aspect of creative approaches is their potential to counter familiarity, and the associated tendency for our research to be 'overshadowed by the enclosed, self-contained world of common understanding' (Mannay, 2010, p 91). Issues of familiarity can be problematic in education settings, where researchers' personal experiences of school, learning and student identities mean that they see 'only the things that are conventionally "there" to be seen' (Becker, 1971, p 10) or, like Geer (1964, p 337), are 'bored by the thought of studying undergraduates'. As researchers and, in many cases, participants have had extended engagement with education systems, education studies are arguably more prone to issues of over-familiarity than other fields and topics of study (Delamont and Atkinson, 1995).

Creative methods of data gathering can disrupt this familiarity because they engender forms of reflexivity and have participatory potential. Reflexivity refers to the process of actively reflecting on experiences, rather than simply reflecting. It is important for researchers to be reflexive about their data gathering and processes of interpretation; and it is also useful to engender opportunities for participants to be reflexive about the topics being studied. For example, when participants are asked to 'make' something, rather than simply answering questions defined by the researcher, the participant needs to think about and produce something that represents aspects of their life and the associated research themes. This space for thinking and reflexivity can lead to defamiliarisation, where participants slow down, engage with metaphors and representations and see their own everyday educational lives in new ways.

In this chapter we present some examples of creative research data gathering with adults in education settings, including LEGO, sandboxing and artefacts. Case studies are provided to illustrate different research questions, designs and techniques, and to offer the reader an insight into possible ways of conducting research with adults in relation to their educational experiences and practices. We invite you to consider:

- different creative techniques of data gathering;
- the potential of creative techniques for attending to the issue of familiarity;
- the affordances and limitations of using creative techniques with adults; and
- ethical considerations for data gathering.

LEGO: not just a construction toy for children

LEGO is a line of plastic construction toys that are manufactured by the LEGO Group. LEGO consists of mostly interlocking plastic bricks and mini-figures that can be pieced together and assembled to construct objects such as vehicles, buildings and scenes from popular culture such as films. You may have played with it yourself as a child, or as an adult with children. However, beyond this everyday use construction bricks have moved into mainstream creative research through the LEGO SERIOUS PLAY® movement.

The LEGO SERIOUS PLAY methodology was developed by the LEGO Group between 1998 and 2010 and consists of a progressive sequence of model-building exercises that encourage participants to think abstractly about complex problems using the iconic plastic bricks. Participants then share their models with others sitting around the table, creating opportunities for both self-expression and shared learning. The methodology aims to deepen the reflection process and support an effective dialogue. In this model, communication is purposefully designed to allow time for individual reflection and provide opportunities for all participants to express their thoughts on an equal footing.

LEGO SERIOUS PLAY has been used as a tool in the world of business and international development. Its opportunities to encourage experiential forms of expression and analysis, which can help participants see and experience familiar situations in a new way, have been recognised by social researchers (see Gauntlett and Holzwarth, 2006; Hinthorne and Schneider, 2012). The following two case studies demonstrate how work with LEGO has been used in educational settings. Case study 5.1 involved practitioners employed to deliver widening participation work with potential candidates for higher education. Case study 5.2 involved LEGO construction as a specific form of creative pedagogy with youth work higher education students. The tips, traps and reflective questions that follow the two case studies will help you to think about the strengths, limitations and opportunities of working with LEGO as a creative technique for data gathering.

CASE STUDY 5.1: THE EFFECTIVENESS OF CREATIVE LEGO® METHODS IN QUALITATIVE INTERVIEWS WITH PRACTITIONERS OF WIDENING PARTICIPATION IN HIGHER EDUCATION

Who and where: This case study reflects on the work of Jon Rainford (2019), who introduced a LEGO-based 'Ladders of Aspiration' task as part of his research with 16 practitioners employed to deliver widening participation work with potential candidates for courses in seven universities in England.

What: Rainford employed creative LEGO-based methods of data gathering in his study to stimulate discussion of everyday practice that allowed for more participant reflection and deeper consideration than a question-and-answer format.

Why: In UK higher education, widening participation is governed by national and local policies, which are often written by individuals who are disconnected from front-line practice and can be subject to varied interpretation and implementation (Forrester and Garratt, 2016). Rainford's study attempted to explore deeper understandings of everyday policy and what they mean in practice, and to make comparisons across types of institutions.

How: Semi-structured interviews were conducted with practitioners. To explore participants' conceptualisations of 'raising aspirations', Rainford designed a 'Typical Student' activity where participants could annotate a figure with drawings and add text answers to prompt questions. Of interest here is his second activity, the 'Ladders of Aspiration' task, where participants were provided with a LEGO ladder and ten figures representing a range of different jobs as illustrated in Photo 5.1. After arranging these representational LEGO figures, participants discussed the rationale for their ordering in an elicitation discussion around the 'Ladders of Aspiration' task.

Rainford had a very positive reaction to the LEGO tasks that created laughter and increased the rapport between him and the participants. Participants found the experience enjoyable because, although it had a level of creativity, they did not require any technical or artistic skills to complete the task. Comparatively, the activity involving drawing was less popular, as the adult participants felt that producing a drawing put them outside their comfort zone. Participants felt that the LEGO task acted as a support for the interview discussions and allowed them time to reflect on their initial assumptions; in some cases, this involved working and reworking the model. This space to think and reflect enabled both the discussion of issues around aspiration and a deeper understanding of participants' decision-making processes in their roles of delivering widening participation work with potential candidates for higher education.

Photo 5.1: 'Ladders of Aspiration'

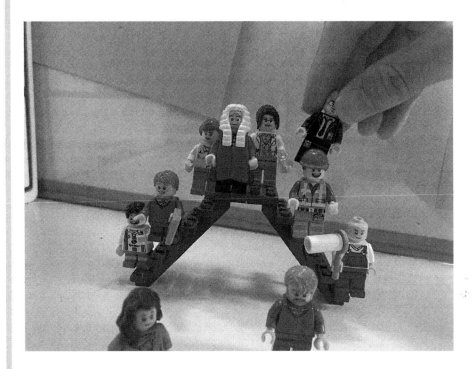

Source: Photo taken by Jon Rainford, 2020

CASE STUDY 5.2: MODELLING 'PROFESSIONAL LOVE' WITH LEGO® – ENGAGING YOUTH AND COMMUNITY WORK STUDENTS IN HIGHER EDUCATION

Who and where: This case study features the work of Martin Purcell (2018), who introduced LEGO as a pedagogical tool with 37 youth and community work students in higher education in England.

What: Purcell aimed to provide students with a learning experience that reflected the transformative agenda of their chosen area of professional practice. He drew on the creative medium of LEGO to enable an exploration of concepts that was not entirely reliant on language-based reflection.

Why: Transformative education is a pedagogical approach that encourages a change in participants' world-views and perceptions, as well as changes in their actions and behaviours, to bring about greater social justice and equality. Purcell was interested in helping students to overcome barriers to their engagement with a particularly complex concept, the transformational capacity of 'professional love' within youth and community work practice. 'Professional love' is demonstrated when practitioners embrace kindness, empathy and intimacy as part of their relationship with young people (Loreman, 2011). As the concept of 'professional love' occupies the affective realm and is open to conflicting interpretations, using a creative teaching approach was positioned as a way to overcome these challenges.

How: Students were provided with a LEGO SERIOUS PLAY kit comprising 129 disparate pieces and invited to create a bridge and an animal, which they were later asked to modify to represent an element of their personality. These warm-up activities familiarised students with the modelling process and different ways of thinking. Students were then asked to represent themselves, their professional philosophy and then 'professional love' in their practice. Each student explained their models to the group.

Overall, Purcell found that the LEGO technique was successful in helping students to articulate their thoughts about their practice in a more engaged manner than in conventional talk-based sessions. In feedback forms students said they liked the fact that the sessions were interactive, providing them with thinking time, and commented that they could see the potential for using LEGO in their own work with young people. However, some students found working in this mode problematic. For example, one student had never played with any construction toys as a child and found the building process challenging. Other students were concerned that the LEGO-based activities brought previously concealed or disturbing sides of their personality to the fore, which was difficult in a group-discussion context with their peers.

For case studies 5.1 and 5.2

Tips
- The two case studies highlight a difference in the suitability of LEGO for working with adults. In Rainford's study all participants enjoyed working through the medium of LEGO, but in Purcell's teaching sessions some students found this approach challenging. You may find it useful to have an alternative creative technique in sessions for participants who do not wish to work with LEGO.
- Using LEGO may engender new ways of thinking and raise unexpected issues for participants. Therefore, you may want to consider the participants you will work with and whether individual or group discussion and reflection is more suitable.
- LEGO construction requires adequate space and flat surfaces, and time must be built in for both building models and reflexive discussions. This should be taken into account when selecting and booking the venue for data gathering.
- In his study, Purcell included warm-up construction activities before focusing on the main point of interest, 'professional love'. You may want to think about whether it would be better to introduce participants to using LEGO with initial tasks before asking them to address your central point of interest.
- Before asking participants to engage with LEGO construction tasks you should trial the activities yourself and involve friends or colleagues as a pilot to see

how the available equipment works to support the creation of models pertinent to your research questions or teaching objectives.

Traps

- Pre-made LEGO pieces limit what can be visualised and this can create issues around the representation of gender, disability and ethnicity. You may want to consider what LEGO pieces you provide to participants and whether it would be preferable to use sets without figurines representing people so as to avoid stereotypical representations and interpretations.
- Using LEGO can bring unexpected issues to the surface. Therefore you will need to ensure that you can signpost participants to sources of external support if necessary.

Reflective questions

1. How might LEGO be useful as a tool to counter familiarity in education research?
2. What do the case studies tell us about the usefulness of LEGO-based activities to engender time and space for reflection?
3. Why is it important not to take a 'one size fits all' position when asking participants to engage with LEGO construction?
4. In what ways is the introduction of unexpected issues elicited by constructing LEGO models both an advantage in data gathering and a potential source of ethical concern?

Sandboxing: from psychoanalytical practice to education research

In qualitative research, there is often a need to understand individuals as 'simultaneously the products of their own unique psychic worlds and shared social worlds' (Gadd and Jefferson, 2007, p 4). Consequently, it is important to engage with research methods that allow space for subjectivities, listening to individual accounts to offer the opportunity to develop more accurate, complex and differentiated understandings. For Hollway and Jefferson (2013), conventional interviews based on the question–and–answer method are thin, rationally driven accounts that omit more than they reveal. In their own psychoanalytically informed work, employing free-association narrative interviews, they emphasise the importance of biography and the usefulness of open-ended questions, understood through participants' meaning frames, which are not predetermined by the researcher.

Sandboxing is also a psychoanalytically informed research technique; however, the term 'sandboxing' is used to distinguish the distinct development of this approach as a tool for qualitative education research inquiry (Mannay et al, 2017). Drawing from the psychoanalytical therapeutic tool the 'world technique' (Lowenfeld, 1950), sandboxing helps participants to represent metaphorically their ideas and experiences. The technique enables participants to create three-dimensional scenes, pictures or abstract designs in a tray filled with sand and a range of miniature, realistic and fantasy figures and everyday objects (Photo 5.2). Lowenfeld (1950) suggests that the collection of objects should represent the ordinary themes found in particular cultures. She defines no strict formula but classifies themes which should appear in any collection: namely people, houses, trees, fences, animals, transport, street signs and miscellaneous (such as sticks, stones, broken parts of objects). This patterning of themes is consistent in applications of the sandboxing technique.

Once this creative activity is completed, the researcher and participants engage in an audio-recorded elicitation interview in which participants describe what they have produced and explain the subjective meanings attached to each element in the completed sandscene. The sandscenes are also photographed for reference when analysing the data.

Despite the technique's association with psychoanalytical practice, it is important to note that in its adapted form sandboxing is a tool of qualitative data gathering. There have been strong objections to taking practices used in psychoanalysis out of the clinical situation of the 'consulting room' (Frosh, 2010). Consequently, it is important for researchers and participants to be clear about the nature of the activity and its aims and purpose. We will return to this point in the traps section of the following case study, which focuses on the educational experiences of mature students.

Universities are crucial sites of identity work, where some will feel comfortable while others will feel like fish out of water (Busher and James, 2018). Mature students face a number of complex psychological and structural barriers to entering higher education (Mannay and Morgan, 2013). Therefore, it is imperative to seek opportunities to create a more inclusive environment so that access is not

Photo 5.2: Sandboxing example

Source: Photo taken by Victoria Timperley (née Edwards), 2013

simply widened at the point of entry; rather, that universities ensure that mature students are supported to complete their undergraduate studies. Case study 5.3 drew on sandboxing as a technique to attend to the imperative to better understand and support mature students in the context of higher education.

CASE STUDY 5.3: 'UNIVERSITY CHALLENGE' – UNDERSTANDING THE LEARNING JOURNEYS OF MATURE STUDENTS IN HIGHER EDUCATION

Who and where: This case study features a study conducted by Dawn Mannay and Victoria Edwards[1] that explored the everyday experiences of nine mature higher education students in Wales (Mannay, Staples and Edwards, 2017).

What: Mannay and Edwards had both undertaken their undergraduate degrees as mature students, making them 'transient insiders' (Roberts, 2018). Therefore, it was important to guard against familiarity and the potentially deceptive assumption of shared understanding (Delamont and Atkinson, 1995). Consequently, the research incorporated the sandboxing technique as a tool to enable participants to represent their subjective experiences of higher education with minimal direction from the researchers.

Why: Mannay and Edwards were interested in the perspectives of mature students, including the challenges and barriers they had encountered and their ideas about how support systems could be improved. The study was designed in relation to action research (Lewin, 1946; Howard and Eckhardt, 2005), which allows practitioners to identify an issue of study so as to determine whether and how changes can be implemented to improve processes, procedures and programmes.

How: Participants created three-dimensional scenes, pictures or abstract designs in a tray filled with sand, using a range of miniature figures to represent their subjective experiences of being a mature student in higher education. Participants completed the sandboxing activity independently while the researcher either left the room or moved to a different part of the room and read a book. They then described what they had created in an elicitation interview with the researcher, using their own subjectively contingent schemas and metaphors to provide a narrative for the objects in their sandscenes. The figures selected evidenced a number of difficulties. For example, one student used the figure of a dinosaur aligned with a series of identical cats to communicate their feelings of difference and isolation. Feeling 'different' was a key theme across the students' accounts and was related not only to age but also to socioeconomic status and classed positioning. The evidence base from the study was used to set up a Mature Students' Coffee Club where students could meet weekly and build social networks to combat the isolation and difference reported in participants' accounts.

Tips

- Sandboxes can be wooden or plastic. Although the latter are lighter, with the sand and accompanying figures the sandboxing sets can be difficult to transport, so this will need to be factored into data-generation fieldwork plans.
- Manufactured kits are available for purchase. However, in this study the researchers created their own sandbox from a wooden drawer and collected the figures from their children's spare toys and everyday objects in the home. This can be a useful alternative to purchasing a kit when there is little or no budget for projects.
- In this study, sandscenes were created only by the participants. More recent work has encouraged joint sandboxing where the researcher and participant each make a sandscene in relation to a research question and then share their interpretations with each other (see Mannay et al, 2018, 2019). Joint sandboxing was introduced to engender a more participatory approach and to disrupt the often hierarchical relationship between researchers and participants.

Traps

- Sandboxing is a relatively open task and participants respond to a research theme rather than a set of rigid research questions. This means that the data generated may move away from the intended area of study, which could be problematic if a study needs to be completed to a tight deadline and specific research questions need to be attended to from the interview data. The interview itself can be used to bring in additional questions and discussions if these are not addressed in participants' sandscenes.
- Although the sandboxing technique is psychoanalytically informed, it is not a form of therapy. Participants may recognise the miniature figures and sand as signifiers of therapeutic practice, so it is particularly important to communicate that this is a research study, not a form of counselling, before entering into data gathering.
- As noted in relation to the LEGO case studies, there can be limitations with gender and ethnicity in relation to the miniature figures available, particularly in existing prepopulated kits (see Mannay and Turney, 2020). It is useful to consider what kits contain, particularly in relation to figurines of people, and consider if adaptions should be made or figures added or excluded in relation to the participants you will work with and the research aims.

Reflective questions

1. If there is no funding to purchase a sandboxing kit what other free or low-cost options could be available to you?
2. How would you ensure that participants in a sandboxing study were clear about the differences between education research and therapeutic practice?
3. What are the advantages and disadvantages of participants completing the sandboxing activity alone, as compared to a joint venture where participant and researcher each build a response to a research theme?

4.   Why might the use of metaphors, reflexivity and participant-led data production in sandboxing be particularly useful when the researchers are transient insiders?

Artefacts: the usefulness of everyday objects as tools of inquiry in education research

Sandboxing kits and LEGO construction supplies may have an associated cost but there are alternative creative approaches and you can source your data–gathering materials for free by using artefacts and everyday objects. The importance of everyday objects for understanding people's lives is a central feature of archaeological study, and museum collections and exhibitions often display material culture, curating and presenting an account of lives in other times and places. However, the usefulness of objects is not confined to exploring the past and it is a technique of data gathering that can be considered as a way of exploring more contemporary issues.

In therapeutic work, objects – sometimes referred to as 'third things' or 'third objects'– have traditionally been used to provide a point of reference for the patient or client to focus on, which can enable a more comfortable environment for communication and disclosure (Winnicott, 1968). Looking together is centralised, and the object facilitates an enactment of joint attention. In therapeutic work the technique has been reported to reduce the stress and anxiety associated with talking about personal or sensitive issues.

Objects can also be introduced into the interview space by education researchers to generate and extend conversations in the research process. The use of objects in research can be effective in creating a more relaxed and less intense atmosphere, as the researcher and participant are both focusing on the object(s) rather than on each other. Objects provided by participants can be revealing, as participants often bring things to an interview where they have an emotional connection or an accompanying story to share. In cases where the researcher provides the objects, they can be used as signifiers and metaphors that link with the participant's experiences. In this way objects become more than a stagnant thing – rather, they are containers of possible meanings and springboards for conversation.

Objects are usually photographed so that there is a record to refer to in the analysis of the data. Sometimes, when it is not convenient to bring an object, participants or researchers may take photographs of objects which are then used in a process of photo–elicitation, where they form the basis of interview discussions (see Collier, 1957). Additionally, the chosen object can sometimes be a photograph that is shared in hard copy or on a mobile phone or laptop (see Rose, 2010).

The following two case studies demonstrate how work with everyday objects has been used in educational settings. Case study 5.4 involved education researchers who curated and reflected on their own objects to understand more about their professional practice in the field of education. Case study 5.5 involved the use of a collection of cufflinks to engage Black male higher education students in discussing their experiences of higher education in elite universities. The tips, traps and reflective questions follow the presentation of the two case studies.

CASE STUDY 5.4: WORKING COLLABORATIVELY WITH VISUAL ARTEFACTS FOR SELF-STUDY

Who and where: This case study introduces the work of two education researchers and university educators based in South Africa, Kathleen Pithouse-Morgan and Linda van Laren (2012), who were interested in understanding their own professional practice.

What: Pithouse-Morgan and van Laren took a collaborative self-study approach to their inquiry, using artefact retrieval as a visual method to re-examine their own research interests.

Why: Pithouse-Morgan and van Laren were responding to the critique that much education research generates knowledge but that it is not enough to 'know'; rather, academic staff should be concerned with how they can contribute to positive change through their research and teaching. To address this concern, Pithouse-Morgan and van Laren adopted Ball's (2012) proposal that researchers should engage in a self-reflexive process of reflection, introspection and critique so as to move beyond advocating change and to becoming agents of change.

How: A collaborative self-study approach to inquiry was adopted that positioned Pithouse-Morgan and van Laren as both researchers and participants, gathering data about their own practices and senses of self. They used artefact retrieval as a creative research method. Initially Pithouse-Morgan and van Laren selected, photographed and wrote about their visual artefacts independently, and this was followed by a process of collaborative reflection.

Pithouse-Morgan and van Laren contend that the collaborative artefact retrieval provided them with space and time to consider their work in relation to broader societal concerns. Furthermore, they found that the collaborative nature of the self-study process provided a greater understanding of each other as colleagues and co-researchers and the tools to act as 'critical friends' both within and beyond the study. Overall, the study enabled a heightened awareness of the importance of others in education research, and a platform from which to explore how best to contribute to raising and addressing social concerns in the field of education.

CASE STUDY 5.5: USING OBJECTS TO EXPLORE THE EXPERIENCES OF UNDERGRADUATE STUDENTS

Who and where: This case study draws on the doctoral research of Constantino Dumangane Jr (2016), who was interested in the experiences of 15 Black undergraduate students in ten elite, majority White universities in England and Wales.

What: Dumangane used third objects as a means to encourage young adult participants to feel more comfortable about sharing their personal journeys in higher education.

Why: While record numbers of Black, Asian and other minority ethnic students are attending university, Black student representation in elite institutions remains low. Dumangane was concerned with providing an opportunity for this marginalised group to discuss their everyday educational experiences and any barriers and challenges associated with being the 'other' in leading universities.

How: The 'third objects' selected by Dumangane were sets of cufflinks that he had collected (Photo 5.3). Although some of the cufflinks held a meaning for Dumangane, for the participants the collection had no history. However, participants were able to draw on the properties of the cufflinks – their colours, shapes and patterns – to explore and create metaphors to represent their experiences, relationships and memories. They were asked to choose cufflinks and share the reasons for their selection and what the cufflink meant to them in relation to their mother, father, caregiver or other significant person in their life. The visual and textual properties of the cufflinks evoked a range of memories, reflections and feelings.

Photo 5.3: Collection of cufflinks

Source: Dumangane (2016)

Reflecting on the cufflink activity, Dumangane (2016) contends that the use of these third objects enabled him to access more information than he could have gained in a question-and-answer-style interview where he simply asked participants: 'Can you tell me a bit about your parents or someone in your life who may have had a significant impact on your life?' The cufflinks acted not only as tools of elicitation but as a technique to build rapport and a connection to and with participants who were, until the fieldwork, relative strangers. The cufflinks were also selected to open up spaces of reflexivity, as it is often easier to reflect on and discuss a topic if there is something to look at or hold, rather than being fixed within the gaze of the researcher (see Ross et al, 2009).

For case studies 5.4 and 5.5

Tips
- In the two case studies, objects were sourced and provided by the researchers, but in other studies (see Rowsell, 2011; Grant et al, 2018; Mannay et al, 2018) researchers asked participants to bring personal objects. In this approach it is useful to send a message to participants shortly before the meeting as a reminder to bring objects if they feel comfortable to take part in this aspect of the data-gathering process.
- It can be useful to have a record of the objects provided by participants, so you may want to take photographs that can be used later to support the analysis of the interview data.

Traps
- Objects 'matter to different people for different reasons and in quite different ways' (Wagner, 2020, p 81). Therefore, it is important that when researchers are curating objects to use with participants they remember that what they consider to be a mundane and benign object may trigger uncomfortable or painful associations for others who have their own unique biographies and subjectivities.
- When participants bring their own artefacts these can be used to frame the interview and lead the conversation on the research theme. However, it is important not to become over-reliant on participants bringing their own objects, as they may not want to, or could forget. Therefore, it is important to have an alternative data-gathering plan such as a semi-structured interview schedule or a different creative activity.

Reflective questions
1. Objects can be either selected by the participant or chosen by the researcher – in which ways might these approaches produce different kinds of data?
2. The openness and diversity of the interpretation of artefacts means that what objects trigger may be unexpected. How can you best prepare for unintended consequences in your research?

3. Some artefacts provided by participants could make them identifiable. How would you guard against this in a project where confidentiality is important?

Ethical considerations for data gathering with adults

In exploring the potentialities of creative research approaches with adult participants, it is important to consider the ethical issues that can arise with these techniques of data gathering. As highlighted in the LEGO case studies, there are tensions around the suitability of techniques and whether they engender confidence for participants in the fieldwork process or elicit feelings of uncomfortableness and moving outside zones of safety. It is important to offer a range of options for participants so that they can take part in your study in a way that suits their preferences. This can be achieved by taking a mosaic approach (see Clark and Moss, 2001), where a range of data-gathering techniques are available and participants have some autonomy in the fieldwork process.

Another point to consider when applying creative data-gathering techniques is the ways in which they can be 'sharp tools' (Burnard, 2018). Participants' involvement with objects and visual approaches like sandboxing and LEGO can engender more emotive and emotional engagements and reflexivity. The ways in which these data-gathering activities can provoke such sensitivities may come as a surprise to both participants and researchers. The metaphorical and mnemonic qualities engendered by creative approaches mean that there is less control in the direction of the talk between researcher and participant. For this reason, we would advise researchers to trial these techniques on themselves, and with colleagues and social networks, before they enter the field to work with participants. This attention to carefulness and reflexivity is necessary before and within the process of creative data gathering.

Ethical debates about whether to reveal or conceal the identities of participants are often associated with photographic or film data (Clark, 2020). However, other creative forms of data gathering also need to be considered. While sandboxing and LEGO may be relatively safe options in terms of maintaining confidentiality, when participants bring their own objects to an interview these could make them visible and knowable if photographs of what they bring are shared at conferences or in publications. Importantly, this visibility can extend to other family members, who could become known by association even though they may not be aware of the research study and not party to the processes of informed consent (Mannay, 2014). Therefore, what is photographed, stored and disseminated is an important consideration for those using creative data-gathering techniques that elicit identifiable materials.

Conclusion

In this and the previous chapter we have presented a range of approaches to, and techniques of, creative data gathering. This chapter has demonstrated how innovative research activities are not restricted to studies with children and young people but are also effective resources for engaging and involving adult participants in education research. Creative research methods can be particularly useful for countering familiarity, engendering reflexivity and enabling participants to take a more active role in the data–gathering process. Accordingly, these methods can help to produce rich and nuanced data. In the following chapter we move on from outlining creative forms of data gathering to exploring different techniques of data analysis.

CHAPTER DISCUSSION QUESTIONS

1. Why are creative methods often viewed as data-gathering techniques for children?

2. How might creative modes of data gathering with adults engender reflexivity and defamiliarisation?

3. What could you do to limit feelings of discomfort in adults when they engage with creative techniques?

4. Are there ethical issues that are more pertinent when working creatively?

5. How could you apply creative data gathering with adults in your own education research or practice?

Note

[1] Victoria Edwards changed her surname in 2020. For more recent related publications, please see Victoria Timperley.

6

Data analysis

Chapter summary

The introduction to this chapter distinguishes between analysis of data gathered using creative methods, and creative methods of analysing data gathered using creative or conventional methods. It highlights how embodied approaches to research can help us to look differently at conventional, creative and innovative approaches to analysing data.

The main body of the chapter looks at methods of analysing data using visual techniques, poetic inquiry, play and screenplay writing and mixed methods. Practical examples help us to understand that visual analysis is often a multistage process, and sense checking with participants can be very helpful. We learn that education researchers are beginning to use poetic analysis techniques which utilise the imaginative and expressive skills of researchers and make space for the complexity and uncertainty inherent in research.

When using creative writing techniques such as poetry, play and screenplay writing in analytic work, the needs of the research should always take precedence over aesthetic and entertainment values. Case studies demonstrate how play and screenplay writing can be of use in analytic work by including multiple voices and communicating complexity, among other things.

Mixed-methods analysis can refer to the analysis of different datasets within the same research project; the use of different analytic techniques with the same dataset; or the use of different theoretical perspectives to enrich analytic work. Case studies reflect some of the possibilities this offers for researchers. The chapter ends with a discussion of ethics and data analysis.

Introduction

Data analysis sometimes feels like the 'dark art' of research. It is often poorly understood, scantily taught and barely explained. Yet analysis is the beating heart of our work as researchers.

This chapter outlines creative approaches to analysing data in education research. You will get most benefit from reading this if you already have a good grounding in when and how to use conventional methods of data analysis. If you lack confidence in this area, we would recommend consulting the relevant section(s) of a good methods text, such as Cohen, Manion and Morrison (2018, part 5), ideally before reading the rest of this chapter.

Creative data analysis can refer to the analysis of data gathered using creative methods such as those covered in the previous two chapters. Alternatively, it can refer to creative methods of analysing data gathered using creative or conventional methods (or a combination of the two). This chapter focuses on the latter, as the former is more fully covered in the literature (for example, Rose, 2016; Lenette, 2019).

The use of creative methods in analysing data makes no difference to good practice in research. Analytic work still needs to include meticulous preparation and coding of data, accurate description and representation and appropriate use of power in interpretation. Creative analytic work can be done by hand, using software or with a combination of methods.

In this chapter we invite you to consider:

• the potential role of embodiment in data analysis;
• how to analyse visual data creatively;
• creative ways to analyse data using arts-based techniques;
• creative approaches to multi-modal data analysis; and
• the ethical aspects of analysing data.

Embodied data analysis

The use of creative methods can lead to new perspectives on conventional approaches to working with data. One example is embodied analysis. Analysing data was conventionally thought of as an entirely cerebral activity. Researchers using embodiment to conceptualise their work give us interesting new perspectives on this process.

CASE STUDY 6.1: EMBODIED ANALYSIS

Who and where: Torkild Thanem from Stockholm University in Sweden, and David Knights from Lancaster University in England.

What: Thanem and Knights co-authored *Embodied Research Methods* (2019), which considers (among other things) embodied analysis and interpretation and puts forward the concept of 'analytical buggery'.

Why: To take into account the way we live in our bodies while we analyse data, in ways that help us to move beyond standard explanatory systems (Thanem and Knights, 2019, p 113). 'By confronting our empirical material with our own embodied experiences as well as with existing theoretical concepts, analytical buggery makes it slip out of the established frames of reference that otherwise tend to determine our thinking' (Thanem and Knights, 2019, p 117).

How: Thanem and Knights recommend not using software; rather, work with data in hard copy: print outs, photographs, documents, field notes – whatever you have. Read through, make notes in margins, use highlighters to identify keywords and potentially useful quotes. Use sticky notes too, and index cards. Develop a colour-coding system if that seems helpful. Cut out key quotes and observations. Spread everything out on the floor. Add artefacts from your research. Walk in your material, crawl in it, play with it. Arrange and rearrange things, taking photographs as you go to keep track of connections that emerge. Draw maps, diagrams, sketches. Add them to your data. Keep going until you see your data differently and learn new things. By working in this way, 'analytical buggery makes it possible to untangle our research problems by infusing new sensations, extracting hidden emissions and creating unconventional insights from the empirical material at hand' (Thanem and Knights, 2019, p 117).

Tips
- If you or someone you work with has mobility problems, you could work on a table instead of the floor. Alternatively, you could attach documents to a wall at a height that best suits you.
- If the result is not as surprising and insightful as you would like, you probably haven't done enough; keep working in the same ways until more insights emerge.

Trap
- Analytical buggery can be very time consuming.

Not everyone agrees with the software prohibition. American researcher Laura Ellingson (2017, p 160) writes of digital materiality, pointing out that you can change background and highlighting colours on screen; cut, paste, annotate and highlight digital copies of data; hyperlink between texts, images and web pages to create connections; and so on. Ellingson also focuses on embodiment, and, for her, working digitally is embodied – we use our eyes to see the screen, our hands to operate mouse and keyboard. She also points out that it is easier to manage large volumes of data digitally (Ellingson, 2017, p 159).

Reflective questions
1. What do you think the transgressive nature of Thanem and Knights' use of the term 'buggery' can teach us about research methods?
2. What do you see as the pros and cons of using analytical buggery with hard copy versus digital data?
3. How do you think analytical buggery might work with a dataset including both hard copy and digital data?
4. In what other ways could an embodied approach support you in analysing data?

Visual analysis

Conventional methods of analysing visual data may be quantitative or qualitative (Cohen et al, 2018, p 702). One widely used conventional method of analysing visual data is content analysis (Parry, 2020, p 356), which in a simple form involves devising codes for the data and counting the number of times each coded item appears. Alternatively, you can count the number of images containing one or more instances of the coded item. Another conventional method is essentially to convert the visual data to text by writing a narrative about each image and what it contains and then using standard methods of textual analysis. It is not possible to analyse visual data using purely visual means, but it is possible to take a more creative approach than converting it to text.

Suzanne Culshaw from the UK used collage, alongside interviews, to help explore experiences of struggling as a high school teacher for her doctoral research. She chose to do this because collage stimulates visual thinking, helps reveal what cannot be expressed in words alone and offers the opportunity to express experiences in holistic, non-linear ways (Culshaw, 2019, p 269). In her review of visual analytic techniques she demonstrates that these techniques usually have three stages (Culshaw, 2019, p 275). The first focuses on description, the second takes a more analytic approach and the third involves interpretation.

Culshaw drew on the methods literature to formulate her three-stage analytic approach:

1. descriptive, focusing on how the image is produced, what it contains (factual and expressional representations, content and colour) and how it conveys meaning – its visual impact;
2. analytic, focusing on aspects such as compositional context, spatial relationships, significance of content/colour/placement of items, and 'visual syntax'; and
3. interpretive, beginning with the most obvious reading of the image, then generating alternative readings (Culshaw, 2019, p 275).

Then, drawing on the work of Grbich (2007), she worked to 'intermingle' the analysis of her visual and interview data (Culshaw, 2019, p 276).

Culshaw tells us what she did, though not how she did it. Yet her outline could provide a useful guide for others who want to analyse visual materials.

Culshaw's approach demonstrates that visual material is 'multi-layered and capable of sustaining several interpretations' (Cohen et al, 2018, p 712). Partly for this reason, mixing analytic methods can also be helpful in managing the complexity of visual data. Case study 6.2 outlines an example of mixed analytic methods with three stages similar to those set out by Culshaw, though in this example the interpretive stage comes before the analytic stage.

CASE STUDY 6.2: VISUAL ANALYSIS

Who and where: Reesa Sorin, Tamara Brooks and Ute Haring at James Cook University in Queensland, Australia.

What: Sorin and her colleagues conducted action research using arts-based methods including drawing, collage and storytelling, plus interviews, with over 100 children aged five to nine in urban, rural and remote schools. The aim was to investigate children's environmental understandings. The researchers gathered a wealth of rich material which they analysed using three separate methods.

Why: As there was no consensus about the best way to analyse visual data, the researchers decided to develop their own approach. This was based on a literature review of existing analytic techniques and the researchers also used action research principles in developing their method (Sorin et al, 2012, p 26).

How: Three forms of analysis were employed:

1. content analysis: developing categories based on items in children's artworks (for example, tree, house, animal), counting instances in each category, then labelling categories with high frequencies as 'meaningful';
2. interpretive analysis: inferring latent content such as the mood of an artwork, and gathering impressions of the environment through identifying categories from children's stories and interview responses; and
3. developmental analysis: linking the content and technique of each artwork to the child's chronological age, in line with established developmental theories of artistic expression in children.

This approach enabled the researchers to identify the presence (and absence) of specific features in the children's artwork; to reveal multiple meanings present in that artwork; and to assess all of this in relation to the children's chronological ages.

Tip
*   Work systematically, because this can guard you against accusations of being subjective.

Trap
*   When the same data has been analysed in different ways, it may tell different stories. See the section on mixed-methods analysis later in this chapter for ways to manage this situation.

Reflective questions

1. Why do you think a multi-modal approach seems to work best in analysing visual data?
2. What problems might result from taking a multi-modal approach to analysing visual data?
3. What do you see as the ethical considerations that arise from visual data enabling multiple interpretations?
4. If you developed your own method of analysing visual data, what would it involve?

Poetic inquiry

Until recent years, poetry was sidelined in education research, partly because it is thought of as 'exclusive and technical' and partly because it is not seen as scientific (Cahnmann-Taylor, 2009, p 14). However, education researchers are beginning to understand that poetic work has a useful role to play in some analytic contexts, for a number of reasons. For one, it makes space for researchers to use and develop their imaginative and expressive skills (Manning, 2018, p 744), and for another, it allows for the complexity and unpredictability inherent in much research (Owton, 2017, p 52). Also, it enables researchers to communicate participants' emotions to research audiences (Stapleton, 2018, p 20). Poetic inquiry has been described as 'a methodological approach that seeks to reveal and communicate multiple truths via intuitive contemplation and creative expression' (Owton, 2017, p 9).

Some researchers elicit poems from participants and then subject them to analysis, but that is much more uncommon than researchers using poetic techniques in analysing other kinds of data (Owton, 2017, pp 31–2). Writing is an inevitable part of data analysis, and clearly that writing does not always have to be prose. However, poetic analytic work 'is not simply the writing of poems, but a systematic creation of poems to demonstrate research findings within a project' (Stapleton, 2018, p 6). Taking a poetic approach to analysis can involve creating poems from data, creating poems about data or even using poetic techniques such as rhythm or rhyme within otherwise prosaic writing. The aim is different from that of literary poetics, where aesthetic quality is the top priority. In poetic inquiry for research, it is more important to stay faithful to participants' meanings than to make a perfect rhyme or maintain a regular rhythm (Owton, 2017, p 44).

Creating or writing poems based in data is in itself a form of analysis (Stapleton, 2018, p 6). Working to express a key concept in a poem, using a comparatively small number of words, is another way to 'slice' qualitative data. A further option is to use conventional qualitative data coding and categorising and then to create poems from those codes and categories.

Stapleton used poetic inquiry in her participatory action research with teachers in low-income urban schools in the US. She had only four participants, who candidly shared some very sensitive information, so she took steps to protect their identities. She used the gender–ambiguous pronouns they, them and theirs. At times she constructed dialogue from phrases and comments which had been spoken on different occasions. To distinguish individual comments and thoughts, she placed each quote or idea from a single participant on a line of its own. However, she blended quotes and anecdotes from different participants within most of her poems (Stapleton, 2018, p 9). Her data had a great deal of emotional content: 'recent and rapidly worsening teaching conditions, impacts of neoliberal policies, lack of administrator support, lack of autonomy, unprofessional treatment, and deep concern for their students' (Stapleton, 2018, p 1). Here are the last two stanzas from one of her poems, 'This Year' (Stapleton, 2018, p 11):

> This year, my doctor noticed a dramatic increase
>   in urinary tract infections
>   among teachers in the district.
> We have no time
>   to even
>   go to the bathroom.
> This year, there were no step-wise
>   or cost of living
>   pay increases.
> This year … and the six years before.

These lines are stark, factual, with great economy of language and few poetic devices apart from the repetition of 'this year'. Yet they invite the reader to empathise. Certainly, any reader who has ever had a urinary tract infection, or a job where they couldn't go to the bathroom as needed, or who has gone without a pay increase for several years, will empathise with these teachers. Even readers who have not had any of those experiences will be able to empathise as long as they have some imaginative capacity.

Although many poetic inquirers agree with Stapleton on the importance of privileging participants' own words, it is also clear that the researcher has a primary role in crafting and shaping analytic poetry (Owton, 2017, p 45; Stapleton, 2018, p 5). Owton (2017, p 45) describes this process:

> I make interpretations and decide how the poem will be constructed, choosing which words and how it takes shape. I may weigh up changing the order of someone's words so that it may rhyme *if* the opportunity is there, as long as this does not change or 'distort' the meaning of their experience.

Another option is the 'multi-voiced' poem (Owton, 2017, p 66). This type of poem includes participants' words and other words too, perhaps researchers' words, words from the literature, words from policy documents – whatever is relevant for the research being conducted. A third option is to use poetic inquiry with a single-voiced secondary dataset, as Canada-based researcher Amber Moore did in her investigation of impostor syndrome in academia, using her own early-stage doctoral writing as data (Moore, 2018, p 46).

Cahnmann-Taylor (2009, p 19) suggests that education researchers should have a method of making notes at all times so they can 'write down images, metaphors, and overheard phrases that may have direct or indirect relationship' to their research. This can help towards 'a fresh way of seeing' and so enable researchers to 'be surprised by unexpected connections and understanding' (Cahnmann-Taylor, 2009, pp 19–20). Also, of course, these notes could themselves become data for future poetic inquiry.

Poetic analysis does not have to be a solitary endeavour. Collaborative work in this area can draw on a range of group members' abilities (Stapleton, 2018, p 6). Working collaboratively with participants can help to redress the power imbalance between researchers and participants (Manning, 2018, p 745). Also, as with visual analysis, poetic analysis can benefit from member checking to ensure that poems reflect participants' perspectives accurately and comprehensively (Stapleton, 2018, p 9).

Literary poems are judged on their aesthetic merit. Research poems, having different priorities, need to be judged on other qualities. Owton (2017, p 106) offers us a 'poetic tick list':

- Artistic concentration: focuses attention on considerations of the history and the presence of craft in poetry.
- Embodied experience: recognises the need for audiences to *feel* with, rather than about a poem, to experience emotions and feelings in situ.
- Discovery/surprise: the poem teaches us to see something familiar in new ways that might be surprising. We learn something new about the human condition and ourselves.
- Conditional: the partiality of the story should also be recognised through poetry, point of view as conditional whilst presenting what we may call narrative truth.
- Narrative truths: the facts presented should ring true, regardless of whether events, feelings, emotions and images 'actually' happened.
- Transformation: is about providing new insight, giving perspective or advocating for social change. (Original emphasis)

Another option would be to use criteria put forward for judging qualitative and/or arts-based research, such as Tracy's 'eight big-tent criteria' (Tracy, 2010) discussed in Chapter 2. A third option is Smith, Sparkes and Caddick's 'characterised traits' – although, as they point out, the relevant criteria may change depending on the context and the purpose of the research (Smith et al, 2014, p 195).

CASE STUDY 6.3: POETIC ANALYSIS

Who and where: Sharon McDonough from Federation University, Australia.

What: As we saw in Chapter 3, McDonough used poetic analysis in her research into the experience of mentoring pre-service teachers.

Why: To communicate what it is like to be a mentor of pre-service teachers; highlight the emotional dimension of the tensions those mentors experience as both supporter and assessor of pre-service teachers; and to offer audiences a chance to connect with the inner turmoil of the mentors.

How: McDonough began by reading and coding interview transcripts, and using the codes to construct categories representing tensions experienced by mentors. Then she selected excerpts from transcripts that represented the identified tensions, and extracted phrases and sentences which highlighted key elements of the tensions and of the mentors' lived experiences. She arranged these phrases and sentences into poetry, using words as they were used by participants, not changing any but sometimes rearranging sentences or repeating phrases for poetic effect (McDonough, 2018, p 103).

Tip
- Aim to convey the emotional dimension of participants' narratives while staying true to their own expression of experience.

Trap
- You may be tempted to insert your own words or experiences to create a poem which is more aesthetically pleasing. For ethical reasons, it is important to resist this kind of temptation and to represent your participants faithfully.

Reflective questions
1. How might poetry help you with your own analytic work?
2. What criteria would you use to judge the merit of a research poem? Why would you use those criteria?
3. Should researchers use their own emotions in their research work? If no, why not? If yes, how?

Play and screenplay writing

Originally, a play script was for a theatrical production to be performed on a stage in front of an audience. This imposes constraints: all of the action has to happen in one place, or the writer has to build in time for cumbersome scene changes or find a venue with a revolving stage. Usually there are only a handful of actors and it is difficult to have them perform actions such as swimming or flying with any credibility. There are also constraints with screenplay writing, which creates the scripts for films, but they are far fewer, particularly in these days of computer-generated imagery. In a film, you can move from one continent to another in seconds, live on Mars or include an army of mermaid soldiers.

Today, we also have television and radio plays, which sit between theatre play scripts and screenplays. However, play writing in research is usually based on the theatre model, and known as 'ethnodrama' if it's a written output or 'ethnotheatre' if performed for an audience (Saldaña, 2011/2016, p 12). For analytic purposes almost everyone who uses this method uses ethnodrama, though a few use ethnotheatre.

There is one key difference between writing for theatre, television, radio and film, and drawing on these methods to write for research. When writing for research, the script is always based firmly in real research data (Saldaña, 2011/2016, p 14). As with poetic inquiry, researchers may use their imaginative and creative skills to guide them as they form and shape their writing, but research findings should always take precedence over dramatic effect.

There are conventions for writing plays and screenplays which are beyond the scope of this book to describe, but the information is freely available online. However, when you're writing ethnodrama, it is not necessary to follow these conventions closely if you have a good reason for doing otherwise.

Screenplay writing can also be useful in analytic work. Lisbeth Berbary, from the University of Memphis in the US, used screenplay writing in her analysis of data from an ethnographic study on Southern sorority women. (A sorority is a social organisation for women in an American college or university.) Berbary made the screenplay out of quotes from interview transcripts and passages from observational field notes, rearranging the quotes and passages to create a script. This was made up of three 'acts', each containing four scenes and addressing one of Berbary's three research questions. Each scene explored the relationships between Berbary's categories of analysis. Here is an excerpt:

Summer
I feel like I'm stuffed in this dress. I can barely breathe.
She begins to adjust the dress in the mirror, pulling it up and re-organizing her breasts.
Summer
My boobs are everywhere. I even have them in the back. Wait till I have to sit down, I'll probably explode.
Roommate S chuckles, recognizing that Summer has a good sense of humor about her size.
Roommate S
Better watch those boobs. How soon you forget your Rush debacle!
Roommate S says half joking, remembering that someone tattled on Summer for having a dress that was too revealing.

Summer
You know I really can't help it. What, do you want me to wear a sack?
Roommate C
Maybe you better. At least pull it up a bit. You don't want people to think
you're trashy or that you're asking for it.
*Roommate C isn't joking. Summer is a little surprised and offended. She feels the need
to defend herself.*
Summer
It's not like I act slutty. The problem is like a combo of dressing and behaviour.
Everyone knows I'm a dead end. I don't sleep around like some people.
(Berbary, 2011, p 192)

Screenplay writing enabled Berbary to incorporate setting, action, dialogue
and 'director's comments', and to combine data from multiple sources into a
single action or interaction. This helped her to convey more fully the systems,
perspectives and interpretations that she perceived within her research. It also
meant that she could show readers the experiences of sorority women, rather
than just telling about them (Berbary, 2011, p 195). Berbary reports that many of
her participants enjoyed reading the screenplay, and non-academic readers found
it surprisingly accessible (Berbary, 2011, p 195).

CASE STUDY 6.4: ETHNODRAMATIC WRITING FOR ANALYSIS

Who and where: Anneliese Cannon and Alissa Blair, educator researchers at the
University of Wisconsin-Madison in the US.

What: Cannon and Blair researched the language learning and educational
trajectories of multilingual immigrant English learners from diverse linguistic
backgrounds in community colleges. They conducted two sets of phenomenological
interviews. Then they analysed the data from four of those interviews, with two
participants from Togo and Laos, using ethnodramatic writing.

Why: To illuminate the nuanced dynamics of participants' experiences; to preserve
the narrative integrity of the interview data; to find an innovative, dialogical way to
share findings; and to help foster useful conversations about working with diverse
English learners in community colleges (Cannon and Blair, 2014, p 315).

How: The researchers used a range of coding techniques, including several recursive
rounds of the dramaturgical coding devised by Johnny Saldaña (2011/2016). This
enabled them to identify participants' emotions and objectives, as well as larger
categories, themes and narrative arcs in participants' lives. They devised scripts with
fictional contexts but using actual data to 'preserve the individual integrity of the

participants' voices' and to enable the presentation of more data than a conventional research report would permit (Cannon and Blair, 2014, p 317).

Tips

- Ethnodramatic writing can 'offer many possibilities for understanding and representing the lives of diverse people and can invite participation in ways that' conventional analytic approaches do not (Cannon and Blair, 2014, pp 309–10).
- Find one or more appropriate theoretical perspectives to connect your work more widely with the world. Cannon and Blair drew on Bakhtinian dialogical theory and postcolonial theory to link their ethnodrama with history and society.

Trap

- While it would be easy to do so, this work should not be done casually or flippantly. The researcher is intimately 'involved in the lived process of responding to and reflecting on the participants' experiences', and so has immense power (Cannon and Blair, 2014, p 329). Thorough reflexive work will be essential to minimise the influence of bias and privilege.

Faithfully using participants' words in ethnodrama is an ethical approach, though it is not the only method. Some researchers have devised scripts from the categories and themes developed through their analytic work.

CASE STUDY 6.5: ETHNODRAMATIC WRITING AND ETHNOTHEATRE FOR ANALYSIS

Who and where: Anne W. Anderson, Patriann Smith, Jenifer Jasinski Schneider and Aimee Frier at the University of South Florida in the US.

What: Doctoral students analysed multimodal videos produced by school pupils in sixth grade (mostly aged 11–12 years) as part of their research training.

Why: Three of the authors – Anne, Patriann and Aimee – were doctoral students in a seminar run by the fourth, Jenifer. Independently, Anne and Patriann chose to analyse the same video. Their analytic work was structured similarly but ended up being different in several respects. Jenifer encouraged them to combine their analyses, but this proved difficult because they had very different writing styles, partly because one was an American English speaker and the other a British English speaker. Anne had some experience of drama and suggested taking a dialogic, ethnodramatic approach to capture the analytic complexity.

How: The researchers used the characters of mythical Greek gods: the rational Apollo and the artistic Dionysus, with their father Zeus as narrator. This helped them to work through and embody their conceptual analytic ideas. Rather than aiming to minimise the differences between the two analytic approaches, they chose to maximise the disparities through oppositional characterisation (Anderson et al, 2015, p 78). They then revised their ethnodramatic work for performance at an academic conference, incorporating a fourth character, the Chorus, which provided more scope for visual and verbal comedy (Anderson et al, 2015, p 79).

Tip

- Analytic work need not stop with ethnodrama. These researchers found that preparing their ethnotheatrical performance enabled them to continue and deepen their analysis. It seems that it may be possible to learn more from dramatising and performing than from reading and discussion.

Trap

- In ethnotheatre, and even in ethnodrama, it can be tempting to give priority to entertainment over research and education. Any such temptation should be resisted.

This case study demonstrates that ethnodramatic methods can be used to explore concepts and ideas as well as relationships or society more broadly (Anderson et al, 2015, p 78).

The researchers who use these methods most comprehensively are those with a background in theatre. Johnny Saldaña, who has used ethnodrama and ethnotheatre extensively and written key texts on the methods, is a playwright, actor, director and designer of theatrical productions, with decades of experience in theatre before he came to research (Saldaña, 2011/2016, p 16). Case study 6.6 shows how some drama educators developed ethnotheatre even further by using a range of performance-focused drama activities as analytic tools.

CASE STUDY 6.6: ETHNOTHEATRE FOR ANALYSIS

Who and where: Jane Bird is a drama educator and researcher at the University of Melbourne in Australia.

What: Jane used ethnotheatre with three drama educator colleagues to study the experiences of women at the University of Melbourne.

Why: To 'investigate the words, stories and images of a range of women who taught, studied and worked at the University' in the past and in the present (Bird, 2011, p 37). Performative methods of analysis enabled the researchers 'to identify with the emotional and visceral components of the participants' lived experiences and to construct an understanding of the cultural world under investigation' (Bird, 2011, p 39).

How: The researchers collected a range of ethnographic data such as interview data, audio-recordings of workshop sessions and historical data. They read their data carefully and discussed emergent themes relating to their research topic. They selected words, phrases and stories from the data which supported those themes. Then they dramatised verbatim text and themes using techniques such as improvisation. This led to further discussions which clarified and deepened their interpretations.

They created short performances, vignette style, using verbatim text, and presented these to individual interviewees. The results of this varied: some interviewees did not recognise the content of the performance as relating to their lives, while others said the performance was emotionally or analytically accurate. The researchers used the discussions generated by these performances to develop or refine the material – and, therefore, their analysis. Alongside the performance vignettes they incorporated a meta-commentary, revealing theoretical perspectives and research methods, as a parallel narrative.

Tips
- For ethnotheatre, you can bypass script writing and go straight to drama activities as your analytic tools.
- Allow plenty of time for this iterative dialogic approach to analysis.

Traps
- Balancing data-based vignettes with meta-commentary, to create a coherent whole, can be very challenging.
- Bird argues that the researchers' 'capacity to shape meaning through the manipulation of dramatic elements was a key tool in analysing the data' (Bird, 2011, p 42). Without some existing skills in drama preparation and performance it would be difficult to undertake ethnotheatric analysis.

Reflective questions
1. How could ethnodramatic writing help in your analytic work?
2. Do you think ethnodramatically written work should always be performable? Why?
3. Given your own level of skill and knowledge of the theatre arts, to what extent could you use ethnotheatrical approaches to data analysis?
4. Which theoretical perspective or perspectives do you use to connect your research with the wider world?

Mixed-methods analysis

Up to now we have focused mostly on arts-based analysis, though some of this has also been mixed-methods, such as the work of Sorin et al in case study 6.2 on visual analysis. However, mixed-methods analysis allows for the incorporation of other methods such as the use of technology. One example is Q methodology, invented in 1935 by the British physicist and psychologist William Stephenson to investigate people's attitudes, beliefs, feelings and opinions (Ellingsen et al, 2010, p 395). This method involves groups of people arranging qualitative statements on a grid, often to rank them in terms such as 'most like my view' and 'least like my view', after which the number and positions of statements are recorded and statistically analysed using software. In research using Q methodology to determine the perspectives and consensus within a physics classroom, Susan Ramlo, from the University of Akron in Ohio, US, used the open source software PQ Method to assist with her statistical analysis (Ramlo, 2008, p 180). In Q methodology, qualitative data is used to aid in the interpretation of the statistical results.

If you have collected different types of data – maybe some numerical data, some text and some images – you will need to use mixed methods of analysis. Mixed-methods analysis can also be conducted with a single type of data, as with the example of Q methodology above, though it is not necessary to use an existing method; you can devise your own. You could use two different types of analysis – say, discourse analysis and narrative analysis – to generate a richer picture of the phenomena under study. Or you could use different theoretical perspectives to enrich your analytic work. These kinds of approaches can also be defined as mixed-methods analysis. This does complicate things somewhat by increasing the complexity of the choices facing researchers when they embark on data analysis.

Mixed-methods researchers of all kinds often want to integrate their findings. This is not always possible. Kate Wall and her colleagues (case study 6.7) found that the results from their deductive and inductive analyses were so different that they could not be integrated. Specifically, the deductive analysis showed a drop-off in positive thinking in secondary schools, while the inductive analysis showed how the learning environment could be tailored to help increase the complexity of pupils' understanding (Wall et al, 2013, p 36). This was not problematic, because both analyses were useful and contributed to new insights. However, Wall et al (2013, p 36) noted that 'if either process were asked to stand alone then it leaves the uneasy conclusion that implications from the data would have remained unknown'.

In our view, it is likely that implications from this huge and complex dataset still remain unknown, despite the researchers using two carefully chosen methods of analysis. Returning to this dataset with other analytic methods may well reveal further insights. However, we agree with their conclusion that choice of analytic method is important because it can significantly influence research findings (Wall et al, 2013, p 37). This means that not only do researchers have a daunting amount of choice in analytic methods but they also need to take great care in making those choices because of the potential influence on their findings.

Mixed-methods analysis, then, is particularly useful with complex datasets – just as mixed-methods research is particularly useful in addressing complex research questions. Whether you are working with one type of data or more than one, you may wish to work towards integrating your findings. The idea of creating a coherent narrative does appeal to many people, but complexity makes this more difficult. Following the work of Haraway and Barad, Uprichard and Dawney propose the use of diffraction as an alternative conceptual model which can be helpful when integration proves difficult or impossible. Diffraction is a term drawn from physics, where it is used to describe the interactions between waves and other waves or objects. Imagine a pebble being dropped into a still pool of water, and the concentric ring of ripples that expands from the point of impact. Then imagine another pebble being dropped into those ripples: the resulting pattern of colliding and overlapping waves is diffraction. For Uprichard and Dawney, this concept is useful because it embodies messiness, disjuncture and instability – all elements that are common in mixed-methods research. They pose the question:

> Given that mixed methods *often* reveal different aspects of the object of study, the question becomes not about how to integrate the data in order to make sense of 'the' object of study, but rather: what evidence is there to suggest that the object of study is not complex, multiple, and messy? (Uprichard and Dawney, 2019, p 28; original emphasis)

CASE STUDY 6.7: MIXED-METHODS ANALYSIS WITH DIFFERENT TYPES OF DATA

Who and where: Jennifer Donovan, from the University of Southern Queensland in Australia.

What: Investigating the interactions of 10- to 12-year-old children with the mass media, and whether (and what) they learn from there about genes and DNA.

Why: At that age, children will not yet have learned about genes and DNA in school.

How: Donovan undertook a quantitative examination of children's engagement with mass media, using questionnaires. She made a qualitative examination of the examples they gave for genetics content. She also used interviews to qualitatively investigate the children's understandings of genes and DNA, and their perceptions of where that knowledge came from. Questionnaire data was analysed using quantitative content analysis, and interview data was analysed using qualitative thematic analysis. Then Donovan cross-compared the datasets, looking for patterns and trends (Donovan, 2016, pp 137–8).

Tips
- Attend to 'the 4 Ms' of mixed-methods research (Donovan, 2016, pp 138–9):
  - *Manipulate* the multiple datasets, using different formats such as spreadsheets, text and tables, and different quantitative and qualitative analytic strategies, as needed.

- *Maintain* a balance of focus between the different types of data.
- *Manage* the cross-referencing; make sure it is accurately recorded, and devise a way to keep track of new findings from the cross-referencing process.
- *Master* the writing up by producing a coherent narrative which would make sense to a naive reader.

Traps

- Mixed-methods research can yield a huge amount of data, which can be burdensome for the researcher.
- It can be tempting to pay more attention to one type of data, particularly if you're more familiar with that kind of data.

CASE STUDY 6.8: MIXED-METHODS ANALYSIS WITH ONE TYPE OF DATA

Who and where: Kate Wall and her colleagues from universities in Durham and Newcastle upon Tyne, UK.

What: As part of a big piece of research called 'Learning to Learn' (L2L) in English schools, the researchers created and used Pupil View Templates (PVTs). These are basic line-drawn black-and-white cartoon depictions of easily recognisable learning situations such as a classroom with a teacher and pupils. Each pupil has a blank face and empty speech and thought bubbles. Participants are asked to draw and write on the template to reflect on their experience of a particular teaching or learning activity. Over 500 PVTs were completed.

Why: The researchers chose mixed-methods analysis of their qualitative data to help them develop better understanding of the new tool they had created: how it worked, and its potential.

How: Wall et al used both deductive and inductive analysis. For the deductive analysis, all written content was transcribed and imported into NVivo software. Documents were categorised by gender and age band. Text was categorised by speech bubble or thought bubble. Statements were categorised as predominantly evidence of cognitive skills (information gathering, building understanding or productive thinking) or of metacognitive thought (strategic or reflective thinking) or both. This enabled quantitative statistical analysis to test hypotheses about relationships between age, gender and thinking skills.

Figure 6.1: One of the Pupil View Templates used by Wall et al

Pupil Response Record – Group Work

The inductive analysis was conducted by an experienced researcher who had no previous involvement with L2L or knowledge of PVTs or the deductive analysis, so as to minimise bias. A sample of 96 PVTs was chosen for this immersive approach. The researcher worked with textual and visual elements of the PVTs in generating constructs which were used to explore prominent trends and themes at school level and for the project as a whole (Wall et al, 2013, pp 28–30).

Tip

• Using two or more methods of analysis can reveal a lot more information than using one method alone.

Trap

• Using two or more methods of analysis requires extra skills and more than double the amount of time because of the need to see what else can be learned by comparing the different results.

Reflective questions

1. What do you think might be the advantages of taking a mixed-methods approach to analysing your own data?

2. What do you think might be the disadvantages?

3. What are the most important considerations for you in choosing how to analyse your data?

4. What are the ethical implications of your answer to question 3?

Ethics in data analysis

Research ethics committees, institutional review boards and the like, which assess researchers' applications for ethical approval, rarely ask questions about data analysis. Yet the work of Retraction Watch has shown that many academic journal articles are retracted due to unethical analytic work. In December 2019 a search of the Retraction Watch database showed 1,941 retractions due to falsification, fabrication or manipulation of data, images or results. Retraction Watch covers all disciplines, and a further search showed that only two of these retractions were from education researchers. However, it is important to remember that Retraction Watch highlights only those ethical breaches that have been discovered; there are likely to be many more that go unnoticed. Also, Retraction Watch was founded by two medical journalists and is, by its own admission, biased towards the life sciences.

We think it would be unusual for a researcher never to have felt tempted to manipulate data or findings. During data analysis researchers are likely to be aware of competing agendas from those with an investment in the research. These may be participants, supervisors, colleagues, managers, communities, funders or others. Some researchers, particularly insider or activist researchers, may feel deep sympathy for some of these individuals or groups. Other researchers may have a strong need for approval from those in positions of power, particularly if the outcome of the research could affect their employment, wages or well-being. These kinds of pulls can increase the temptation for a researcher to add emphasis where emphasis is not warranted or to omit items that should be included.

All researchers need to be aware of these possibilities and work to mitigate their effects. We also need to be as aware as possible of our own biases and how they might affect our analytic work. Working reflexively – in effect, analysing our own analytic work – can help us to do this work more ethically (Ellingson, 2017, pp 163–5; Kara, 2018, pp 117–18).

Data analysis is difficult, taxing work, and some of its processes are tedious. Data should be prepared meticulously and coded thoroughly. Some people enjoy coding data, but for others it is a boring chore. This can lead even the most ethical researcher to make mistakes. Turning again to Retraction Watch, in December 2019 the database listed 657 journal articles retracted due to errors in analyses. Three of these were from education research.

Of course, anyone can make a mistake. Even so, we need to safeguard ourselves and our work, as far as possible, against the possibility of errors in our research. There are a number of ways to do this. If there is a task you find boring, do it in small chunks of time, interspersed with more interesting activities. Keep your mind on the job: by all means play music if it helps you concentrate, but try to keep unhelpful distractions to a minimum. Spot-check your work for accuracy, or ask someone to spot-check it for you.

Technology can be a great help here, but it also carries temptations for misuse. For example, some people who are new to the quantitative analysis software Statistical Package for Social Sciences (SPSS) decide to run all the tests it can do. But this way you are likely to find one or more which gives a statistically significant result – if you're using a 5% level of probability, then five from a hundred will do so by chance. This kind of 'fishing' is highly unethical. The key is to know which statistical test or tests are appropriate to use for your dataset (Davis, 2013, p 17).

On the other hand, technology can also help us to find solutions to ethical problems at the data analysis stage. Data analysis software can improve researchers' well-being by saving time and effort (provided you have invested the time to learn it). Technological tools such as encryption and password protection can help us to store electronic data securely.

Working collaboratively can lead to better ethical practice at the analytic stage. Fully collaborative analytic work is time consuming and in some Euro-Western contexts, such as most doctoral research, is not seen as appropriate. However, even a little time spent working collaboratively with data can widen your perspective, particularly if you can work with someone from a different disciplinary background (Sword et al, 2018, p 499). And in fully participatory research, collaborative analysis is essential (Cole, 2017, p 350).

Where possible, it is helpful to involve participants in the data analysis. In her research on educational inclusion, UK-based researcher Clare Woolhouse used photo elicitation with school pupils and then cartoonised the photos to anonymise them before sharing them with other children and young people for discussion. Woolhouse found that involving her participants in analysing visual materials helped to bridge the gap between child participants and adult researchers (Woolhouse, 2019, p 13). It may not always be possible to involve people so fully in the analytic process, but there are useful methods of re-engaging participants such as 'member checking'. Meagan Call-Cummings and her colleagues from the US used photovoice with English language learners at a school in Virginia. They conducted analysis and wrote a full draft manuscript of their findings, then sent a copy of this to each participant with a request for feedback. The researchers then used this feedback in reviewing their analysis, in recoding data that seemed controversial to participants and in revising their manuscript. This enabled them to reflect and incorporate perspectives they previously had not fully understood (Call-Cummings et al, 2019, p 403).

There are many reasons why academic journal articles are retracted, most of them to do with ethical breaches. In December 2019, the Retraction Watch database gave the total number of retractions in education research as 1,538. So, although few of the retractions from education researchers showed ethical breaches at the analytic stage, we cannot say that education researchers are more ethical than researchers in other disciplines. The onus is on all of us to ensure that our analytic work is ethically conducted.

Conclusion

This chapter has shown that analysing data is one of the most complex parts of the researcher's work. You need to balance competing priorities, such as the voices of your participants, the demands of your superiors, the wishes of other stakeholders and your own feelings and needs. At the same time you have to work systematically, carefully and thoroughly. There are many methodological and ethical decisions to be made. In this chapter we have offered some guidance on creative approaches to data analysis that may be particularly useful in education research. However, it is far from exhaustive, and could not be, as new methods of analysing data are being developed all the time. Perhaps you will develop one yourself.

CHAPTER DISCUSSION QUESTIONS

1. Is data analysis necessarily embodied, or can it be disembodied? Why?

2. In data analysis for education research, what is science and what is art? Why?

3. Which creative methods of analysing data would you like to explore further? What are the implications of your answer?

4. What steps do you take to ensure that you analyse data ethically?

Research reporting

Chapter summary

This chapter introduces the concept that all research reporting is, to some extent, creative. We outline the main principle of good practice in research reporting: to aim to communicate in ways that meet the needs of your audience(s). We also cover some of the key points of good practice, such as using plain language, editing carefully and seeking – and using – feedback on draft versions. A case study demonstrates the utility of including creatively gathered data in research reports. Ways of putting research into practice are considered and advice is given on creating recommendations.

We discuss some ways that fictionalisation has been used in research, including composite quotes and case studies, short stories and fictionalised accounts. We observe the alignment between fictionalisation and mixed methods, and clarify the difference between mixing methods within a research report and mixed-methods reporting on a research project. Two case studies demonstrate how these can work in practice.

We argue for using poetry in research to communicate concisely and engage audiences' emotions. We then consider the relative merits of different poetic forms, with examples to illustrate their practical application. We also argue for the use of comics and graphic novels, which have been shown to engage, motivate and help with comprehension and retention of information. This is illustrated by a case study. Then we consider the use of technology in research reporting, with particular reference to blogging, video, podcasts and animation. We look at collaboration in research reporting with a helpful case study, and we finish by debating some of the main ethical issues in research reporting.

Introduction

Research is conventionally reported in written prose, although other methods such as poetry, story, performance and video are becoming more common. This chapter offers an overview of some of the methods used for reporting education research.

The standard Euro-Western expository method of writing about research is widely regarded as uncreative. We disagree with this; our view is that all writing is creative, because every writer is putting words together to make new sentences, and sentences to make new paragraphs, and ultimately to create new documents. Everyone makes choices as they write, and these choices are 'simultaneously political, poetic, methodological, and theoretical' (Richardson, 1997, p 17). It surprises some people to find that non-fiction writers use many of the same techniques as fiction writers (Stein, 1998, p 7). The more we find out about this, the more the division between 'academic writing' and 'creative writing' seems incomprehensible. After all, some creative writing techniques are almost imperceptible: a metaphor, a change of viewpoint, a sensory phrase can have a subtle but important effect on the reader.

However, the establishment mitigates against the practice of creative research reporting, such as academics being required to publish in academic journals while the majority of academic journals are unwilling to accept creatively written submissions (Rodriguez and Lahman, 2011, p 604). Yet researchers across the social sciences, including education researchers, are increasingly using creative methods to report their research.

The methods we consider in this chapter include fictionalisation and mixed methods, poetry, comics and graphic novels, methods that use technology, collaborative reporting and performative reporting. This is not an exhaustive list; new methods are constantly being devised. Nor are these methods mutually exclusive: performative reporting may also use technology, poetic reporting may be collaborative and so on. Also, it is possible – and sometimes desirable – to use more than one method of reporting. We will see some examples of this later in the chapter.

In this chapter we invite you to consider:

- good practice in reporting research creatively;
- the role of fictionalisation in research reporting;
- mixed-methods reporting of research;
- poetry in research reporting;
- comics and graphic novels;
- collaborative reporting;
- performative reporting; and
- the ethical aspects of reporting on research.

Good practice

As is so often the case, the use of creative methods does not alter the principles of good practice. The primary principle in reporting is to think about your audience or audiences. Do not think only of what you want to convey, think also of who wants to hear what you have to say. How can you reach those people? What will help them to understand the points you want to make? This is not always easy to think through, but it is well worth the effort. You may have to use your imaginative as well as your cognitive faculties. Figuring out, as best you can, answers to these who/how/what questions will help you to decide on the most appropriate reporting method or methods.

There are some key points of good practice in reporting which apply, whoever is in your audience.

- Use plain language whenever possible.
- If you have to use a technical term, provide a brief definition in plain language.
- Use short words and sentences.
- Create a structure that will help your audience understand the points you want to make.
- Seek feedback on drafts and use it to help improve your output.
- Edit carefully to ensure your product is free of errors.
- Avoid clichés.
- Avoid repetition; reiterate points only when necessary for audience comprehension.
- Do not plagiarise other people's work.
- Give yourself enough time to create a good-quality report of your research.

Another good practice point: if you have used creative methods to gather and/or analyse data, such as collage for data gathering or poetry for analysis, where possible use examples of these in your research reports. They will help to breathe life into your work. You will need to use careful judgement about what to include, when and where. Of course, you should not include anything that could reveal the identity of someone who has been promised anonymity. Nor should you simply include the most aesthetically appealing items, or whatever will give most support for a conclusion you want to draw. It can be helpful to formulate a rationale for including examples from your work: this could be to illustrate points made, or to offer a different perspective, or for some other reason. A rationale should help to reduce bias in selection, and you can include it in your report to inform your readers.

Education researchers often seek to apply their findings to practice. This is understandable, sensible and difficult to do effectively. It is very important not to overclaim. For example, your findings may be interesting and potentially useful, but if they are drawn from research in your own institution, community, region or country they may not be applicable elsewhere. Equally, they *may* be applicable elsewhere – but if you start saying they *are* or they *will be*, you are overclaiming. Do not underclaim, either: saying your findings are *not* applicable elsewhere is just as unhelpful (unless you have a very good reason).

One method of applying findings to practice is to make recommendations. These, too, can be difficult to write. They need to be practical and implementable. Your research may have found, unequivocally, unarguably, that small-group cookery lessons should be available weekly for every new family in your district. However, if there are not enough resources to make this happen, there is no point recommending that it should. This does not mean that you should withhold your finding. Also, this kind of finding often leads to research into the resources that are available, so you can report on both together. Then you can make an implementable recommendation, such as that cookery lessons could be provided monthly at a community centre, or that a cooking-buddy system could be set up in the district, or that a recipe book for new families could be produced by local people. This often involves some creative thinking and good local knowledge. Also, it is always worth checking your recommendations with participants and other stakeholders before you finalise them, because those people's ideas may confirm or strengthen your own.

Most reports of research are in writing, so this chapter will focus mostly on the art and craft of writing in education research. Even reports of research in other media, such as comics or video, are often written before the visual elements are created. Writing is an embodied practice (Richardson, 1997, p 49), whether we write by hand or digitally (Ellingson, 2017, p 150). Also, some scholars speak of 'embodied writing', or writing that uses sensory words which can evoke sensation in the reader (Yoo, 2019, pp 152–3). Poetry is often embodied in both senses, and prose may be so too. It is worth aiming for embodied writing where possible, as this will be more engaging for audiences.

CASE STUDY 7.1: USING CREATIVELY GATHERED DATA IN RESEARCH REPORTING

Who and where: Susan Wallace, education researcher and teacher from the UK.

What: Using generated fairy tales in reporting action research with student teachers.

Why: The author's aim was to give an account of her experimental action research to discover whether student teachers' reflection on practice could be enhanced by fictionalising their experience (Wallace, 2010, p 468).

How: Within the action research, student teachers were asked to create and discuss fairy tales focusing on any aspect of their professional experience. This was intended to encourage them to reflect on their practice. In the reporting, some of the generated fairy tales were included, in part or in whole, to illustrate key themes emerging from the analysis of the stories. Here is an example:

The prince put on his armour and tightened his chin strap. 'Once more into the breech,' [sic] he muttered to himself, and taking a deep breath he stepped into the room where the goblins were running riot. When they saw that he was fully armoured and wielding his broadsword most of them cowered away. But one of them, the most gobby goblin of the lot, just turned his back and kept on talking to his mates. 'Turn around,' ordered the prince. But Gobby took no notice. Right that's it thought the prince to himself. They need to know who's boss. And with one sweep of his trusty broadsword he sliced off Gobby's head. This made the other goblins take a bit of notice. (Wallace, 2010, p 473)

It is easy to see this as a metaphor for the classroom, and it is engaging to read. Wallace included excerpts from other stories and from the student teachers' written commentaries on their own stories and those of others, and skilfully wove these into her narrative. She did not give a full rationale for the choices she made about what to include and what to leave out, though she did specify that she privileged the student teachers' interpretations even when her own were different (Wallace, 2010, p 472).

Tip
- Think through your rationale for including creatively gathered data and make this clear for your readers.

Trap
- It can be tempting to privilege your own interpretations. Wallace considered whether adding her own interpretation might be useful, but ultimately decided that in this situation it would be unethical because it would undermine the objective of encouraging student teachers' independent reflection (Wallace, 2010, p 478). This is good ethical practice. As researchers we are trained to make and use our own interpretations, but we must also be able to see when that is inappropriate.

Reflective questions
1. When reporting on research, why is it important to give a rationale for what data you put in and what you leave out?
2. How could you include visual data in your reporting?
3. What might be the disadvantages of using creatively gathered data in research reports?
4. Can you think of a different situation in which a researcher's own interpretation would also be inappropriate?

Fictionalisation and mixed methods

We saw one use of fictionalisation in the work of Wallace (2010) reported in case study 7.1, who asked her participants to generate fairy tales and then used some of these to illustrate her research report. Another option is for researchers to use fictionalisation themselves, rather than eliciting it from participants, and there are a number of ways this can be done. A composite quote or case study may be used to conceal the identity of participants who need to be anonymous by 'selecting representative elements from the data set and composing a new original that is not traceable back to the originals' (Markham, 2012, p 5). Short stories may be written to create an emotional connection between research participants and research audiences (Diversi, 1998, p 133). Creating fictionalised accounts may help researchers to distance themselves from their own experiences (Weibe, 2014, p 552), which can help to reduce bias. These are just some of the ways fictionalisation can be used in research.

Some people still claim that there is no place for fiction in research (Weibe, 2014, p 552). Yet narrative structure and devices are essential for social science writing (Richardson, 1997, p 27). Stories and narrative can help researchers to communicate experience, ideas and emotions concisely, and to make sense of complex situations (Gabriel and Connell, 2010, p 507). It is a very human trait to tell, co-create and learn from stories. They allow us to 'experiment with solutions to problems, try out explanations and interpretations' (Gabriel and Connell, 2010, p 508), and that is the main business of research. So we argue that fiction in general, and stories in particular, have a key role to play in research reporting. This may perhaps be even more so in education research, as storytelling is inextricably linked with teaching (Leggo and Sameshima, 2014, p 542).

In general, fictionalisation can help to make education research reporting more accessible and more engaging (Leggo and Sameshima, 2014, p 540). We agree with Leggo and Sameshima (2014, p 543) that education researchers would benefit from focusing on the value of fiction to represent reality.

Fictionalisation seems often to be present when methods of reporting are mixed. There are many ways in which this can be done, though they can be divided into two main approaches: mixing methods within a research report (case study 7.2), and mixed-methods reporting on a research project (case study 7.3).

CASE STUDY 7.2: MIXING METHODS WITHIN A RESEARCH REPORT

Who and where: Ben Clayton, sports researcher from the UK.

What: Clayton researched male university student football players' discourses around masculinity and gender, to try to understand those men's behaviour. His research report used a combination of techniques from conventional academic writing, fiction and non-fiction.

Why: Clayton adopted this approach to 'show' his readers, rather than 'tell' them about, how his students behave (Clayton, 2010, p 382), while also linking this phenomenon with relevant academic literature and theory.

How: Conventional academic writing provided the report frame: an abstract, an introduction and a conclusion. However, even within this there are allusions to other ways of writing. The abstract begins, 'This paper presents a tale ...' (Clayton, 2010, p 371), which is a clear signal to the underlying storytelling. The heading 'Conclusion' is followed by '(or the final elucidatory pause)', a more literary way of saying the same thing (Clayton, 2010, p 380).

The centre of the article is the tale itself, the story of a ten-minute classroom interaction informed by empirical data. The tale is framed by creative non-fiction-type prose in the third person, interspersed with fictionalised scenes incorporating standard elements of fiction writing such as dialogue, speech tags, description and sensory writing.

Tips

*   If you write a story for research purposes, ask others to read your drafts critically: to test for evocativeness and realism, and to ask questions about how typical or exceptional are the events or interactions you depict (Clayton, 2010, p 373).
*   Tell different but related stories in a variety of ways, to solve the problem of sacrificing detail in favour of increased accessibility (discussed further in Chapter 8).

Trap

*   Showing audiences your participants, through a creatively produced story, is likely to be less conclusive than telling an audience about your findings (Clayton, 2010, p 381). This is because 'a story always opens up more questions than it provides answers' (Leggo and Sameshima, 2014, p 545).

Reflective questions

1.   How could you use fictionalisation in reporting your research?
2.   Which other methods of reporting could you use alongside fictionalisation?
3.   How would those methods improve your reporting?
4.   When do you think researchers should use a single method of reporting research?

CASE STUDY 7.3: MIXED-METHODS REPORTING ON A RESEARCH PROJECT

Who and where: Dawn Mannay and her colleagues at Cardiff University in Wales.

What: They investigated the educational experiences and aspirations of care-experienced children and young people.

Why: They aimed to gather and represent the views of these children and young people on where improvements could be made to their educational experiences, because care-experienced children and young people achieve poorer educational outcomes than their peers.

How: The fieldwork adopted creative, participatory and visual methods. Then – of particular relevance here – the researchers reported on their findings in a wide range of ways to reach a variety of diverse audiences. These audiences included care-experienced children and young people, foster carers, teachers, social workers and other practitioners.

The researchers wrote a conventional research report with three summaries: a standard executive summary, a child-friendly summary and a summary for young people. They produced five short films, three songs with accompanying music videos and three graphic art posters. They also produced two magazines, *Thrive* for young people and *Greater Expectations* for foster carers. These 'translated the findings and recommendations into a magazine format with problem pages, features and advice sections, which resonate with other popular print press publications and are ... accessible for ... foster carers and young people' (Mannay et al, 2019, p 56).

Tips
- Mixing methods of reporting research is particularly useful when you want to reach a range of diverse audiences.
- The use of creative methods is often helpful when you want to involve participants in research reporting.

Trap
- Mixing methods of research reporting is often resource intensive. Mannay and her colleagues needed to secure funding from a few different sources. They were also dependent on support from several individual and organisational collaborators. While very worthwhile, this approach is also difficult and demanding, and should not be undertaken lightly.

Reflective questions
1. How can mixing methods in research reporting help researchers to reach more diverse audiences?
2. Why is it important to make research reports accessible to a wide range of people?
3. When might researchers choose to involve participants in research reporting?
4. How could researchers mix methods in research reporting without needing so many resources?

Poetry

Some people argue that there is no place for poetry in research reporting. Our view is different. Poetic writing offers a way to sum up, to get to the heart of the matter, to communicate concisely and with intensity. This applies particularly with shorter poems (Lahman et al, 2011, p 894). Poetry demonstrably makes people think and feel differently (Dark, 2009, pp 182–3). Therefore, poems can have considerable impact on audiences (Yoo, 2019, p 153).

Poetry may be most useful in reporting research based on verbal data such as that gathered through interviews or focus groups. This is partly because written speech is usually represented in prose, yet speech is often more like poetry (Carter, 2004, p 10). Some scholars have demonstrated how identical passages have a different effect when rendered as prose and as poetry (Patrick, 2016, p 395; Kara, 2020, pp 173–4). Lisa Patrick is a literacy researcher at the University of Ohio who is interested in poetic methodologies. Drawing on her own earlier research, she gives an example of this (Patrick, 2013, p 234, cited in Patrick, 2016, p 395).

The data arranged as prose:

   Jenny: Through my choices of lines to use in my poem, I realized what parts of the story meant the most to me and how the story really impacted me and helped me to grow as a reader and as a person.

The data arranged as poetry:

Jenny
Through my choices of lines to use in my poem,
I realized
what parts of the story
meant the most
to me
and how the story really
impacted me and
helped me
to grow as a reader
and as a person.

Patrick does not argue that poetry is better than prose, but that 'each form offers a unique way of viewing the data' (Patrick, 2016, p 395). At times, therefore, it may not be necessary to choose between prose and poetry; it may be more helpful to use both. Patrick does this throughout her article, using 'found poetry' – that is, poetry compiled from other people's words and phrases – alongside prose to report on her research into creative writing with prospective teachers. She even concludes with a 'found poem' she compiled from the words and phrases in the list of references for her article (Patrick, 2016, p 403).

   Poetry demonstrates that writing to evoke emotion, and writing with precision, are not mutually exclusive. Yet most poetry is more open than most prose to 'multiple and open readings' (Richardson, 1997, p 143). This means that while poetry is potentially useful for any researcher, it may be particularly useful for researchers working from standpoints such as postmodernism, feminism or Deleuzian theory, which prioritise multiplicity.

Much research poetry is written in free verse, though established poetic forms may also be used, or new ones devised (Fry, 2005, p xviii). Maria Lahman and her colleagues in the US studied the graduate school experiences of international doctoral students, using in-depth narrative interviews, and reported their findings in a conventional research article written in prose. Then they composed three research poems in different styles: free verse, elegy (a structured rhyming poem of mourning) and senryu (a type of haiku that focuses on human relationships rather than the environment). The researchers then reread and reflected on the conventional article and the three different poems. They considered which was the most appealing and why, and also what unique knowledge they gained from each form and how the different renditions informed and enriched each other (Lahman et al, 2011, p 891, drawing on the work of Laurel Richardson, 2002, p 942). They did not come to any firm answers to those questions. However, they did conclude that poetry makes research findings more accessible for some people (though not for all, as some people are unfamiliar with, or daunted by, or alienated by poetry). Also, short forms of poetry, such as haiku and senryu, can carry a powerful message (Lahman et al, 2011, p 894). We would add couplets, quatrains and limericks to the options here.

Some researchers use poetry alone, or primarily, to report their findings. Again, they may use free verse or established or new poetic forms. If we are constrained into apparently factual prose by the requirements of an academic journal, that limits the perspectives we can present. This helps us to understand that 'How we are expected to write affects what we can write about' (Richardson, 1997, p 42). Similarly, trying to fit a message into an established poetic form can reduce our options for multivocality or expressing complexity. On the other hand, though, the boundaries of different genres of writing can enable ideas and insights to arise that may not appear in any other way.

CASE STUDY 7.4: POETIC RESEARCH REPORTING

Who and where: Darlene Drummond from the University of Miami in Florida, US.

What: Drummond published 'White American Style in Rhyme', which is an academic journal article made up of a short prose abstract and three poems.

Why: This was situated as an experiment in unconventional reporting. The information was taken from Drummond's research into the intra-racial experiences of White college women, and 'the author used the poetry styles to address serious issues of racial identification, identity negotiation, and enactment' (Drummond, 2011, p 332).

How: The poems were written using established forms: a villanelle, a rondeau and a roundel. Drummond used these forms effectively to convey her material.

Tips

- Even if you use established poetic forms, do not worry too much about the poem's aesthetic appeal. When you use poetry in research reporting, the aim is to write a poem that is 'good enough' (Lahman and Richard, 2014, p 345, drawing on Lawrence-Lightfoot, 1983). This means a poem that is fit for purpose – the purpose being to communicate your points to your audience.
- In academic publications, using poetry alongside prose to report research is likely to reach a wider audience than using poetry alone or using mostly poetry with a little prose.

Traps

- Using established poetic forms can be challenging. For example, the villanelle has 19 lines grouped in five stanzas of three lines each plus a final quatrain, with a complex prescribed sequence of rhyme and repetition. The rondeau and the roundel have similar structures and also specify the number of syllables per line. Finding the right words to communicate research findings within such constraints can be very difficult.
- Unconventional research reporting can struggle to find an audience. At the time of writing in early 2020, Drummond's article from 2011 had been cited only twice, in 2015 and 2016.

Reflective questions

1. How much skill in poetry writing do you think you need to use poetry in research reporting? Why?
2. What do you see as the pros and cons of using established poetic forms or free verse?
3. Do you think poetry alone can adequately report on research? Why?
4. How do issues of power affect the use of poetry in research reporting?

Comics and graphic novels

Research has demonstrated that the use of pictures together with text, as in comics, graphic novels, zines and animation, aids comprehension and retention of information (Duncan et al, 2016, p 44; Aleixo and Sumner, 2017, p 79; Botes, 2017, p 1). In education, comics are primarily used as resource materials (Aleixo and Norris, 2010, p 72), perhaps because they are known to engage and help to motivate students (Hosler and Boomer, 2011, p 309; Blanch and Mulvihill, 2013, p 38). Because comics and graphic novels demonstrably engage and motivate, and help with comprehension and retention of information, we argue that there is a place for them in reporting on education research. One scholar who agrees is the American Nick Sousanis, who created a pioneering doctoral dissertation, in graphic novel format, arguing for the importance of visual thinking in teaching and learning. His dissertation, 'Unflattening', was published by Harvard University Press (Sousanis, 2015) and won the 2015 Lynd Ward Graphic Novel Prize.

Researchers from across the social sciences are beginning to see the potential of comics and graphic novels for reporting research. As yet, this seems to be in its infancy in education research, though there are a small number of examples.

CASE STUDY 7.5: RESEARCH REPORT IN COMIC FORM

Who and where: UK-based education researcher Katy Vigurs.

What: Vigurs conducted research into the impact of student debt for the Society for Research into Higher Education and wrote a conventional research report. She then decided to create a comic based on that report: *Higher Fees, Higher Debts: Greater Expectations of Graduate Futures? A Research-Informed Comic.*

Figure 7.1: The cover of *Higher Fees, Higher Debts* (Vigurs et al, 2016)

Why: Vigurs had become aware of comics as 'a powerful, engaging and efficient way to communicate an important message that stemmed from research findings' (Priego, 2016, p 4). Many of the student participants' descriptions of their financial worries were very visual. Colleagues from the arts faculty advised her to create a comic.

How: A BA degree in Cartoon and Comic Arts ran at Vigurs' institution, Staffordshire University. She was able to secure funding for a creative dissemination output and hired four students to work with her on the comic, which can be downloaded from the Staffordshire Online Repository.

Tip

- Seek help from others if you're unsure of how to go about working to create a comic or graphic novel (Priego, 2016, p 7).

Trap

- Creating a comic or graphic novel can be more time consuming than you might at first expect. While this may seem counter-intuitive, working collaboratively can actually make the process even more time consuming (Priego, 2016, p 7).

Reflective questions

1. What do you think are the most useful qualities of comics and graphic novels for reporting research?
2. When do you think it might not be a good idea to use a comic or graphic novel to report on research? Why?
3. Do you think a comic or graphic novel alone could report adequately on research? Why?

Using technology to report on research

As well as text and text with visuals, there are ways to report research findings using technology, such as through blogging, video, podcasts and animation.

A blog post is a short piece of 500–1,000 words, typically with at least one illustration and several hyperlinks in the text. Some education researchers have their own blogs, such as Sam Sims' Quantitative Education Research Blog from the UK and Deborah Netolicky's the édu flâneuse from Australia. Other education researchers choose to write occasional guest posts for institutional or other blogs.

A blog post can be a great way to publicise research findings fast. Having your own blog means that you have total control, but it is a big commitment. Blogs are content heavy, so you need to be an enthusiastic writer to have a successful blog. Millions of blog posts are published every day (Carrigan, 2020, p 2), so bloggers have to compete hard for readers. Then again, blogs can be useful places to try out ideas and store thoughts and resources (Carrigan, 2020, p 203). Also, they can enable you to reach a wide variety of people: participants, practitioners, policy makers and others (Carrigan, 2020, p 100). Writing a guest post for a high-profile blog may reach more people than publishing in the mainstream media. There are high-profile blogs dedicated to education research, such as EduResearch Matters from Australia and the Institute of Education London blog from the UK, as well as more general social science blogs and mainstream blogs which accept guest posts.

Video is an increasingly popular way to report on research. This is partly because it is becoming easier to make video; in theory, you can do it with a smartphone. In practice, for best results you may need other tools, but it is possible even for amateurs to create decent videos with inexpensive equipment. And some education researchers have access to institutional resources to help them create videos.

Some institutions are setting up their own programmes of video research reports. The American Institutes for Research has a playlist on YouTube, 'Education Research and Findings', containing short videos. In other cases, individual researchers publish videos reporting on their research. Dr Susan Bruce has published a video on 'Action Research in Special Education', giving examples of action research projects at Perkins School for the Blind in the US.

A small but increasing number of academic journals are accepting and peer-reviewing video articles. There is even a dedicated Video Journal of Education and Pedagogy, founded in 2016, which publishes only video articles.

Podcasts are audio files which people can download to listen to offline, and they are increasing in popularity. Podcasts can be any length and can be in various formats such as monologue, interview or conversation. You can make a one-off podcast using the recording equipment in your smartphone, laptop or other device and upload it to your website, blog or a platform such as SoundCloud. Alternatively, you could try to get yourself interviewed on a hosted podcast. Like blogs, these are content heavy and hosts are often happy to hear from people with interesting content to discuss. At the time of writing, Player FM keeps a list of education research podcasts with dozens of options for you to explore.

Figure 7.2: A still from 'Flying While Fat', by Stacy Bias

Stacy Bias is a fat activist and freelance animator who used animation to report on her research into the impact of flying on fat people. She wanted to find a way of reporting which used the voices of some of her research participants (that is, those who consented) and could educate others about fat people's experience of travelling by plane. Her animation 'Flying While Fat' is six minutes long, and she made it available online. Within weeks it had hundreds of thousands of views; within months it had millions (Phillips and Kara, 2021, p 112).

Animation is a skilled and time-consuming process so it is not an easy option. Of course, it helped that Bias was already an animator. However, she also used some creative thinking: she was not deterred by the fact that research projects are rarely reported using animation. The extent of the reach of her animation shows that this is an effective reporting method for researchers with the skills and/or resources to make it happen.

This also shows that innovation in research reporting can pay dividends. Do you have a skill that is not conventionally used to create reports, but could be? Or do you have access to resources – skilled colleagues, skilled students or funding – that could help you take an innovative step in research reporting, like Katy Vigurs with her comic or Stacy Bias with her animation?

Collaborative reporting

It is common in the education discipline for academic articles to have more than one author. However, this may not indicate that the writing process itself was collaborative. A co-author could have written one section of an article and given feedback on the rest. Occasionally someone may be named as a co-author without having written any of the article, such as when they have carried out the analytic work from which the reported findings are drawn.

Actual collaborative writing for research reports is quite rare, but there are examples. However, one of the difficulties in writing this chapter was that education researchers who report collaboratively in writing focus much more on *what* they are reporting than on *how* they collaborated in the reporting process. Case study 7.6 is no exception, but it does provide some useful clues.

Reporting research using methods other than writing is often a collaborative process, as we have seen in several of the examples in this chapter. We would like to see more education researchers explaining their reporting methods. We agree with Leggo and Sameshima that it is important to elucidate the ways in which we narrate the stories we tell (Leggo and Sameshima, 2014, p 545).

CASE STUDY 7.6: COLLABORATIVE RESEARCH REPORTING

Who and where: John Adamson and Theron Muller, Euro-Western language teacher scholars working at universities in Japan.

What: Adamson and Muller collaborated on autoethnographic research into working peripherally: in the geographic periphery rather than the Euro-Western centre; in the academic periphery where language education resides; and in the linguistic and ethnic periphery they occupy as Euro-Westerners in Japan.

Why: They wanted 'to show how academics exploring and representing their (our) own stories and experiences can contribute to the ongoing conversation regarding academic migration in the context of globalized higher education' (Adamson and Muller, 2018, p 207).

How: The authors' universities are 250 km apart, so they used documents in Google Drive to collaborate on their autoethnography, together with occasional meetings online and face to face. This provided a 'conversational third space' (Adamson and Muller, 2018, p 211) for both of them to reflect on their practices and experiences. This third space bridged their countries of origin (first space) and Japan/workplaces (second space). Adamson and Muller wrote dialogically, co-creating narratives which they revisited and analysed. They do not explain how they collaborated in writing their report of their findings, but it seems reasonable to surmise that they would have used a similar system.

Tips
- Remember that writing is a research method and, where appropriate, reveal your writing methods. This is particularly important when you are using a creative approach such as genuinely collaborative writing.
- Collaborative writing can be a very supportive process (Richardson, 1997, pp 99–100).

Trap
- Collaboration can be difficult and the stakes may be high (Lemon and Salmons, 2021, p 5). Careful thought and self-care are essential.

Reflective questions
1. Under what circumstances might collaboration hinder the reporting process?
2. What do you think are the principal advantages of collaborating on research reporting?
3. When is it important to reveal your writing methods, and why?
4. What ethical issues might arise from collaborating on research reporting?

Performative research reports

Performative reporting doesn't involve actual performance, though it may form the basis of performative presentation and/or dissemination. Performative reporting refers to the use of methods including many of those we have already seen in this chapter such as poetry, scripts and screenplays – those methods which could, in principle, lead to performance. Again, storytelling is fundamental.

Also, performative methods link with several of the approaches we have covered in this chapter. Fictionalisation can be used in dramatising participants' stories, research encounters and so on. Creating characters is an embodied approach which can help to make your work more engaging for readers (Weibe, 2014, p 552). And performative reporting is very often collaborative.

While a performative approach may be useful for any researcher, it is perhaps particularly useful for researchers who are drawing on theories that prioritise performativity, such as those of Derrida, Lyotard or Butler.

CASE STUDY 7.7: PERFORMATIVE REPORTING OF RESEARCH

Who and where: Katrina Rodriguez and Maria Lahman, education researchers in Colorado, US.

What: Rodriguez and Lahman created a dramatic performative text using fictionalisation to report their research into the experiences of Latina college students.

Why: They wanted to illuminate participants' life stories, particularly participants' own views of their ethnic identities and educational values.

How: The researchers created fictitious exchanges between student characters, and combined these with direct quotes from interview and focus group transcripts to produce a dramatic text incorporating performative dialogue (Rodriguez and Lahman, 2011, p 602).

Tips
- Dramatic texts are useful for portraying complexity through multiple narratives (Rodriguez and Lahman, 2011, p 604).
- The use of different voices can help us to 'show' rather than 'tell' (Richardson, 1997, p 73).
- Even if you plan never to have your drama performed, it may be useful to enlist the support of others in reading a draft aloud, to help ensure the dialogue is authentic (Rodriguez and Lahman, 2011, p 611).

Traps

- Dramatic text may sit uneasily alongside conventional research reports, such as academic journal articles, which usually require a single narrative arc (Rodriguez and Lahman, 2011, p 604).
- It is difficult to write a dramatic text that others find authentic (Rodriguez and Lahman, 2011, p 611).

Reflective questions

1. Under what kinds of circumstances do you think performative reporting would be most useful?
2. What do you think are the potential disadvantages of performative reporting?
3. Why do you think it can be difficult to write a dramatic text that others find authentic?
4. How might you use performative reporting in your own research?

Ethical issues in research reporting

Reporting on research is a powerful act. We must make choices in this process, and each choice we make has ethical implications (Richardson, 1997, p 34). All the creative methods of reporting research based on text – poetry, fiction, dramatisation – are difficult to deploy effectively, whether for research or otherwise (Weibe, 2014, p 552). Yet researchers, like others, can 'learn the intricate challenges that comprise the craft and art' of creative writing in the service of research (Leggo and Sameshima, 2014, p 545). And our reporting, if we are sufficiently skilled and persuasive, may influence others. We cannot control the precise effect of our research reports on others, but we can control the content and structure of those reports (Richardson, 1997, p 117). With this power, though, comes responsibility, and it comes from several sources.

External factors may affect the ways in which we report our research findings. These include the influences of funders and other stakeholders, so it is important that we explain these influences, and how we think they have affected our work, within our reports (Brooks et al, 2014, p 164). There may also be tension between the need to report accurately and the need to care for participants' well-being (Brooks et al, 2014, p 165). We also need to act ethically in respect of researchers whose work we build on, by citing their work correctly and not plagiarising (Löfström, 2011, p 263). Each responsibility puts pressure on researchers, and balancing them can feel like a juggling act at times. Therefore, it is also part of our ethical duty to take care of ourselves amid these competing priorities (Kara, 2018, p 162).

Writing and other forms of reporting can conceal much more than they reveal. Academic journal articles reporting empirical research typically present a neat account of a process which was anything but neat (Kara, 2018, p 123). This may, at times, be acknowledged, but usually still within a tidy narrative. As ethical education researchers, we need keen awareness of what we are revealing in our research reports, what we are concealing and why.

As well as telling and showing our work to others, writing also brings us new insights and ideas (Richardson, 1997, pp 87–8). Sometimes these new thoughts are easy to use and incorporate; sometimes they are disruptive or tangential. This creates an ethical difficulty for a writer. Tangential and disruptive thoughts can be very useful, but when time is limited (as it usually is for Euro–Western education researchers) it is not easy to know when to pay attention to new ideas and when to let them go. At a minimum, we would advise that you keep a record of ideas and insights that occur as you write. This should help you to maintain the flow of your writing and enable you to assess your new ideas and insights separately from the writing process. That way you are likely to make better decisions about what to include, and how to do so.

Conventional social science writing aimed to be 'disembodied' (Ellingson, 2017, p 6), privileging the values of detachment and objectivity. We argue that education researchers today have an opposite ethical imperative for their reporting: to engage audiences intellectually and emotionally (Richardson, 1997, p 167; Pickering and Kara, 2017). Or, at least, to try our best to do so.

Conclusion

This chapter has outlined some creative ways of reporting research. Of course, others are also used in education research, such as zines (Boatwright, 2019) and textiles (Photo 7.1), and no doubt more will be invented in time.

Photo 7.1: Part of Clare Danek's 'stitch journal' of her PhD research: one sewn square per day

There is a danger here in that the appeal of a method may override other considerations. If you are a poet, it will be tempting to use poetry; if you are an avid reader of graphic novels and have good drawing or computer skills, it may be tempting to produce a comic. However, it is essential to select methods in the interests of the research, not in the interests of the researcher. Of course you must take your own abilities into account. Trying to create an animation to report on your research will be much more challenging and time consuming if you have no animation skills or experience. Do take care to ensure that you choose the methods which will best serve the research and its audiences.

CHAPTER DISCUSSION QUESTIONS

1. Do you agree that all research reporting is, to an extent, creative? Why?

2. What do you see as the relationship between fictionalisation and truth?

3. Some people argue that using creative methods in reporting research is a distraction from the real issues. What is your view of this, and why?

4. Which skills do you have that link to the methods covered in this chapter? How could you put those skills to use in your own research?

5. Which method of reporting do you find most appealing? What potential dangers could that attraction hold for your own research?

8

Presentation

Chapter summary

After a brief introduction to set the scene, we discuss good practice in presentation. This includes working to meet the needs of your audience or audiences and using more than one method of presentation. Then we look at the role of creativity in presenting research in writing, particularly presenting data and participants. We consider ways in which quantitative and even some qualitative data can be presented visually, using graphs and charts. We review ways of presenting participants using quotes and screenplay scripts, and offer an example to show how this can work in practice.

Then we turn to creative uses of technology, particularly in presenting research findings: video, digital storytelling and whiteboard animation. Case studies and an example show how these methods have been used in education research. We discuss the role of collaboration in performative presentation, and offer case studies to demonstrate that this can be done in both small-scale and large-scale ways. The chapter concludes with a discussion of the ethics of presentation.

Introduction

In this chapter we look at creative ways to present our research to audiences. We begin by considering good practice in research presentation. Then we look at representation of data, participants and findings. We discuss some creative methods of presenting research in person, which is always, effectively, a performance. Dissemination – circulating research outputs more widely – is covered in Chapter 9. We also review the ethical dimensions of presenting research.

As we saw in Chapter 7, research is most often reported in writing, though researchers are also using visual, performative and poetic methods to report on their work. Here we look in more detail at how written reports can be presented creatively on page and screen.

Performative presentation is embodied; there is no way to perform without using our bodies (Ellingson, 2017, p 1). Conventional performative presentation can be incredibly boring, such as when someone reads text from a page (Cutcher, 2013, p 39; Evergreen, 2014, p 5). Conversely, using creative performative methods can engage audiences intellectually and emotionally.

Storytelling is at the root of the presentation process, whether in prose, drama, film, dance or any other form of presentation. A good story will inform and entertain an audience. Stories have been described as 'the creative conversion of life itself to a more powerful, clearer, more meaningful experience' (McKee, 1999, p 27). As this suggests, a story is an effective way of making sense of complexity. Also, a story is an accessible way to present information (Kovach, 2009, p 131).

It seems that education researchers rarely use poetry in presentations. There is clearly scope for doing this, because poetic inquiry can help researchers to understand and communicate their findings in other ways than those promoted by their disciplinary training (Cahnmann-Taylor, 2009, p 24). Also, presenting participants' experiences in poetic form can help people to identify and empathise with those participants (Dumenden, 2016, p 227). Conversely, research poems can be easily understood by, and so make findings accessible to, participants themselves (Stapleton, 2018, p 19).

Education researchers do use a range of other creative methods for presenting their research, including imaginative uses of technology and performance. We cover these later in the chapter, but first we consider the principles of good practice in presenting research.

In this chapter we invite you to consider:

- the needs of your audience(s);
- how best to meet those needs;
- presentation in writing;
- using technology in presentation;
- collaborative presentation;
- performative presentation;
- mixing methods in presentation; and
- the ethical issues associated with presentation.

Good practice in research presentation

Presentation methods should be chosen with your audience in mind. Think about their characteristics and attributes: ages, genders, ethnicities, cultural backgrounds and other characteristics. If you are not sure, use your best guesses or estimates. Then select the methods you think are most likely to help you communicate effectively with your audience (Kelleher and Wagener, 2011, p 826; McNiff, 2019, p 34). Presentation is a relational process, whether written or performative; you are working together with your readers, viewers and audiences to create meaning (Kirk, 2016, p 22).

It is good practice in research presentation to use more than one method at a time, whether in writing or performance. There are two main reasons for this. First, evidence shows that audience members retain more information if presentation includes more than one method (Evergreen, 2014, p 18). Second, using more than one method enables you to present more of the complexity of research (Mandlis, 2009, p 1358). So, a written report should contain pictures or diagrams, a performative presentation can be accompanied by images on slides or video. Written reports online can also include links to audio or video content. An image or video clip can liven up a statistical presentation and make the research seem more relevant, while a graph or a diagram can clarify specific aspects of complex qualitative data (Fielding, 2012, p 127). There are many options here, which can seem daunting, but remember to think first of what your audience will find most useful, and that will help you to narrow them down. Also, always remember to use visual elements to clarify and enhance, not to confuse and obscure.

To make your presentations more accessible, tell your story in everyday language as far as possible. It is important to connect with the language that is appropriate for your audience. If you need to include any technical or other unusual terms, then give brief, audience-friendly definitions unless your audience is made up of specialists who will know what you mean. In performative presentation, speak slowly and clearly, and use pauses to help the audience digest your messages. To ensure your presentation is easy to follow and understand, begin by writing a summary of what you want to communicate, in as few words as possible. Then use that to help you stay on track as you prepare your presentation.

In performative presentation, read aloud only briefly and when absolutely necessary. If you use visual aids such as PowerPoint, do *not* read the words from the slides. Use as few words as possible on your visual aids; pictures, diagrams, infographics and maps are more useful for your audience. However, we suggest you do not take this further, as one presenter did in a presentation attended by an author of this book. The presenter played a funny video on a screen while giving a verbal presentation on a different topic. The attending author remembers the funny video rather well, but remembers very little of the verbal presentation.

Diagrams can enable researchers to show complex and simultaneous relationships more clearly than text alone (Buckley and Waring, 2013, p 149; White et al, 2014, p 396). There are many kinds of diagram such as the flow chart, spidergram, schematic diagram and culturegram (Kara, 2020, pp 193–4). Diagrams are particularly useful for conceptualisation and, used together with text or narrative, enable audiences to understand more fully (Buckley and Waring, 2013, pp 168–9). Some researchers worry that diagrams can be reductive, but this risk is mitigated by using them with other forms of communication. However, it is possible to overdo the use of diagrams (or indeed any visual aid); they are most effective when they can add real value to your presentation (White et al, 2014, p 397).

Like diagrams, infographics are good for showing connections and explanations.

You can see that the infographic in Figure 8.1 tells a story on an interesting topic, based on research evidence, and helpfully supported by appealing and relevant visual information. This shows another good point of infographics: they are useful for understandable presentation of complex information. Many other examples of education-related infographics are readily available online.

Also available online are tools to help you create infographics such as Infogram, Piktochart and Visual.ly.

Figure 8.1: Student performance in collaborative problem solving – infographic

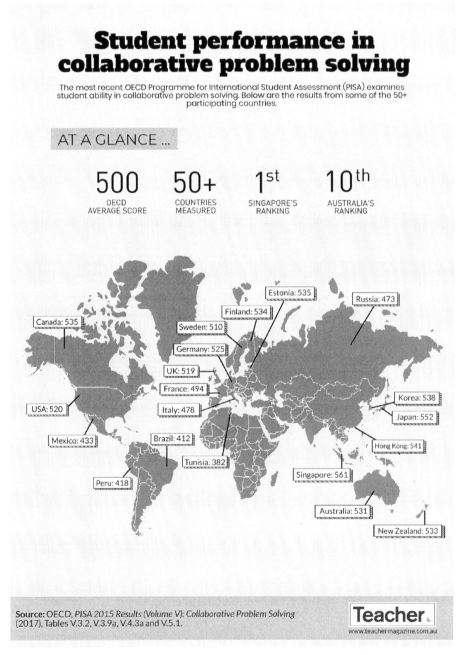

Student performance in collaborative problem solving

The most recent OECD Programme for International Student Assessment (PISA) examines student ability in collaborative problem solving. Below are the results from some of the 50+ participating countries.

AT A GLANCE ...

500 OECD AVERAGE SCORE

50+ COUNTRIES MEASURED

1st SINGAPORE'S RANKING

10th AUSTRALIA'S RANKING

Estonia: 535
Finland: 534
Russia: 473
Canada: 535
Sweden: 510
Germany: 525
UK: 519
France: 494
Korea: 538
USA: 520
Italy: 478
Japan: 552
Mexico: 433
Brazil: 412
Hong Kong: 541
Tunisia: 382
Singapore: 561
Peru: 418
Australia: 531
New Zealand: 533

Source: OECD, *PISA 2015 Results (Volume V): Collaborative Problem Solving* (2017), Tables V.3.2, V.3.9a, V.4.3a and V.5.1.

Teacher.
www.teachermagazine.com.au

Source: Infographic by Dominique Russell, *Teacher* magazine, April 2018. Reproduced by permission of The Australian Council for Educational Research Ltd.

Maps are most helpful for showing relationships. People may most commonly think of geographic or road maps, which show the relationships between geographic features and places. Maps are also useful for showing other relationships more relevant to much research, such as relationships between data and ideas (Powell, 2010, p 539; Newman, 2013, p 228) or between people. These maps can be very simple; a series of concentric circles can be used to map the closeness or distance between people and groups, and this method has been used successfully in various disciplines to gather data from children (Eldén, 2012, p 71). Or they can be much more complex, such as the large-scale Ordnance Survey maps, which give incredibly detailed information about the whole of the UK. And there are many other kinds of map. Think about a street map of your local area, a floor plan of your house and a weather map such as you might see on television. They are all different. And, as with many creative methods, you can devise your own. Software is available to help, such as My Maps by Google or MapInfo.

Using large posters for presentation is common in academia. They may be as big as four feet by six feet (or approximately 125 × 185 cm) and can be dull or dramatic (Saldaña and Omasta, 2018, pp 324–5). For an engaging poster presentation, use a good-sized font and keep detailed information, such as graphs or tables, to a minimum. Thoughtful use of colour and images will help. Also, as always with presentation, your poster should tell a story. If you have, or can recruit someone with, the relevant skills, posters in comic form have been shown to be particularly engaging and 'are well suited to convey the multidimensionality of real life' (Darnhofer, 2018, p 1).

Technology often plays a role in presentation. We have already mentioned the ubiquitous PowerPoint. Internet platforms enable researchers to present their work directly to audiences in other locations, such as through webinars or remote online conference presentations. This can help to reduce the costs and burdens of travel. The increasing accessibility of audio and video recording can be used to improve equality in presentations, such as by overcoming some of the barriers to collaborative presentation (Douglas et al, 2019, p 537; and see the later section 'Collaborative performative presentation' for more on this topic). It is good practice to use technology to help with presentation whenever it will lead to improvements over the non-technological options. We will discuss some more creative ways of using technology later in this chapter.

A great way to make presentations more interactive, as long as your audience members are likely to have personal digital devices such as smartphones or tablets, is to use an app to collect questions or take on-the-spot polls. At the time of writing, Slido is perhaps the best-known app for collecting questions during presentations, though alternative apps are available. On Slido, people can post questions anonymously if they wish. Also, everyone can see all the posted questions on their device and upvote those of interest. Another advantage of this is that it saves time in fixed-time presentations. Polling apps include Mentimeter and iClicker. They enable presenters to take real-time surveys of audience responses and present their findings straight back to the audience. Education researchers have an advantage here, as many classroom settings around the world are now using these kinds of tools. Also, online meeting apps such as Zoom sometimes have built-in polling options, though these may require extra costs to use.

Written presentation

There are many creative ways to represent data, participants and other stakeholders, and findings in written reports. Quantitative and even some qualitative data can be represented creatively using graphs and charts, as in the following examples.

- Line graphs use a line to show how values change where one variable is continuous, such as changes in population health over time. Line graphs are useful for showing trends.
- Bar graphs use columns to display relationships between discrete categories, such as the number of respondents to each question in a survey or the percentage of people involved in different leisure activities. Bar graphs are useful for making comparisons.
- Scatter graphs show relationships between two variables, such as chronological age and reading level. They use dots to show where each individual participant sits on the graph to demonstrate trends and outliers.
- Pie charts display parts of a whole. They use a circle divided into slices, often of different colours, to illustrate proportions.
- Pyramid charts can compare three variables, such as income distribution between people in two different countries. You could use a central column for daily income with a value against each row, for example, $0–$9.99, $10–$10.99, and so on. Then you could use rows extending out on each side showing the numbers of people earning at that level in India and the US.
- Radar charts look like the centre of a bicycle wheel, with a number of spokes radiating out from a central point. Each spoke represents a category, and its length shows the level of an attribute such as achievement or involvement. These are useful for 'within and between' presentations. If you had done research on involvement in extra-curricular activities in four high schools, you could make a radar chart for each school with spokes for relevant activities such as extra-curricular sports, music, drama and science. Each spoke would have a length relative to the proportion of pupils involved in that activity at that school. Then displaying these charts together would show the within-school and between-school variations.
- Flow charts are useful when you want a visual way to depict a process or a structure. These can be simple, such as a student's progress through three years of college, or complex, such as the staffing structure of a big university.
- Timelines are, as the name suggests, a line with time divisions used to display historical data or future projections.

These are probably the most common charts and graphs used in educational research, but there are many other options, and information can be found online by searching for 'types of charts' or 'types of graphs'. The use of graphs and charts involves considerable creativity in the choice of what to display and how. There are an enormous range of options for using different colours, fonts, layouts, sizes and combinations of information. This makes data visualisation quite a daunting prospect for some people, and exciting for others. Again, data visualisation is a huge subject which could – and does – take up entire books in itself (see Kirk, 2016).

Representing participants and other stakeholders is a more complex qualitative process. Until quite recently researchers used to think and talk in terms of 'giving participants a voice' in written and other research outputs. Now it is regarded as more ethical to recognise that participants have their own voices, which are not researchers' to bestow, though researchers may at times have a role in amplifying those voices. One way that researchers have done this is to include quotes from participants in presentations. This must be done with great care where anonymity and confidentiality have been assured; it is essential in these cases that any potentially identifying information is removed. Also, it is a good idea to have, and make clear to your audience, a rationale for including quotes. Including quotes to illustrate findings, or to demonstrate a range of views, or for some other defined reason is fine. Cherry-picking quotes to reinforce the points you want to make is not such a great idea.

There are other creative ways to represent participants in writing. We saw in Chapter 6 that Lisbeth Berbary from the US researched Southern sorority women and used screenplay writing in her analytic work, creating composite characters and depicting their interactions. She presented her screenplay scripts to participants and others. Many of her participants 'indicated that they enjoyed following along with the characters and looking for bits of their own experiences in the scenes' (Berbary, 2011, p 195). Non-academics were surprised by how accessible research was in this form. Berbary's conclusion (2011, p 195) was that this kind of creative approach 'changes our expectations of research because rather than disconnect and reduce experiences, it instead encourages involvement, inspires curiosity, creates inclusivity, and constructs depictions that remain in the thoughts of readers in ways that traditional representations sometimes do not'.

There are also creative ways to represent findings, such as through creative uses of technology. Education researchers are using technology to present their research and findings in a range of creative ways. Here we review the use of video, digital storytelling and whiteboard animation.

Video

Video has been, and is, used in various ways in education research. It can help to enhance democratic practices by engaging diverse voices such as those of teachers, students, faculty, administrators and community members, as well as legislators, policy makers and others (Friend and Militello, 2015, p 85). Like all good presentation methods, video is based on storytelling. Friend and Militello (2015, p 91) say: 'Rather than a peer–reviewed research publication, the final product of a research investigation utilising filmmaking methodology uses images and sound to share a story with a much wider audience about the participants, the context, and the themes explored through the video production, data analysis, and editing processes.' And video also has a role to play in the evaluation of educational work (Friend and Militello, 2015, p 86). Video can engage an audience's emotions and intellect, which helps them to retain information (Rogers and Coughlan, 2013, p 298).

Video has huge potential for co–creating and co–producing educational research together with participants, resulting in the 'co–generation of knowledge through inclusion of authentic voices that can be shared with a wide audience' (Friend and Militello, 2015, p 91). However, the use of video makes significant demands on resources of money and time. Also, there are ethical issues to consider, such as how to avoid introducing bias and how to manage intellectual property rights (Friend and Militello, 2015, p 97). Not all research ethics committees or institutional review boards have the necessary expertise to assess a project proposal that includes video (Friend and Militello, 2015, p 98). Nevertheless, education researchers are finding some very creative ways to use video for presenting research aims and findings.

CASE STUDY 8.1: VIDEO PRESENTATION IN DOCTORAL EDUCATION

Who and where: Daniel Rogers and Paul Coughlan at the Innovation Academy in Trinity College, Dublin, Ireland.

What: Rogers and Coughlan encouraged doctoral students from a range of disciplines to plan, shoot, edit and present a short video about their doctoral research.

Why: They aimed to 'enable the doctoral student to contribute to knowledge and society in different ways, and to develop within the doctoral researcher new and different skills and perspectives', and 'to explore the potential for innovation in their thesis research and to communicate this potential to academics, employers, funding agencies and other non-expert audiences' (Rogers and Coughlan, 2013, p 296).

How: Rogers and Coughlan organised a week-long, 40-hour module designed to enable doctoral students to produce research-based video content. On the final day of the module each student presented their work to their peers and supervisors, outlining their experience of video production before presenting their video (Rogers and Coughlan, 2013, pp 303–4).

Tips

- It is not enough just to shoot footage; editing skills must be applied and developed.
- All of the skills required for video production – idea generation, scriptwriting, storyboarding, filming and editing – are transferable to other contexts.

Traps

- Good-quality video editing is time consuming.
- Producing research-based video content is a complex and potentially daunting process that will take most people out of their comfort zone.

Reflective questions

1. What skills and equipment would you need to create a short video?
2. How would you ensure that a video about your research was as accessible as possible?
3. In what ways, other than through video, could student research contribute to knowledge and society?
4. What are the benefits and disadvantages of working outside your comfort zone?

Digital storytelling

As we have seen in previous chapters, one video technique that has gained considerable traction in education research is digital storytelling. This has been used in a wide range of educational settings and with a variety of topics (Friend and Militello, 2015, p 84). Digital storytelling is a process of creating a 'first-person mini-movie' (Willox et al, 2013, p 312) using images (photographs, artwork, video) and sound (music, voiced narrative, naturally occurring sounds). It has broad utility for education, particularly to enhance people's learning and understanding of others' lived experience (De Vecchi et al, 2016, p 190). Nadia De Vecchi and her colleagues in Australia conducted a scoping review to assess how digital storytelling is used in mental health around the world. They found that digital storytelling is demonstrably effective in capturing the lived experience of people with mental health problems (De Vecchi et al, 2016, p 188). They also found that the presentation of digital stories has proved useful for a variety of mental health–related educational interventions in school settings with young people (De Vecchi et al, 2016, pp 188–9). Education researchers have also found that digital storytelling is useful for capturing the lived experience of participants, which can then help to educate others.

Digital storytelling has been used with marginalised groups such as refugees (Lenette, 2019) and Indigenous people (Willox et al, 2013). Although Lenette works primarily in Australia, and Willox and her colleagues in Canada, there is a high degree of alignment between their work. Lenette agrees with Willox et al that digital stories can provide richer data than standard qualitative methods.

She suggests that presenting digital stories to policy makers may be effective in creating change (Lenette, 2019, p 119), a point echoed by Willox et al. They also agree that there is scope for digital storytelling to pathologise, romanticise, glamorise or neutralise participants and their situations (Willox et al, 2013, p 140; Lenette, 2019, p 132). Lenette (2019, p 133) suggests that researchers can mitigate these risks by working collaboratively, valuing participants' uniqueness and their culture, and embracing unconventional modes of storytelling. However, though worthwhile, these kinds of measures will not eradicate such risks entirely (Willox et al, 2013, p 141).

CASE STUDY 8.2: DIGITAL STORYTELLING

Who and where: Ashlee Cunsolo Willox from McGill University, Sherilee Harper and Victoria Edge from the University of Guelph, in Canada, and residents of the small coastal community of Rigolet in the Nunatsiavut region of north-eastern Canada. Rigolet is the southernmost Inuit community in the world and has a population of around 270.

What: A transdisciplinary team of Indigenous and non-indigenous people worked to support people from Rigolet to create digital stories about their experience of climate change.

Why: The aim of the research project was to investigate the links between climate change and Rigolet residents' physical, mental, emotional and spiritual health and well-being. The researchers used digital storytelling to complement the more standard qualitative methods of questionnaires, interviews and focus groups to reflect, preserve and promote the community's culture, histories, and narratives (Willox et al, 2013, p 131).

How: Through week-long digital storytelling workshops in Rigolet where researchers supported community members in developing and reviewing their own digital stories. At the end of each workshop, participants presented their stories to each other. Some stories were subsequently presented at academic conferences, community events, story nights and a Nunatsiavut-wide youth and Elder storytelling camp.

Tips
- Digital storytelling gives participants a great deal of control: they can 'tell their own stories, in their own words, in the manner in which they want others to hear' (Willox et al, 2013, p 136).
- Participants' presentation of digital stories enables deep sharing within groups and communities.
- Some stories may be emotionally demanding to witness when presented, so explicitly prioritising self-care for everyone involved is essential.

Traps

- Digital storytelling is a resource-intensive method, requiring access to technological resources and the skills and time to use them. Also, researchers require time and skills to build trusting relationships with individuals and communities.
- In some Indigenous communities, audio and video recording of people is not regarded as an appropriate practice, therefore digital storytelling cannot be used with these communities.
- Some participants may need to share personal stories rather than stories on a topic set by researchers.

Reflective questions

1. When and why might it be important for Indigenous and non-indigenous people to work together on research?
2. Can research ever truly be led by participants? Why?
3. What are the kinds of research topics that you think would be best served by digital storytelling?
4. Could you see yourself using digital storytelling in your own research work? Why?

Whiteboard animation

Digital storytelling is not the only technological approach to presentation that can be culturally appropriate for marginalised people. The work of Canada-based public health researchers Lori Bradford and Lalita Bharadwaj shows that whiteboard animation can also serve this purpose.

CASE STUDY 8.3: WHITEBOARD ANIMATION

Who and where: Lori Bradford and Lalita Bharadwaj at the University of Saskatchewan in Saskatoon, Canada

What: Bradford and Bharadwaj used collaborative whiteboard animation to present research findings.

Why: The researchers wanted to find ways to inform and educate communities and policy makers about environmental changes identified by Indigenous peoples in northern Canada.

How: The researchers conducted 11 ethnographic interviews with Elders and local people from the region to find out about environmental changes in their lifetimes. Analysis of this interview data yielded five themes:

1. Where we came from;
2. Development and disease;
3. Our food is changing;
4. Our water is changing;
5. The balance is off.

These themes and the data were used to develop a single encompassing narrative of environmental change in the region over 'a lifetime' (Bradford and Bharadwaj, 2015). This was converted into a script including quotes from participants. Then a sequence of images was created. A fourth-year fine arts student with Indigenous ancestry was recruited to draw key images on a whiteboard, in front of a high-quality camera capturing five images a second. Preparatory images were shared with Indigenous partners to confirm their accuracy before they were drawn for the camera. Draft segments from the animation were shared with Indigenous partners, research scientists and supporting agencies before editing was completed. The final version was presented to the community in an arranged public viewing, after which community members decided to make it available on YouTube.

The use of whiteboard animation enabled the researchers to condense a large amount of information into an accessible 13-minute video. The video was well received by Indigenous partners and has been used in schools and a health clinic as an educational tool (Bradford and Bharadwaj, 2015). However, the researchers do not explain the extent to which their presentation was delivered to, or used by, policy makers.

Tips
*   Allow plenty of time for making a whiteboard video because it is physically demanding to draw on a whiteboard for long periods of time.
*   Working collaboratively on this kind of project also requires a generous allowance of time.

Trap
*   Technical issues such as camera 'bounce' and the memory limitations of devices need specialist support to resolve.

Reflective questions
1. Why do you think the researchers chose an artist who had Indigenous ancestry?
2. Why do you think the researchers shared preparatory images and draft segments with Indigenous partners?
3. What other kinds of data, apart from interview data, do you think could be presented through whiteboard animation?
4. What makes animation so useful as an educational tool?

Collaborative performative presentation

Researchers may give presentations together with participants, colleagues or others. This can be an effective way to reflect the multivocal nature of education research, and has been done in some creative ways.

There are some barriers to collaborative presentation. Some people may not want to take part. Others may not be able to take part for any number of reasons, including inaccessible events or caring responsibilities. Funding may solve some of these problems but is not always available. Fitting a collaborative presentation into a short time period may be even more challenging than for a solo presentation. And large-scale collaborative presentation is resource intensive. Nevertheless, there are many potential benefits from presenting collaboratively, as you will see from the following case studies. It is always worth considering whether a presentation could be collaborative.

CASE STUDY 8.4: COLLABORATIVE PRESENTATION – SMALL SCALE

Who and where: Cate Watson, education researcher from the UK.

What: Watson gave a presentation on constructions of the 'home-school partnership' at a research seminar on professional development for inclusion in education. Within this, she drew on the narrative of a mother whose child had been diagnosed with Attention Deficit Hyperactivity Disorder (ADHD).

Why: There was a clear difference in perspective between the mother's view of her child's ADHD diagnosis, which seemed to her to be based on a series of trivial events, and the view of the professionals, who saw a deviant family (Watson, 2011, p 402).

How: Watson wrote a series of satirical scenes to highlight the relationship between the rational and irrational, in the narrative in particular and in society in general. Then she asked audience members at her conference presentation to volunteer to take the roles in the scripts she had written and play them out, unrehearsed, for the rest of the audience. This was well received, with audience members describing the presentation as 'powerful' (Watson, 2011, p 402).

Tip
- Volunteer 'actors' will bring their own ideas to the performance, which creates possibilities for more interpretations.

Trap
- If you expect volunteer 'actors' to perform roles exactly as you intended them, you may be disappointed.

While creative, Watson's is quite a simple, low-key approach to collaborative presentation. It is also possible to take a much bigger and higher-profile approach.

CASE STUDY 8.5: COLLABORATIVE PRESENTATION – LARGE SCALE

Who and where: Tara Goldstein and Jocelyn Wickett at the University of Toronto in Canada.

What: Goldstein and Wickett adapted a four-volume, 595-page health and safety report into a 30-minute stage play which was performed at a Safe Schools Conference attended by 500 teacher candidates.

Why: The health and safety report was the result of an investigation into school safety prompted by the fatal shooting of 15-year-old Jordan Manners in his school in Toronto. The findings and conclusions of the report were very important for schools in Toronto, but in its written form it was quite inaccessible. Goldstein was a teacher educator and experienced playwright, Wickett was a master's student in education and a theatre artist. They worked together to adapt the report and create the performance (Goldstein and Wickett, 2009, pp 1552–3).

How: The researchers defined the intended audience: teacher candidates and teacher educators. They included public responses to the report, as well as the report itself. Goldstein created characters – a media reporter and a group of five new teachers – which were included to help the intended audience relate to the performance. She also created a narrator role to emphasise that the performance was just one interpretation, and she decided which stories from the report to tell in the performance. Wickett kept the staging simple. The researchers held 'three different "validation" readings with educators and parents working in and with Toronto public schools' before the performance (Goldstein and Wickett, 2009, p 1556). The third validation reading was conducted by the people who would perform the script at the conference, who were themselves all teacher candidates and education professionals. Goldstein and Wickett revised the script after each validation reading.

Tip
- This kind of large-scale collaborative presentation can be an excellent way of communicating complex information.

Trap
- You are unlikely to be able to do this well without some relevant professional theatre skills or support from others with such skills.

Reflective questions
1.   What do you see as the disadvantages of performative presentation?
2.   What are the barriers to collaborative performative presentation of your own research?
3.   How might you overcome those barriers?
4.   How do you think power imbalances between collaborators could affect performative presentation?

The ethics of presentation

The ethics of presentation are rarely addressed in the academic literature or in research ethics guidelines. Yet methods of presenting research, like all research methods, are not neutral or value free (Ellingson, 2009, p 6). All presentation simultaneously reveals and conceals (Tamas, 2009, p 617). It is important to keep this in mind when planning and preparing presentations: what will you reveal, what will you conceal? And how ethical are the choices you are making? What will be their consequences? (Ellingson, 2009, p 39). There are always compromises to be made, and choice of method is aligned with choice of compromise. Written presentation allows for more detail but is less likely to engage readers' emotions; performative presentation can communicate emotionally and intellectually, but is likely to include fewer facts (Pickering and Kara, 2017, p 306). Performative presentation has more impact; written presentation has a longer reach. It is good ethical practice to be explicit about the choices and compromises you make as you prepare your presentation (Pickering and Kara, 2017, p 307).

Cultural sensitivity can be important when using visual methods because some colours and shapes have different meanings in different cultures (Evergreen, 2014, pp 106–7). In China, red denotes good luck, while in Europe it means danger and is often used for traffic warning signs. For some of the Indigenous peoples of Canada and Alaska, the circle is sacred and must be treated with reverence (Blodgett et al, 2013, p 319). Colours of mourning differ around the world: black in many Euro-Western countries, white in many Asian countries and purple in Brazil, where it is considered inappropriate to wear purple unless you are attending a funeral. While nobody can be expected to know the cultural background of every single person who may be in their audience, where there is a significant presence from a particular culture it is both ethical and sensible to find out about the meanings of colours and shapes in that culture, and to prepare your presentation accordingly.

Truly ethical presentation includes enough information to enable the audience to make their own judgements about the quality and value of the research. In the Indigenous research paradigm this may be facilitated by existing community methods for communicating information such as, in some communities, the sharing circle. Also in the Indigenous paradigm it is generally held to be essential to present research to participant communities (Kovach, 2009, p 149; Okalik,

2013, p 245; Wilson and Wilson, 2013, p 349; Lambert, 2014, p 215; Land, 2015, p 27). (We would also regard this as good ethical practice in Euro–Western research.) Other projects include actions such as embedding First Nations researchers and knowledge holders throughout the research process as co-researchers (Somerville, 2013; Treloyn and Charles, 2014, 2015; Tuck and McKenzie, 2014), creating Indigenous advisory boards, and empowering the Indigenous ownership of knowledge databases by using Indigenous cultural heritage licences and labels such as Mukurtu. These practices can situate research presentation in different ways, as it may become collaborative knowledge sharing with reciprocity. Co-presenting and knowledge exchange are closely aligned with the relational ethic which is widespread in Indigenous research (Bowman et al, 2015, p 351).

Promises of anonymity and confidentiality can carry specific problems for some education research. Educational institutions are close communities, which means that people carrying out research in those institutions may be able to guarantee anonymity and confidentiality to participants only in respect of people outside their institutions. It may be impossible to render data unidentifiable when it comes from, and is presented to, people who know each other very well. Even explaining this to potential participants, and obtaining their informed consent on that basis, may not prevent upset when research is presented (Reiss, 2005, p 127).

Another issue to consider in education research is how your participants are likely to receive your presentation. Education is itself about continuous improvement, and this often influences the work of education researchers, leading towards questions of what works, when, where and how. This almost inevitably implies critique which can upset participants and other stakeholders more than researchers expect (Brooks et al, 2014, p 138). Teachers, in particular, often react negatively to presentations of education research (Reiss, 2005, p 129), though other stakeholders may also exhibit adverse reactions (Carroll, 2018, pp 102–3).

This can even apply in explicitly evaluative research. Helen Kara, one of the authors of this book and an independent researcher, evaluated an education project in the early 2000s. This was an innovative project at the time and Helen's client was keen to publish the evaluation to inform work in other locations. The evaluation was overwhelmingly positive. Helen made ten recommendations in which, broadly speaking, nine said 'all going very well with this aspect of the project' and one said 'some room for improvement here', with suggestions for how that improvement could be made. She shared a draft report with her client, who then called three separate meetings to argue for the tenth recommendation to be taken out. Helen maintained that it should be left in because it was fully supported by the data she had gathered. In the end, the client grudgingly accepted the recommendation, but refused to publish the evaluation because they felt it was so critical that it reflected badly on the project.

It is good ethical practice to share presentations in draft with participants and other stakeholders when possible (Brooks et al, 2014, p 140). This is particularly so if those presentations are intended for publication. However, as Helen Kara's experience above shows, this does not provide a foolproof safeguard against all difficulties. Even so, wherever possible, it is ethically important to present your research to your participants. It is not always easy or straightforward to do this; barriers can include time, distance and power imbalances (MacKenzie et al, 2015, pp 106–7). However, it can be easier in education than in some other disciplines, particularly if your participants come from one or more institutions, though it will still be a challenge at times. In the Indigenous paradigm, presenting research to participants is often regarded as essential (Wilson, 2008, p 48; Lambert, 2014, pp 215–16). This is due to the Indigenous ethical principle of benefit sharing, which states that participants and other stakeholders should benefit from research equally with researchers.

Conclusion

We have demonstrated in this chapter that creative methods of presenting research are more accessible, engaging and memorable than conventional methods. There are a wide range of creative methods that can be used for presenting research, including some that we have not covered here, such as music and song (Fournillier, 2010). Also, new creative methods of presenting research are constantly being devised. Maybe you will devise one yourself.

Whether or not you use creative methods at other stages of the research process, the increasing evidence of their efficacy makes a compelling argument for their use in presentation. The next chapter will show that this also applies to dissemination.

 CHAPTER DISCUSSION QUESTIONS

1. How would you try to meet the needs of the audience(s) when you present your research?

2. What do you think are the main issues to consider when involving participants in creative presentation?

3. Can there be too many methods in creative presentation? Give reasons for your answer.

4. Is technology essential for creative presentation? Why?

9

Dissemination

Chapter summary

This chapter focuses on conventional and creative forms of dissemination. First it discusses the emphasis on text-based outputs and sets out how creative methods can connect with audiences in different ways. This is followed by a closer examination of chapter writing, blogs, participatory video, museum curation and multimodal online resources. Each of these approaches to dissemination is outlined and then case studies are introduced to demonstrate how researchers have applied these creative methods to disseminate their own research approaches and findings. The case studies reflect on writing a conventional academic chapter, blogging, artefact- and audio-based work in a museum context and the development of an online community of practice. A case study from South Africa provides an insight into the use of video to connect with communities and raise awareness of social issues. The case studies are followed by tips, traps and reflective questions that examine the strengths, limitations and opportunities of creative methods of dissemination. The chapter then offers an account of ethics and ethical practice. It invites you to consider how you could draw on creative forms of dissemination in your own research projects to increase the reach of your research findings, connect with diverse audiences and engender impact and changes in practice.

Introduction

'There is no best way to tell a story about society ... the world gives us possibilities among which we choose' (Becker, 2007, p 285). However, strategies of dissemination often follow a conventional path, which involves writing up findings and recommendations in a dissertation, thesis or final report, often followed by peer-reviewed journal articles and other scholarly publications such as books or chapters in edited collections. The narrowness of this dissemination strategy may mean that findings and recommendations from studies in education do not reach people who would benefit from hearing these key messages. Consequently, the implications of education research studies often have little impact on practice, policy or communities, limiting opportunities for change and improvement.

In Chapter 8 we explored different ways to present research findings – given in person, either face to face or online – and illustrated the diverse ways that audiences can be engaged with innovative, creative and multimodal presentations that go beyond the formulaic standard 'talk'. In this chapter, we consider forms of dissemination that go beyond the formulaic print-based outputs. However, this does not mean that conventional forms such as reports and academic outputs have no value. Research and publishing is the oxygen of academic life (Vale and Karataglidis, 2016) and it is important to engage with a range of dissemination strategies and see these as complementary processes rather than being in competition.

This chapter reflects on some conventional formats of dissemination before considering creative ways to disseminate education research that have the potential to reach wider and more diverse audiences and engender impact. We present illustrative case studies that draw on multimodal techniques to offer the reader an insight into possible ways of disseminating research. As Keen and Todres (2007, np) contend, 'research, done well, is worth disseminating'. Both students and more experienced academics and practitioners produce research 'done well', which should be widely shared. We invite you to consider:

- different creative techniques of dissemination;
- reaching diverse audiences; and
- ethical considerations in disseminating research.

Writing for dissemination

Universities centralise the importance of research output, and education researchers are expected to write and to publish at speed so as to keep their accounts relevant before they become obsolete (Mannay and Morgan, 2015). Despite this pressure to publish, there are arguments that the majority of academic journal publications are uncited and underused (Rawat and Meena, 2014). This position supports the adoption of more creative and engaging forms of dissemination that move beyond the dense prose that forms much academic writing. However, text-based outputs continue to retain their value as an effective method of disseminating research and they are an essential tool for communicating the findings and recommendations from studies in education.

In Chapter 7 we emphasised the importance of good writing and reporting practice. One reason why text-based outputs are important is that they provide a platform for contextualising the meaning of more transient and edited forms of dissemination such as conference presentations. Chapter 8 offered an insight into a range of arts-based methods of presentation including visual, textual and performative techniques. However, it is essential not only to engage audiences but to ensure that there are resources available to promote a holistic understanding of research projects. Avenues for the promotion of research through theatre, film, exhibitions and images 'often lack contextualizing information' (Banks and Zeitlyn, 2015, p 142). However, if these forms of presentation and creative dissemination can be linked to a written output, audiences have the opportunity to find out more about the background, methods, findings and recommendations of research studies. As we saw in Chapter 2, exhibitions and installations can also be mixed with performative methods (Cole and McIntyre, 2006).

Writing is very much part of the academic journey in educational studies. Undergraduate and postgraduate students write essays, exams and dissertations as part of formal assessments, doctoral students produce a thesis and educational practitioners may be involved in writing reports from their classroom-based research. For academic researchers, writing is centralised and projects will be communicated via reports, book chapters, books and journal articles. Importantly, the writing of students, practitioners and academic staff can be disseminated and made accessible to interested readers. As the following examples illustrate, students can draw on the research they conduct to move from the assessed outputs of the assignment, essay, dissertation or thesis towards other forms of dissemination. Work designed and carried out by students generates valuable information that is worth sharing. The following case studies discuss how students have used the text-based dissemination strategies of chapter writing and blogging to communicate their work to a wider audience base. Case studies 9.1 and 9.2 focus on an undergraduate dissertation and an aspect of doctoral research; however, these examples are also applicable for postgraduate students at master's level and educational practitioners. The tips, traps and reflective questions follow the presentation of the two case studies.

CASE STUDY 9.1: 'ONLY INSIDE THE CLASSROOM?' MOVING FROM AN UNDERGRADUATE DISSERTATION TO AN ACADEMIC CHAPTER PUBLICATION

Who and where: Non Geraint (2016) conducted research for her undergraduate dissertation project with students in a comprehensive secondary school in north Powys, an area located close to the border between Wales and England.

What: Geraint facilitated focus groups with two mixed-gender groups of Year 8 pupils from the school (aged 12–13). The school taught through the mediums of Welsh-language and English-language in separate classes and each focus group represented students from one of the language streams.

Why: A body of research has been conducted on Welsh-language use and attitudes among young people (Scourfield et al, 2006), but the internal diversity in Wales requires further clarification. Geraint's research aimed to contribute to the existing literature by exploring the views of young people in a geographical area that is often neglected in language research.

How: Geraint's research was documented in her undergraduate thesis but it had not been published. Following the premise that 'research, done well, is worth disseminating' (Keen and Todres, 2007, np), Geraint's dissertation supervisor contacted her when the edited collection *Our Changing Land: Revisiting Gender, Class and Identity in Contemporary Wales* (Mannay, 2016b) was in the proposal stage. Geraint's study aligned with the book's aims and she was invited to submit a chapter. Geraint's chapter 'Only inside the classroom? Young people's use of the Welsh language in the school, community and peer group' was published, demonstrating that undergraduate research can go beyond assessed work tasks and become part of the academic literature.

CASE STUDY 9.2: THE 'CASE OF ETHICS' – GETTING OUT MESSAGES FROM RESEARCH BEFORE COMPLETION OF THE DOCTORAL THESIS

Who and where: Victoria Edwards[1] (2019) conducted research with young people across two special schools and one mainstream school in Wales, UK.

What: Edwards was interested in young people's engagement with digitally mediated gaming cultures, with a particular focus on young people who are identified as having additional learning needs. In her doctoral research she employed a range of visual and creative methods of data gathering to enable opportunities to gain an understanding of young people's subjective experience of online gaming and digital cultures.

Why: The everyday lives of young people with additional learning needs or disabilities is an under-researched area (Curran and Runswick-Cole, 2014), and Edwards set out to understand aspects of their digital and online experiences. Edwards developed the 'Case of Ethics' as a way to materialise consent in her research with young people and engender deeper understandings about what it means to participate in research.

How: Aligning with some of the creative forms of presentation documented in Chapter 8, Edwards (2019) presented the 'Case of Ethics' at a Childhood and Youth Research Group seminar at her university as a form of 'show and tell'. At this presentation it was suggested that Edwards should share this work with a wider audience and she was invited to submit a blog to the online community of practice website ExChange: Family and Community. Edwards created an illustrated blog focused on the 'Case of Ethics' and this was tweeted and retweeted, receiving hundreds of views. The short blog post led to interest from other universities, where Edwards gave presentations and workshops. The blog has also been cited by academics writing about ethical practice (for example, Lomax, 2019); and other doctoral researchers have created their own 'Case of Ethics' materials based on Edwards' design. The dissemination of the 'Case of Ethics' is one example of why it is important to take up opportunities to share work from doctoral projects and how a short blog piece can act as a vehicle for connecting wide audiences with innovative ideas and practices.

For case studies 9.1 and 9.2

Tips

- If you are interested in publishing from your undergraduate or postgraduate studies, speak to your supervisors and other academic staff about possible opportunities for disseminating your research literature review, methodology or findings.
- Conferences often have an attached output that invites contributions from conference presenters. These can include the format of an edited book, a special issue journal or a set of conference papers. If you give a paper at a conference or seminar, then this may provide an opening for sharing your work more widely.
- There are many specialised websites for different topics related to education that have a blog section. They are often keen to keep up with and publish emerging work in the field and you can contact them directly to suggest a blog piece.
- When you have a blog or paper published you can widen its reach by using social media sites and online academic repositories such as Twitter, Academia. edu or ResearchGate. However, you will need to get permission from and acknowledge the original publisher when sharing your blog, to ensure that you comply with laws governing intellectual property.
- It is important to remember that not everything submitted for publication gets accepted. All academics will have experiences of their articles, chapters or conference papers being rejected. This is part of the academic publishing process and you should not feel too disappointed if you submit work that is not included in a particular output. Seek out advice and support when considering where, how and when to publish.

Traps

- It is important to be careful about where you publish from your research. There has been a rise in what are referred to as 'predatory publishers' (Gogtay and Bavdekar, 2019; Poff and Ginley, 2019). These predatory publishers often have similar characteristics and undertake practice such as e-mailing invitations that offer a quick turnaround for publication. They may charge fees for publishing and lack robust processes for quality assurance. Therefore, it is useful to discuss publishing plans with supervisors or other colleagues who have experience of the publishing world before submitting your work for publication.
- Another area for consideration is whether there are any restrictions around publication. For example, if you are undertaking a doctoral study jointly funded by a university and an external partner you may need permission to publish from the partner organisation, or they may expect to read and sign off any external publications. Each case is different, so it is important to check.
- If your original research was not publicly accessible it is worth checking that the strategies to maintain confidentiality and anonymity applied in the original output – for example, an undergraduate dissertation – are robust enough for wider dissemination. New forms of dissemination mean a wider readership

base and it can be difficult to retract information from materials that have been made available online if there are errors with pseudonyms or images that could identify participants.

Reflective questions

1. Why are text-based forms of dissemination important?
2. What do you feel are the key messages from your research that should be disseminated to a wider audience?
3. Who can you go to for advice on where to publish and how to avoid 'predatory publishers'?
4. Which specialised websites in your topic area are you aware of, and do they have a blog that you could contribute to?

Using film to communicate messages from research

The history of film dates back to the invention of the medium in the 1890s. Anthropological and ethnographic filmmaking has existed since film cameras emerged, and by the 1920s researchers were producing cinematic projects communicated through image and sound (Chapman, 2020). Film has been a central tool for gathering data, and researchers have drawn on the medium of film to shift the position from which the researcher sees and to record the nuances of interactions, places and communities. In contemporary practice, technological advances have seen the development of ethnographic knowledge through film-based methods becoming more widespread as researchers engage in new image-making practices such as interactive documentaries, and work with equipment that can video-record social interaction, often alongside conventional fieldwork (Bates, 2015).

Film is an attractive medium for researchers because it creates knowledge through the production of an audio–visual artefact that evokes a social reality and fosters an appreciation of the practical, sensual and affective dimensions of individuals' everyday worlds (Vanni, 2020). These elements make film not only a useful mode for data gathering but also one that becomes attractive when considering creative ways to disseminate research findings.

Films promoting the main messages from research studies can include participants or actors, or be animated using cartoons or other forms of graphic art. One good example that you can find online is the animation discussed in Chapter 7, 'Flying While Fat' by Stacy Bias, based on her undergraduate research into experiences of aeroplane travel. This animation received millions of views within weeks of being placed online (Bias, 2021). Films can sometimes be directly linked to journal article publications; for example, the *Video Journal of Education and Pedagogy* offers a facility for hosting video content alongside written text. The *Journal of Embodied Research*, established in 2019, goes further: it is the first peer-reviewed, open access academic journal to accept only video articles. Films can be used for public screenings, hosted on websites, shared on social media and sent out as e-mail attachments or online repository links. The digital age has meant that film is far more portable and has the potential to reach wide audiences and a broad geographical spread.

Although films can be made specifically for data gathering or explicitly for the purposes of disseminating the findings of research projects, these distinctions are sometimes blurred. For example, in case study 9.3 films were produced as part of the fieldwork process but there was an a priori decision that these films would be used to communicate messages to an educational audience. This approach aligns with Dan Silver's (2016, np) position that researchers should take 'audience … as a starting point' and explore visual methods not simply as a means of data gathering, but also as a possible vehicle for dissemination, engagement and impact.

CASE STUDY 9.3: CRITICAL TAKE ON PUBLIC ENGAGEMENT WITH RESEARCH AND ACHIEVING RESEARCH IMPACT USING PARTICIPATORY VIDEO IN A SOCIAL ACTION FRAMEWORK

Who and where: Claudia Mitchell and Naydene de Lange (2020) undertook a community-based participatory video and social action project with young people in educational contexts in South Africa.

What: Mitchell and de Lange facilitated video-making workshops with 19 senior secondary school students, three teachers, three community healthcare workers and several parents. The participants considered the question 'What are the key issues affecting your daily lives in your community?' Students identified rape and gender violence as the key issues and created a storyboard that was developed into three films.

Why: Mitchell and de Lange were interested in facilitating a dialogue between students, schools and wider communities and exploring the possibilities for social action. This was particularly important in the context of rural South Africa, where social issues such as gender-based violence are so prevalent.

How: Mitchell and de Lange published journal articles following the standard conventions of education research outputs. However, one of the key purposes of utilising community-based participatory video was to engage the community in 'making visible' those issues which are 'hidden' – issues which were unlikely to have been effectively shared with these communities through journal articles. The film screenings brought together a wide range of community members. The video work enabled hidden issues to be discussed and to be viewed from different perspectives, providing opportunities for communities to open up to the possibilities of addressing HIV and AIDS. Mitchell and de Lange also developed a booklet to accompany the video, and conducted workshops with the teachers and students on ways of sensitively using the composite video and booklet on gender-based violence. This ensured that ongoing use and dissemination of the film would be accompanied by materials to add context and develop the understanding of future audiences.

Tips

- Filmmaking requires video cameras, access to editing equipment and training in the use of editing equipment. This may be beyond the scope of student research projects, but an alternative could be Cellphilm, which is simply using a smartphone to make short films (MacEntee et al, 2016). Many people use smartphones in their everyday lives; using the video function does not require as much training and short films can be created that could be used in disseminating messages from research.

- When making a film consider interference of surrounding noise levels, including wind if you are recording outside.

- Films can be constructed without participants, researchers or actors. They can use animation, still images and written text to communicate key messages and findings from research projects.

Traps

- It is vital to consider the ethics of film content and whether or not film outputs should include footage of participants. Participants may not feel comfortable or safe to share their experiences publicly and need sufficient time to decide on issues of anonymity and visibility in film outputs developed for dissemination. Remember, it is very difficult to retrieve film footage once it is shared on social media or hosted online.

- There is an assumption that everyone has access to equipment to watch videos or connect with the internet. However, this is not the case and some communities may find this a barrier to engaging with film-based dissemination outputs.

Reflective questions

1. How might visual media such as film help to shift consciousness and behavioural practices in ways that would not be achievable through text-based forms of dissemination?
2. What access to equipment and technical skills would you need to produce a film to disseminate the key messages from your research?
3. How will you ensure ethical practice, and what strategies would you apply in producing a film if participants involved in the project wanted to be assured of anonymity?
4. In providing context for a film output, which supplementary materials would be most useful for supporting the understanding of your intended audiences?

Disseminating research messages with artefacts

Film evokes motion and movement. However, static media (Reavey, 2011b) can also be an effective resource for engaging viewing publics, disseminating research findings and generating impact. Works of art such as sculpture and painting can encourage us to slow down our perception, to linger and to notice. They can also be political and be used to communicate messages of revolution, acceptance, alignment and rejection. For example, nationhood and 'imagined communities' are often constructed and reconstructed through the symbolism of artworks through which a common identity is assumed (Anderson, 1983).

The power of artefacts used for dissemination was recognised in a school-based participatory activist project with young people on gender-based and sexual violence, where participants made a range of collaborative art pieces to communicate girls' experiences of oppressive sexual cultures and practices (Libby et al, 2018). Similar to the films in case study 9.3, which were tools of both data gathering and dissemination, EJ Renold (2017, p 37) conceptualised these art pieces as 'da(r)ta', emphasising the blurred boundaries between what is seen and viewed as research data and how this combines with art to communicate research findings. One of the pieces in the collection included a skirt made from rulers: every ruler contained a written message from the participants documenting issues of sexual harassment, and the ruler skirt was a poignant symbol of how girls were often subject to male pupils lifting up their school uniform skirts using the institutional stationery accessory of the ruler. These arts-based objects were displayed in local galleries, academic conferences and commissioned films, as well as being shared and discussed in school assemblies (see http://agendaonline. co.uk/ruler-heart/).

Photo 9.1: The ruler skirt

Source: Photo taken by EJ Renold, 2020

Artefacts are also the lifeblood of museum exhibitions because of their ability to communicate how it felt to live in particular points in history and how individuals endured and survived sometimes traumatic experiences, and to help make sense of all this as the emotional landscapes of the past recede from living memory (Tout-Smith, 2018). Similar elements of artefact and art-based communication and exhibition were discussed in Chapter 8 in relation to more transient forms of the presentation of research findings. However, as illustrated in case study 9.4, work with artefacts can feature in more permanent projects of dissemination, which create forms of legitimate legacy.

CASE STUDY 9.4: USING ARTEFACTS AND AUDIO TO COMMUNICATE ALTERNATIVE GENDER DISCOURSES TO AUDIENCES AT A MUSEUM

Who and where: Kayte McSweeney and Jay Stewart (2017) worked with young people to disrupt the power balance of gender 'norms' within the Science Museum in London, England.

What: In a process that McSweeney and Stewart describe as 'hacking', they worked in the museum with young people who challenged and troubled the understanding of gender by displaying their own objects with accompanying audio-recordings explaining the meanings they ascribed to the objects. These forms of display enabled objects to be understood from the perspectives of those outside the institution, reconfiguring what counts as knowledge through co-production. The project also drew on ethnographic qualitative research techniques, including interviews with young people and staff and participant observation.

Why: Museums often present politically safe, sterile and authoritative representations of culture, while maintaining an impression of objectivity and neutrality. This can create barriers when museums try to promote trust with the communities they serve (Barrett and Sutter, 2006). Such critiques have led to calls for a democratisation of knowledge, where there is an opportunity to make clearer connections between the objects displayed and the meaning making of those who have designed and used the curated material culture. McSweeney and Stewart responded to this call for democratisation in their work with young people.

How: In terms of dissemination, McSweeney's and Stewart's work illustrates how to move beyond temporary displays on the sidelines to achieving a legitimate legacy. The project created a knowledge-based legacy in the form of conventional academic publications. Additionally, the participant-chosen objects and artefacts and the accompanying audio recordings became part of the museum's permanent collection. The curation of young people's objects gave some recognition to trans identities, which had previously been made invisible, marginalised, medicalised or stigmatised.

In this way, dissemination is afforded both through conventional textual means and in the ongoing interface between the museum and its visitors who are the audiences for these artefacts and the messages they present about the complexity of gender.

Tips

- It may not be possible to arrange a display, particularly a permanent collection in somewhere like a national museum, as in this case study. However, there are other ways to bring together artefacts and use them as tools of dissemination. For example, in her doctoral research Curie Scott (2018) produced a booklet to accompany her thesis. The booklet had images of creative objects and drawings that participants had made during the research. Copies of the booklet were produced for all participants and distributed further to illustrate the work of the doctoral study.
- As discussed in the introduction to this section, another way to increase the impact and longevity of a collection of artefacts is to use film, as in EJ Renold's (2017) work. The collection of participant-created objects documenting issues of sexual harassment was filmed so that it could be circulated widely and reach audiences who were not able to be involved in the original exhibitions.

Traps

- If artefacts are used as tools of dissemination it is essential to consider ownership. If they belong to or were created by the researcher, then this poses fewer concerns than if they are provided by participants. If artefacts belong to other people, then it is best practice to ask if they want them returned and, if so, when, how they will be stored, transported and displayed, and what contingency measures would be put in place in case of theft, loss or damage of an object.
- If you work with community partners, schools or heritage organisations, it is important for them to have an accurate idea of the individual artefacts within a collection. While you may feel that all objects are suitable for display, there may be differences of opinion about 'suitability' for particular audiences.

Reflective questions

1. Are there objects and artefacts associated with your project that could be useful in disseminating key research findings and messages?
2. This section offered the case study of the museum, but also discussed how artefacts had been used in art exhibitions and school assemblies – where could you reach your intended audiences?
3. If these displays were transient presentations, how could you develop a more permanent record of the artefacts and contribute to forms of legitimate legacy?

Disseminating research messages via websites

In the earlier sections we considered dissemination in multimodal forms, including book chapters, blogs, films and artefacts. The advantage of a dedicated website is that it can house all these different forms of material and provide links to other web pages and online resources. They also offer the opportunity to move beyond local audiences and share methods and techniques, research findings and recommendations on a global scale.

Web pages are often designed to accompany project reports. For example, Sarah Wilson and E.J. Milne (2013) created open access web pages about their project Young People Creating Belonging. The project was interested in young people's experiences of being in care and the objects, places and people that fostered feelings of belonging. Wilson and Milne worked with 22 care-experienced children and young people aged 10–23 in Scotland, drawing on qualitative methods. The website documents the creative techniques used in the fieldwork as well as the research findings and messages from children and young people. Going beyond the limitations of a purely textual output, this online form of dissemination offers viewers an opportunity to see still images and film footage from the project. Arguably, this multimodal output enables audiences to immerse themselves in the project visually and aurally, bringing it alive and communicating a more nuanced insight into, and emotional connection with, the accounts of children and young people.

The work of EJ Renold (2017) was introduced in the previous section on artefacts. In addition to the exhibitions, conferences, workshops, films and academic papers discussed in the previous section, this work also resulted in the online output AGENDA. The AGENDA online resource (http://agendaonline. co.uk) provides teachers, youth workers and other educational practitioners with a range of interactive and accessible activities to support children and young people to safely and creatively speak out on issues that matter to them. The web pages host a number of freely accessible workshop- and class-based activities and films, and information about forthcoming events and opportunities. Again, this example illustrates the range of creative outputs that can be brought together within a website.

As well as being a platform to disseminate materials about a particular project, websites can also be used to create an online 'community of practice' around a wider topic of interest. The concept of a 'community of practice' was developed in post-Vygotskian, sociocultural approaches and it refers to 'a set of relations among persons, activity, and world, over time' (Lave and Wenger, 1991, p 98). Through membership, individuals become full participants in the community and learn through mutual engagement in an activity that is defined by the negotiation of meaning both inside and outside the community.

An online website resource can offer an opportunity to build a 'community of practice' where practitioners, academics, policy makers and other key stakeholders can share resources, exchange cases of best practice and keep up to date with developments in the field. There are existing networks, which can be seen as interlinked communities of practice. However, to provide a platform to ensure that excellent practice is identified, promoted and shared, wherever it exists, there needs to be an accessible, comprehensive and dynamic online resource that can work alongside existing, more localised and organisational networks. Case study 9.5 illustrates how a website can act as an online 'community of practice' that brings people and ideas together and disseminates the work from numerous projects and stakeholders, creating a one-stop shop for viewers, contributors and those with an interest in the field of social care.

CASE STUDY 9.5: A MULTIMODAL ONLINE COMMUNITY OF PRACTICE TO REACH DIVERSE AUDIENCES AND ENGENDER CHANGE IN THE FIELD OF SOCIAL CARE

Who and where: The Children's Social Care Research and Development Centre (CASCADE) developed two online communities of practice resources – ExChange: Care and Education and ExChange: Family and Community.

What: In 2016, the Welsh Government commissioned CASCADE to build a community of practice, ExChange: Care and Education, where practitioners, academics, policy makers and other key stakeholders could share resources, exchange cases of best practice and keep up to date with developments in the field of care-experienced children and young people. In 2019 a second site, ExChange: Family and Community, was created to cover the wider remit of supporting the Welsh Government's commitment to children, young people, families and communities in Wales.

Why: The team at CASCADE had been involved in a range of research projects and produced multimodal forms of dissemination including reports, journal articles, book chapters, artwork, music videos, films and magazines (Mannay et al, 2019; Mannay, 2020). This track record in creative forms of dissemination and research impact led the Welsh Government to contact CASCADE to design, maintain and develop an evolving and interactive website targeted at developing and sharing best practice. The aim was to bring resources together that were hosted in different locations and to seek out new research, policy and best-practice case studies to share with key stakeholders. The websites were a response to calls for democratising knowledge, improving accessibility to new ideas, policies and practices, involving multiple stakeholders and responding to the impact agenda – so that changes and improvements could be enabled (Esroy, 2017).

How: The websites feature invited blogs from academics, practitioners, foster carers and young people, a repository of policy, international practice and academic publications, events, workshops, consultations and job opportunities, multimodal materials and a forum. These online communities of practice have been developed with the input of a steering group of key stakeholders to ensure that they remain attuned to current developments and requirements. The team have followed developments in the field and alerted stakeholders to key updates via social media and newsletters. These online communities of practice act as sites of knowledge transfer and dissemination for a diverse range of projects and developments in the field of social care.

Tips

- It is important to ensure that website pages are clear and engaging. Make sure that there is an accessible and well-defined contents page and use images (where publication rights have been secured) so that web pages are attractive to viewers.
- One way of attracting audiences to a website is through social media. When a new blog, event or project report is added to a website, sending a tweet that tags in other associated organisations can help to attract visitors.
- It may not be possible to develop and host a website from a small, unfunded project. However, many universities have departmental or research group web pages, and there are various websites concerned with central topics in education. Accordingly, it may be possible to contribute a blog, as discussed earlier and illustrated in case study 9.2, or to have a featured page on an existing website.

Traps

- Websites require work to update pages, source new materials and ensure that links to outside materials are maintained and in working order. If you begin a website but no longer have capacity to continue with regular updates, the website should be marked as an archive on its homepage so that any visitors are aware of when active engagement was curtailed.
- Many websites have a forum or pages where viewers can add a comment. These facilities have the potential to be subverted or used inappropriately. Consequently, it may be useful to have some kind of delay mechanism where contributions are checked before they 'go live', to ensure that the reputation of the website is not compromised.

Reflective questions

1. Does your university or workplace have an existing website or web pages where they host information about projects conducted by staff and students?
2. What topic-based websites do you use to find information, and could there be an opportunity to showcase your own research?
3. Who would you want to visit your web pages? What strategies would you use to raise awareness and engage those audiences with your online materials?

Ethical considerations for dissemination

Publication ethics describes 'a series of moral issues related to appropriate and inappropriate behaviour that can occur in the context of the dissemination of research' (Poff and Ginley, 2019, np). As in undergraduate essays, dissertation projects and doctoral theses, the issue of plagiarism continues to be of central importance. Plagiarism occurs when published work and ideas are appropriated without acknowledgement through references, and sources need to be acknowledged in all outputs to ensure ethical dissemination. In written texts, such as chapters, journal articles, blogs and magazines, this can be ensured through footnotes or the use of other standardised referencing systems. In the case of films, artefacts and visual images, this is often achieved through acknowledging sources and linking to other text-based published works.

A further ethical consideration is anonymisation. Anonymisation is the process of rendering personal data non-personal, but, despite this simple definition, in practice decisions about how and when to anonymise data can be complex (Mackey, 2019). In student research, the process of obtaining informed consent from participants will often include information about how their data will be stored and anonymised, and where the research will be published. At that point it may be envisaged that the work will only be in a dissertation or project report that is not necessarily publicly available. However, if this work is followed by other forms of dissemination, the researcher's ideas about anonymisation may change and develop. If this was not covered in the initial consent process, then to retain ethical practice participants may need to be consulted about the further use and circulation of their data.

In some cases, artists are named with consent in education research where the artwork is distinctive and anonymisation is not appropriate. However, issues of anonymity and identification can be particularly problematic when they are related to visual and creative materials (see Wiles et al, 2008; Kara, 2018; Mannay, 2019). Additionally, once data is made public through a website or shared via social media, it is extremely difficult to control, and participants' data may be available for time immemorial (Brady and Brown, 2013). Therefore, when we are considering creative forms of dissemination and connecting with wide and diverse audiences, it is important to keep reflecting on the best interests of research participants and ask questions about what represents 'the unsayable and the unspeakable', 'who to represent and how' and 'what to omit and what to include' (Ryan-Flood and Gill, 2010, p 3). The ethics of dissemination are complex, and it is important to work through issues on a case-by-case basis and balance the ethical imperative to share research findings with respect for the participants who were involved in research studies.

Conclusion

This chapter has considered conventional text-based and multimodal forms of dissemination that can be used to share research practice and key findings in the field of education. In relation to the question 'what impact does voice have if no one is listening?' (Alexandra, 2015, p 43), we have argued for the importance of sharing research and for the value of work being undertaken by student researchers. If research is not effectively disseminated, then it cannot contribute to the knowledge base in educational studies, nor can it have an influence on future research and practice. Researchers and practitioners can draw on imaginative ways of reporting to communicate with wide and diverse audiences and, just as we need to consider vigour in the process of generating and analysing data, this also needs to translate into what we do with the data in terms of strategies of dissemination (Mannay, 2016a). Therefore, at the outset of a project it is important to consider how project findings will be shared and to make this integral to the research process.

CHAPTER DISCUSSION QUESTIONS

1. Why are written forms of dissemination still important in the field of education research and practice?

2. Who are your key audiences to share your research messages with? Do you think that they would read conventional outputs such as dissertations, project reports, chapters or journal articles?

3. Are there ethical issues that are more pertinent when working with particular modes of creative dissemination?

4. How could you apply creative forms of dissemination to share key findings and messages from your own education research projects?

5. What do you feel are the advantages and limitations of engaging with creative dissemination strategies?

Note

[1] Victoria Edwards changed her surname in 2020. For more recent related publications, please see Victoria Timperley.

10

Where to next with creative research methods

Chapter summary

In this concluding chapter we illuminate our vision and how the text we have created is a starting point to inspire you, as educators, to work with creative methods across all stages of research. This book demonstrates how creative research methods can be used in education contexts, taking a broad definition of education to include formal and informal education across the life course. We connect with the notions that your learning will be forever continuing and, no matter the stage you are at or the experiences you have had, everyone can be creative and engage with creative ways of being and knowing. We conclude this book with some activities to support you to keep investigating and exploring the ideas we have presented. And we invite you to continue to build your knowledge and transfer this into practice.

Introduction

Everyone is creative and has the capacity to work in creative ways. You may be an educator, future educator, teacher–researcher, artist–teacher, education researcher or any other professional working in a formal or informal education setting. Whatever your role, we want to inspire you to embrace working in creative ways and approach this work in ways that suit you right now. This is what we intend this book to provide.

We wrote this book to be accessible for those considering creative methods for the first time who may be unsure where to begin, as well as to provide inspiration for those who are more experienced in using such methods. Our first aim was to demonstrate the practical applications of creative research methods for education research. As such, we have provided a plethora of case studies to offer numerous examples of creative research methods in education practice. We have offered reflective and discussion questions throughout to facilitate individual thought and collaborative discussion to support learning. These have been provided to spark ideas and support possibilities. This approach has been carefully aligned with our second aim, to provide you with an opportunity to engage with creative methods in consideration of your designing of research. This book bridges theory and practice, to inform and inspire you as educators and education researchers to conduct more creative research. We offer a starting point for the opportunity to be inspired and to be creative in your approach to research through all aspects of research.

What comes next

Creative research methods include arts-based research, digitally mediated research, mobile methods, embodied research, mixed-methods research, place-based research and transformative research frameworks such as participatory, feminist and activist research. As you will have discovered while you read this book, there are many different approaches and influences. We are not advocating the use of creative research methods instead of conventional methods. There will be times when one or more conventional research methods are just what you need. However, we are advocating the use of creative research methods, where appropriate, alongside conventional methods. Moreover, we emphasise the need to consider both conventional and creative methods whenever you are designing research.

Creative methods are particularly helpful in addressing complex contemporary research questions that are hard to answer using conventional methods alone (Kara, 2020, p 6). The field of creative research methods is comparatively new, fast growing and relevant for quantitative, qualitative and mixed-methods researchers. This inspired us as researchers to write this book for you. We all engage with creative methods in different ways ourselves and, as such, we wanted to share the value we see in working this way. Our primary audience encompasses undergraduate and postgraduate education students and practitioner-researchers in education who are considering creative research methods for the first time. We also intend this book as a helpful resource for educators in any context who have some familiarity with creative methods and would like to extend their use.

Education is a large discipline. It is complex, involving many different age ranges, areas, fields and sectors, while also catering for millions of students and employing hundreds of thousands of teachers and other professionals around the world. Most of those students, and many of the professionals, have to conduct and use research. Education is an inherently creative activity, as shown by the number of books on creativity in education (see, for example, Boys, 2010; Sefton-Green et al, 2012; Adams and Owens, 2015; Sannino and Ellis, 2015; Thomson and Hall, 2016; Zhou, 2016). Accordingly, we felt that education students and professionals would welcome, and benefit from, a book on creative research methods for their field. We hope that you feel the same and have been inspired to reflect on lessons learned. We also hope that you will explore further opportunities to embrace the excitement and challenges of working with creative techniques in the field of education, both as a qualitative research tool and as a pedagogic approach to learning and development.

As you have read each of the chapters in this book, you will have engaged with the key aspects of a research project. We constructed the book this way to support you in developing your own research plan. The stages of research design, context setting, data gathering, analysis, reporting, presentation and dissemination have all been covered. As we unpacked each of these areas and presented case studies together with reflective questions, we invited you to consider ways of working with creative methods. We hope that you have engaged with the material that inspires you and that this engagement has motivated you to think about designing research that enables you to take action and explore a creative method that resonates with you. Finding the right research techniques for you and your project aims will engender the best outcomes for you, your participants, the context and your contribution to the field. Your next steps will be to decide what you want to do and to find ways to investigate further while still drawing on creative methods where appropriate.

At different points of your research journey as an educator or education researcher we invite you to move back and forth between the chapters, ideas, case studies and reflective questions. The chapters are written for you to read closely or flick through and find what resonates with you, inspires you or even ignites you to create a new approach or combination of approaches.

Next steps

To help you think about your own next steps, we have compiled four activities that will assist you to begin your project.

Activity 1: Find out more

- Choose a case study that has resonated with you.
- Find the publication(s) we have referred to and download them to a digital platform that allows you to annotate, highlight and really connect with this work. Alternatively, you may wish to print the publications and use sticky notes, highlighters and pencils to annotate them.
- Use the reflective questions connected to this case study as a starting point and begin to interrogate the publications further. What did the researchers do? Why? How? When? How did this support working within a context, with participants, in a field? What understandings were generated? What is happening here? Record your notes, thinking and insights.
- Look at the reference list that the researcher(s) compiled and now find and interrogate some of those publications. Once again, connect to the questions we have provided to inspire you, and also now begin to form your own opinion and ideas.

Activity 2: Not sure what to do next

- Find a case study that you engaged with – it could be because you are fascinated and would like to try the method, or are not sure and would like to find out more.
- Talk with someone about the approach taken in the case study, using the conversation as a connection point to articulate what you are interested in and how you are making links to what you would like to do. As you have a conversation about your idea, consider other perspectives. What feedback do you receive? What ideas are developed? What is reinforced? What requires more work and further investigation?

Activity 3: Making links

As you read this book, multiple ideas were probably coming to mind. Take these ideas and make links.

- Find a large space. Work with a whiteboard, butcher's or flip chart paper or a blank wall where you can place sticky notes or tape up small pieces of paper.
- Use this large space to support your ideas, so set it up in a way that works best for you. Stand back, look and reflect from a distance as well as getting up close.
- Now mind-map your ideas. Honour each individual idea with one sticky note or piece of paper. You can capture these visually with icons, drawings or photographs and/or with text in prose or poetry. Create these in any order, allowing your ideas to flow.
- Place these in your space, knowing that you can move them around, group, reorder, add to, cross out and extend.
- Look at all these ideas and begin to make links and connections.
- What might you place on one side that might not work this time? What might you need to tweak? Where are there overlaps? What stands out and engages you?

Activity 4: Thinking differently

- Now that you have explored a variety of ways of working with creative methods across various stages of research, take one of your ideas and express it in five different ways (think in ways that you can reword, refocus and reframe). What do you notice? How does this change your thinking? How do you consider your audience? How does it connect to the research question? How could it support a research question? How does it impact on the outcomes of the research?

Each of these activities can be a starting point on your journey into exploring and using creative methods. You may use all of a method, or some, parts of it, or adapt it. You might even devise a whole new method. Enjoy the process of discovery.

Ethics

No matter where you start, everyone will need to consider ethical standards and behaviour. We have emphasised ethical practice throughout this book and have provided you with some points to consider. This is not exhaustive, however, and we highly recommend that as you design your research you also consider ethical practice at each stage of the process. A great place to start is to look at university and workplace policy together with wider guides on ethical practice such as those referred to in Chapter 1 of this book. Another option is to follow up some of the literature referred to in the ethics sections of this book – perhaps the literature cited on points that you find particularly thought provoking. As well as reading and considering these policies, guides and literature you may also embrace the opportunity to discuss ethics with others who have used, or are thinking of using, creative methods in education research.

Conclusion

Throughout this book we have explored the ways in which creative research methods are, and could be, used by people around the world who are studying and working in education. Our vision was to collect and collate evidence of the use of creative research methods in education settings, to identify the opportunities presented by existing cases and to convey this information clearly: to undergraduates and postgraduates who are studying education, and to professionals working in education settings. So, as you embark on your next steps, we encourage you to think about what it is that you are investigating. What do you want to find out? Whom do you want to share your findings with? And how can creative methods support your work?

We wish you luck in, and enjoyment from, your own education research.

References

Adams, J. and Owens, A. (2015) *Creativity and Democracy in Education: Practices and Politics of Learning through the Arts*, London: Routledge.

Adamson, J. and Muller, T. (2018) 'Joint autoethnography of teacher experience in the academy: exploring methods for collaborative inquiry', *International Journal of Research & Method in Education* 41(2): 207–9, DOI: 10.1080/1743727X.2017.1279139.

Agbebiyi, A. (2013) 'Tiers of gatekeepers and ethical practice: researching adolescent students and sexually explicit online material', *International Journal of Social Research Methodology*, 16(6): 535–40.

Alexandra, D. (2015) 'Are we listening yet? Participatory knowledge production through media practice: encounters of political listening', in A. Gubrium, K. Harper and M. Otanèz (eds) *Participatory Visual and Digital Research in Action*, Walnut Creek, CA: Left Coast Press, pp 41–56.

Aleixo, P. and Norris, C. (2010) 'The comic book textbook', *Education and Health*, 28(4): 72–74.

Aleixo, P. and Sumner, K. (2017) 'Memory for biopsychology material presented in comic book format', *Journal of Graphic Novels and Comics*, 8(1): 79–88, DOI: 10.1080/21504857.2016.1219957.

Anderson, B. (1983) *Imagined Communities*, London: Verso.

Anderson, J. (2004) 'Talking whilst walking: a geographical archaeology of knowledge', *Area*, 36(3): 254–61.

Anderson, A.W., Smith, P., Jasinski Schneider, J. and Frier, A. (2015) 'Live! From Mount Olympus', *Creative Approaches to Research*, 8(1): 75-96.

Ashkanasy, N.M. and Dasborough, M.T. (2010) 'Emotional awareness and emotional intelligence in leadership teaching', *Journal of Education for Business*, 79: 18–22.

Avolio, B., Walumbwa, F. and Weber, T.J. (2009) 'Leadership: current theories, research, and future directions', *Management Department Faculty Publications*, 60(1): 421–49, https://doi.org/10.1146/annurev.psych.60.110707.163621.

Babbie, E. (2015) *The Practice of Social Research* (14th edn), Boston: Cengage Learning.

Bach, H. (1998) *A Visual Narrative Concerning Curriculum, Girls, Photography etc.*, Edmonton, Alberta, Canada: Qual Institute Press.

Bach, H. (2001) 'The place of the photography in visual narrative research', *Afterimage*, 29(3): 7.

Bagnoli, A. (2009) 'Beyond the standard interview: the use of graphic elicitation and arts-based methods', *Qualitative Research*, 9(5): 547–70.

Bahn, S. and Weatherill, P. (2013) 'Qualitative social research: a risky business when it comes to collecting "sensitive" data', *Qualitative Research*, 13(1): 19–35.

Ball, A.F. (2012) 'Presidential Address: To know is not enough: knowledge, power, and the zone of generativity', *American Educational Research Association Annual Meeting*, Vancouver, Canada, 15 April.

Banks, M. and Zeitlyn, D. (2015) *Visual Methods in Social Research* (2nd edn), London: Sage.

Barad, K. (2007) *Meeting the Universe Halfway: Quantum Physics and the Entanglement of Matter and Meaning*, Ann Arbor: Duke University Press.

Barone, T. and Eisner, E. (2012) *Arts Based Research*, Washington, DC: Sage Publications.

Barrett, E. and Bolt, B. (eds) (2010) *Practice as Research: Approaches to Creative Arts Enquiry*, London: I.B. Tauris.

Barrett, M.J. and Sutter, G.C. (2006) 'A youth forum on sustainability meets the human factor: challenging cultural narratives in schools and museums', *Canadian Journal of Math, Science and Technology Education*, 6(1): 9–23.

Bates, C. (ed) (2015) *Video Methods: Social Science Research in Motion*, London: Routledge.

Becker, H. (1971) 'Footnote', in M. Wax, S. Diamond and F. Gearing (eds) *Anthropological Perspectives on Education*, New York: Basic Books, pp 3–27.

Becker, H. (2007) *Telling About Society*, Chicago, IL: University of Chicago Press.

Berbary, L. (2011) 'Poststructural writerly representation: screenplay as creative analytic practice', *Qualitative Inquiry*, 17(2): 186–96.

Bias, S. (2021) 'Your stories are moving: animation and affect in creative research dissemination', in R. Phillips and H. Kara (eds) *Creative Writing for Social Research*. Bristol: Policy Press, pp 144-9.

Biesta, G. (2018) 'What if? Art education beyond expression and creativity', in C. Naughton, G. Biesta and D.R. Cole (eds) (2018) *Art, Artists and Pedagogy: Philosophy and the Arts in Education*, Abingdon: Routledge, pp 11–20.

Bird, J. (2011) 'Performance-based data analysis: a dynamic dialogue between ethnography and performance-making processes', *NJ*, 34(1): 35–45.

Bishop, C. (2012) *Artificial Hells: Participatory Art and the Politics of Spectatorship*, London: Verso Books.

Blanch, C. and Mulvihill, T. (2013) 'The attitudes of some students on the use of comics in higher education', in C. Syma and R. Weiner (eds) *Graphic Novels and Comics in the Classroom: Essays on the Educational Power of Sequential Art*, Jefferson, NC and London: McFarland & Company, Inc. Publishers, pp 35-47.

Blodgett, A., Coholic, D., Schinke, R., McGannon, K., Peltier, D. and Pheasant, C. (2013) 'Moving beyond words: exploring the use of an arts–based method in Aboriginal community sport research', *Qualitative Research in Sport, Exercise and Health*, 5(3): 312–31.

Boatwright, T. (2019) 'Flux zine: Black queer storytelling', *Equity & Excellence in Education*, 52(4): pp 383–95.

Bochner, P. and Ellis, C. (2003) 'An introduction to the arts and narrative research: art as inquiry', *Qualitative Inquiry*, 9(4): 506–14, DOI: 10.1177/1077800403254394.

Bolt, B. (2010) 'The magic is in the handling', in E. Barrett and B. Bolt (eds) *Practice as Research: Approaches to Creative Arts Enquiry*, London: I.B. Tauris, pp 27–34.

Bolt, B., MacNeill, K., McPherson, M., Ednie Brown, P., Barrett, E., Wilson, C., Miller, S. and Sierra, M. (2017) 'What is "Value" when Aesthetics Meets Ethics Inside and Outside of the Academy', ACUADS annual conference proceedings. Retrieved from: https://acuads.com.au/conference/article/what-is-value-when-aesthetics-meets-ethics-inside-and-outside-of-the-academy/

Botes, M. (2017) 'Using comics to communicate legal contract cancellation', *The Comics Grid: Journal of Comics Scholarship*, 7(1): 14, DOI: https://doi.org/10.16995/cg.100.

Bowman, N., Francis, C. and Tyndall, M. (2015) 'Culturally responsive Indigenous evaluation: a practical approach for evaluating Indigenous projects in tribal reservation contexts', in S. Hood, R. Hopson and H. Frierson (eds) *Continuing the Journey to Reposition Culture and Cultural Context in Evaluation Theory and Practice*, Charlotte, NC: Information Age Publishing, pp 335–59.

Boys, J. (2010) *Towards Creative Learning Spaces: Re-thinking the Architecture of Post-Compulsory Education,* London: Routledge.

Bradford, L.E. and Bharadwaj, L.A. (2015) 'Whiteboard animation for knowledge mobilization: a test case from the Slave River and Delta, Canada', *International Journal of Circumpolar Health*, 74(1): 28780, DOI: 10.3402/ijch.v74.28780

Brady, G. and Brown, G. (2013) 'Rewarding but let's talk about the challenges: using arts-based methods in research with young mothers', *Methodological Innovations Online*, 8(1): 99–112.

Braidotti, R. (2013) 'Posthuman humanities', *European Educational Research Journal*, 12(1): 1–19.

Bray, R. (2014) 'Layers of watching and protection in research with children', in D. Posel, and F. Ross (eds) *Ethical Quandaries in Social Research*, Cape Town, SA: HSRC Press, pp 27–40.

Brooks, R., te Riele, K. and Maguire, M. (2014) *Ethics and Education Research*, London: SAGE.

Bryman, A. (2016) *Social Research Methods,* Oxford: Oxford University Press.

Buckley, C. and Waring, M. (2013) 'Using diagrams to support the research process: examples from grounded theory', *Qualitative Research* 13(2): 148–72.

Burnard, P. (2018) 'Arts-based research methods: a brief overview', *Creative Research Methods Symposium*, 2 July 2018, University of Derby.

Busher, H. and James, N. (2018) 'Struggling for selfhood: non-traditional mature students' critical perspectives on access to higher education courses in England', in R. Waller, N. Ingram and M.R.M. Ward (eds) *Higher Education and Social Inequality: University Admissions, Experiences and Outcomes*. Oxford: Routledge, pp 22–36.

Cahnmann-Taylor, M. (2008) 'Arts-based research: histories and new directions', in M. Cahnmann-Taylor and R. Siegesmund (eds) *Arts-Based Research; Foundations for Practice*, Routledge: New York, pp 3–15.

Cahnmann-Taylor, M. (2009) 'The craft, practice, and possibility of poetry in educational research', in M. Prendergast, C. Leggo and P. Sameshima (eds) *Poetic Inquiry: Vibrant Voices in the Social Sciences*, Rotterdam: Sense Publishing, pp 13–29.

Cahnmann-Taylor, M. and Siegesmund, R. (eds) (2008) *Arts-Based Research in Education: Foundations for Practice*, New York: Routledge.

Call-Cummings, M., Hauber-Özer, M., Byers, C. and Mancuso, G.P. (2019) 'The power of/in photovoice', *International Journal of Research & Method in Education*, 42(4): 399–413.

Cancienne, M.B. and Snowber, C.N. (2003) 'Writing rhythm: movement as method', *Qualitative Inquiry*, 9(2): 237–53, DOI: 10.1177/1077800402250956.

Cannon, A. and Blair, A. (2014) 'Dramatic data: the possibilities of ethnodramatic writing for understanding the experiences of English learners in community college settings', *Critical Inquiry in Language Studies*, 11(4): 307–33.

Carrigan, M. (2020) *Social Media for Academics* (2nd edn), London: Sage.

Carroll, K. (2018) 'Approaching bereavement research with heartfelt positivity', *Emotion and the Researcher: Sites, Subjects and Objectivities*, pp 97–111, DOI: 10.1108/S1042-319220180000016007.

Carter, R. (2004) *Language and Creativity: The Art of Common Talk*, London: Routledge.

Chapman, J. (2020) 'Researching film and history: sources, methods, approaches', in L. Pauwels and D. Mannay (eds) *The Sage Handbook of Visual Research Methods* (2nd edn), London: Sage, pp 452–62.

Chilisa, B. (2012) *Indigenous Research Methodologies*, Thousand Oaks, CA: Sage.

Clark, A. (2020) 'Visual ethics beyond the crossroads', in L. Pauwels and D. Mannay (eds) *The Sage Handbook of Visual Research Methods* (2nd edn), London: Sage, pp 682–93.

Clark, A. and Moss, P. (2001) *Listening to Young Children: The Mosaic Approach*, London: National Children's Bureau Enterprises.

Clayton, B. (2010) 'Ten minutes with the boys, the thoroughly academic task and the semi-naked celebrity: football masculinities in the classroom or pursuing security in a "liquid" world', *Qualitative Research in Sport and Exercise*, 2(3): 371–84, DOI: 10.1080/19398441.2010.517043.

Cohen, L., Manion, L. and Morrison, K. (2018) *Research Methods in Education* (8th edn), Abingdon: Routledge.

Cole, A. and McIntyre M. (2004a) 'History', *Mapping Care* [website], Available from https://legacy.oise.utoronto.ca/research/mappingcare/history_alz.shtml [Accessed 2 February 2020].

Cole, A. and McIntyre M. (2004b) 'The Alzheimer's Project', *Mapping Care* [website], Available from https://legacy.oise.utoronto.ca/research/mappingcare/alzproject_exhibit.shtml [Accessed 2 February 2020].

Cole, A. and McIntyre, M. (2004c) 'Research as aesthetic contemplation: the role of the audience in research interpretation', *Educational Insights*, 9(1), Available from www.ccfi.educ.ubc.ca/publication/insights/v09n01/articles/cole.html [Accessed 20 February 2020].

Cole, A. and McIntyre, M. (2006) *Living and Dying with Dignity: The Alzheimer's Project*, Toronto, Ontario: Backalong Books and Centre for Arts-informed Research.

Cole, P. (2017) 'An Indigenous research narrative: ethics and protocols over time and space', *Qualitative Inquiry* 23(5) 343–51, DOI: 10.1177/1077800416659083.

Coleman, K. (2018) 'Mapping the nomadic journey of becoming in digital portfolios: digital way finding in art education [online]', *Australian Art Education*, 39(1): 91–106.

Collier, J. (1957) 'Photography in anthropology: a report on two experiments', *American Anthropologist*, 59(5): 843–59.

Collins, C.S. and Stockton, C.M. (2018) 'The central role of theory in qualitative research', *International Journal of Qualitative Methods*, 17(1): 1–10.

Coulter, C.A. and Smith, M.L. (2009) 'The construction zone: literary elements in narrative research', *Educational Researcher*, 38(8): 577–90, DOI: 10.3102/0013189X09353787.

Cox, A.M. (2017) 'Space and embodiment in informal learning', *Higher Education*, 75(6): 1077–90.

Craft, A. (2001) 'Little c Creativity', in A. Craft, B. Jeffrey and M. Liebling (eds) *Creativity in Education*, Bloomsbury: London, pp 45–61.

Craft, A. and Jeffrey, B. (2008) 'Creativity and performativity in teaching and learning: tensions, dilemmas, constraints, accommodations and synthesis', *British Educational Research Journal*, 34(October (5)): 577–84.

Cram, F., Chilisa, B. and Mertens, D. (2013) 'The journey begins', in D. Mertens, F. Cram and B. Chilisa (eds) *Indigenous Pathways into Social Research: Voices of a New Generation*, Walnut Creek, CA: Left Coast Press, pp 11–40.

Creswell, J.W. and Poth, C. (2017) *Qualitative Inquiry and Research Design: Choosing among Five Approaches* (4th edn), Thousand Oaks, CA: Sage Publications.

Culshaw, S. (2019) 'The unspoken power of collage? Using an innovative arts-based research method to explore the experience of struggling as a teacher', *London Review of Education*, 17(3): 268–83, DOI: https://doi.org/10.18546/LRE.17.3.03.

Curran, T. and Runswick-Cole, K. (2014) 'Disabled children's childhood studies: a distinct approach?', *Disability & Society*, 29(10): 1617–30.

Cutcher, A. (2013) '[In]accessibilities: presentations, representations and re-presentations in arts-based research', *Creative Approaches to Research*, 6(2): 33–44.

Dalton, J.E., Hall, M.P., Hoyser, C.E. and Jones, L.F. (2019) 'An ancient monastic practice: reviving it for a modern world', in J.E. Dalton, M.P. Hall. and C.E. Hoyser (eds) *The Whole Person: Embodying Teaching and Learning through Lectio and Visio Divina*, Lanham, MD: Rowman and Littlefield, pp 1–10.

Dark, K. (2009) 'Examining praise from the audience: what does it mean to be a "successful" poet-researcher?' in M. Prendergast, C. Leggo and P. Sameshima (eds) *Poetic Inquiry: Vibrant Voices in the Social Sciences*, Rotterdam: Sense Publishers, pp 171–86.

Darnhofer, I. (2018) 'Using comic-style posters for engaging participants and for promoting researcher reflexivity', *International Journal of Qualitative Methods*, 17: 1–12, DOI: 10.1177/1609406918804716.

Davis, C. (2013) *SPSS for Allied Sciences: Basic Statistical Testing*, Bristol: Policy Press.

Delamont, S. (2012) 'Milkshakes and convertibles: an autobiographical reflection', *Studies in Symbolic Interaction*, 39: 51–69.

Delamont, S. and Atkinson, P. (1995) *Fighting Familiarity: Essays on Education and Ethnography*, Cresskill, NJ: Hampton Press.

Derry, C. (2005) 'Drawings as a research tool for self-study: an embodied method of exploring memories of childhood bullying', in C. Mitchell, S. Weber, and K. O'Reilly-Scanlon (eds) *Just Who Do We Think We Are? Methodologies for Autobiography and Self-study in Teaching*, New York, NY: RoutledgeFalmer, pp 34–46.

De Vecchi, N., Kenny, A., Dickson-Swift, V. and Kidd, S. (2016) 'How digital storytelling is used in mental health: a scoping review', *International Journal of Mental Health Nursing*, 25: 183–93, DOI: 10.1111/mm.12206.

Diversi, M. (1998) 'Glimpses of street life: representing lived experience through short stories', *Qualitative Inquiry*, 4(2): 131–47.

Donovan, J. (2016) 'Meandering in the maze of mixed methods: navigation strategies of a researcher into the influence of the mass media on children's science understandings', in D. Rossi, F. Gacenga and P. Danaher (eds) *Navigating the Education Research Maze: Contextual, Conceptual, Methodological and Transformational Challenges and Opportunities for Researchers*, Cham, Switzerland: Palgrave Macmillan, pp 131–44.

Douglas, K., Carless, D., Milnes, K., Turner-Moore, T., Tan, J. and Laredo, E. (2019) 'New technologies of representation, collaborative autoethnographies, and "Taking it Public": an example from "Facilitating Communication on Sexual Topics in Education"', *Qualitative Inquiry*, 25(6): 535–8, DOI: 10.1177/1077800418806607.

Drummond, D. (2011) 'White American style in rhyme', *Qualitative Inquiry*, 17(4): 332–3, DOI: 10.1177/1077800411401189.

Dumangane, C. (2016) 'Exploring the narratives of the few: British African Caribbean male graduates of elite universities in England and Wales', PhD thesis, Cardiff University, Available from http://orca.cf.ac.uk/86927/1/Constantino%20Dumangane%20-%20Final%20Thesis%20%28January%202016%29.pdf [Accessed 12 December 2019].

Dumenden, I.E. (2016) '"If you believe, if you keep busy, you can develop yourself": on being a refugee student in a mainstream school', in K. Galvin and M. Prendergast (eds) *Poetic Inquiry II – Seeing, Caring, Understanding*, Boston, MA: Brill Sense, pp 227–36.

Duncan, R., Taylor, M. and Stoddard, D. (2016) *Creating Comics as Journalism, Memoir and Nonfiction*, New York, NY: Routledge.

Eber, D.E. (2002) 'The student's construction of artistic truth in digital images', in C. Beardon and L. Malmborg (eds) *Digital Creativity: A Reader*, Lisse: Swets and Zeitlinger, pp 45–60.

Edwards, V. (2019) '*How might we work more ethically with children and young people: the 'Case of Ethics'*. Available from https://www.exchangewales.org/how-might-we-work-more-ethically-with-children-and-young-people-the-case-of-ethics/ [Accessed 19 October 2020].

Egg, P., Schratz-Hadwich, B., Trubswasser, G. and Walker, R. (2004) *Seeing beyond Violence: Children as Researchers*, SOS-Kinderdorf: Hermann Gmeiner Akademie.

Eisner, E. (2002) *The Arts and the Creation of Mind*, New Haven, CT: Yale University Press.

Eldén, S. (2012) 'Inviting the messy: drawing methods and "children's voices"', *Childhood* 20(1): 66–81.

Elkins, J. (2001) *Why Art cannot be Taught: A Handbook for Art Students*, Champaign, IL: University of Illinois Press.

Ellingsen, I., Størksen, I. and Stephens, P. (2010) 'Q methodology in social work research', *International Journal of Social Research Methodology*, 13(5): 395–409.

Ellingson, L. (2009) *Engaging Crystallization in Qualitative Research: An Introduction*, Thousand Oaks, CA: SAGE.

Ellingson, L. (2017) *Embodiment in Qualitative Research*, Abingdon: Routledge.

Ellsworth, E. (2005) *Places of Learning: Media, Architecture, Pedagogy*, New York: RoutledgeFalmer.

Emdin, C. and Adjapong, E. (2018) *#HipHopEd: The Compilation on Hip-hop Education: Volume 1: Hip-hop as Education, Philosophy, and Practice*, Boston, MA: Brill Sense.

Emmel, N. and Clark, A. (2009) 'The methods used in connected lives: Investigating networks, neighbourhoods and communities', ESRC National Centre for Research Methods, NCRM Working Paper Series, 06/09, Available from http://eprints. ncrm.ac.uk/800/ [Accessed 27 February 2020].

Ersoy, A. (2017) 'Conclusion', in A. Ersoy (ed) *The Impact of Co-production: From Community Engagement to Social Justice*, Bristol: Policy Press, pp 201–12.

Evans, J. and Jones, P. (2011) 'The walking interview: methodology, mobility and place', *Applied Geography*, 31(2): 849–58.

Evergreen, S. (2014) *Presenting Data Effectively: Communicating Your Findings for Maximum Impact*, Thousand Oaks, CA: Sage.

ExChange: Care and Education, Available from www.exchangewales.org/careandeducation [Accessed 26 January 2020].

ExChange: Family and Community, Available from www.exchangewales.org/familyandcommunity [Accessed 26 January 2020].

Fernández-Giménez, M.E., Jennings, L.B. and Wilmer, H. (2018) 'Poetic inquiry as a research and engagement method', *Natural Resource Science, Society and Natural Resources*, 1–13, Available from www.ars.usda.gov/ARSUserFiles/51815/6.%20Poetic%20Inquiry%20as%20a%20Research%20and%20Engagement%20Method%20in%20Natural%20Resource%20Science.pdf [Accessed 27 February 2020].

Fielding, M. (2001) 'Students as radical change agents', *Journal of Educational Change*, 2(2): 123–41.

Fielding, N. (2012) 'Triangulation and mixed methods designs: data integration with new research technologies', *Journal of Mixed Methods Research* 6(2): 124–36.

Flicker, S. and MacEntee, K. (2020) 'Digital storytelling as a research method', *The Sage Handbook of Visual Research Methods* (2nd edn), London: Sage, pp 267–81.

Forrester, G. and Garratt, D. (2016) *Education Policy Unravelled* (2nd edn), London: Bloomsbury.

Foster-Fishman, P., Nowell, B., Deacon, Z., Nievar, M.A. and McCann, P. (2005) 'Using methods that matter: the impact of reflection, dialogue, and voice', *American Journal of Community Psychology*, 36(3/4): 275–91.

Fournillier, J. (2010) 'Plus ça change, plus c'est la même chose: an Afro Caribbean scholar on the Higher Education Plantation', *Creative Approaches to Research*, 3(2): 52–62.

Freire, P. (1972) *Pedagogy of the Oppressed*, New York, NY: Penguin.

Freire, P. (1993) *Pedagogy of the City*, New York, NY: Continuum.

Friend, J. and Militello, M. (2015) 'Lights, camera, action: advancing learning, research, and program evaluation through video production in educational leadership preparation', *Journal of Research on Leadership Education*, 10(2): 81–103, DOI: 10.1177/1942775114561120.

Frosh, S. (2010) *Psychoanalysis outside the Clinic: Interventions in Psychosocial Studies*, Basingstoke: Macmillan.

Fry, S. (2005) *The Ode Less Travelled: Unlocking the Poet Within*, London: Arrow Books.

Gabriel, Y. and Connell, N. (2010) 'Co-creating stories: collaborative experiments in storytelling', *Management Learning*, 41(5): 507–23, DOI: 10.1177/1350507609358158.

Gadd, D. and Jefferson, T. (2007) *Psychosocial Criminology*, London: Sage.

Gauntlett, D. (2007) *Creative Explorations: New Approaches to Identities and Audiences*, London: Routledge.

Gauntlett, D. (2011) *Making is Connecting: The Social Meaning of Creativity, from DIY and Knitting to YouTube and Web 2.0*, Cambridge: Polity Press.

Gauntlett, D. and Holzwarth, P. (2006) 'Creative and visual methods for exploring identities', *Visual Studies*, 21(1): 82–91.

Geer, B. (1964) 'First days in the field', in P.E. Hammond (ed) *Sociologists at Work*, New York: Basic Books, pp 372–98.

Geraint, N. (2016) 'Only inside the classroom? Young people's use of the Welsh language in the school, community and peer group', in D. Mannay (ed), *Our Changing Land: Revisiting Gender, Class and Identity in Contemporary Wales*, Cardiff: University of Wales Press, pp 41–62.

Gogtay, N.J. and Bavdekar, S.B. (2019) 'Predatory journals – can we stem the rot?', *Journal of Postgraduate Medicine*, 65(3): 129–31.

Goldstein, T. and Wickett, J. (2009) 'Zero tolerance: a stage adaptation of an investigative report on school safety', *Qualitative Inquiry*, 15(10): 1552–68.

Grant, A., Mannay, D. and Marzella, R. (2018) '"People try and police your behaviour": the impact of surveillance on mothers' and grandmothers' perceptions and experiences of infant feeding', *Families, Relationships and Societies*, 7(3): 431–47.

Gravetter, F.J. and Forzano, L.B. (2018) *Research Methods for the Behavioural Sciences*, Boston, MA: Cengage.

Gray, B., Hilder, J., Macdonald, L., Tester, R., Dowell, A. and Stubbe, M. (2017) 'Are research ethics guidelines culturally competent?' *Research Ethics*, 13(1): 23–41.

Hall, M.P. (2019) 'Embodying deep reading: mapping life experiences through Lectio Divina' in J.E. Dalton, M.P. Hall and C.E. Hoyser (eds) *The Whole Person: Embodying Teaching and Learning through Lectio and Visio Divina*, Lanham, MD: Rowman and Littlefield, pp 11–21.

Hamilton, J. (2004) 'Digital camera explained', *Classroom Magazine*, 24–25.

Hammersley, M. (2009) 'Why critical realism fails to justify critical social research', *Methodological Innovations Online*, 4(2): 1–11.

Haraway, D. (1991) 'A cyborg manifesto: science, technology, and socialist-feminism in the late twentieth century', in D. Haraway (ed) *Simians, Cyborgs and Women: The Reinvention of Nature*, New York, NY: Routledge, pp 149–81.

Harper, D. (2002) 'Talking about pictures: a case for photo elicitation', *Visual Studies*, 17(1): 14–26.

Harper, D. (2012) *Visual Sociology*, New York: Routledge.

Harris, A. (2014) *The Creative Turn: Toward a New Aesthetic Imaginary*, Rotterdam: Sense.

Hayton, J. (2019) 'Academic writing: context is everything', [online] 8 May, Available from https://jameshaytonphd.com/quick-tips/context-is-everything [Accessed 27 February 2020].

Hickey-Moody, A.C. (2018) 'Materialising the social: art practice as a transversal Methodology', *RUUKKU*, 9. Available from www.researchcatalogue.net/view/371583/371584 [Accessed 20 February 2020].

Hickey-Moody, A.C. (n.d.) 'About', *Interfaith Childhoods Project* [website] Available from www.interfaithchildhoods.com/. [Accessed 20 February 2020].

Hinthorne, L.L. and Schneider, K. (2012) 'Playing with purpose: using serious play to enhance participatory development communication in research', *International Journal of Communication*, 6: 2801–24.

Hollway, W. and Jefferson, T. (2013) *Doing Qualitative Research Differently* (2nd edn), London: Sage.

Hosler, J. and Boomer, K. (2011) 'Are comic books an effective way to engage nonmajors in learning and appreciating science?' *CBE – Life Sciences Education*, 10(3): 309–17.

Howard, J.K. and Eckhardt, S.A. (2005) 'Why action research? The leadership role of the library media specialist', *Library Media Connection*, 24(2): 32–34.

Hughes, J., Roy, A. and Manley, J. (2014) *Surviving in Manchester: Narratives on movement from the Men's Room, Manchester*, Research report (March).

Inkpen, K. (2001) 'Designing handheld technologies for kids', in *Proceedings of Conference on Human Factors in Computing Systems, Seattle, WA: USA, March 31–April 5*.

Irwin, R.L. (2013) 'Becoming a/r/tography', *Studies in Art Education*, 54(3): 198–215.

Isa, B. and Forrest, D. (2011) 'A qualitative case study of the implementation of education programs at the National Gallery of Victoria (NGV), Australia', paper presented at the 2nd International Conference on Education and Educational Psychology 2011, Istanbul Turkey, 19–22 October 2011,in Z. Bekirogullari (ed) *Procedia-Social and Behavioral Sciences*, 29, pp 1905–13.

Jackson, A. and Mazzei, L. (eds) (2008) *Voice in Qualitative Inquiry: Challenging Conventional, Interpretive, and Critical Conceptions in Qualitative Research*, New York, NY: Routledge.

Johnson, K. (2008) 'Taking children to use visual research methods', in P. Thomson (ed) *Doing Visual Research with Children and Young People*, London: Routledge, pp 77–94.

Johnson, L., Adams, S. and Witchey, H. (2011) *The NMC Horizon Report: 2011 Museum Edition*, Austin, TX: The New Media Consortium.

Kahneman, D. (2011) *Thinking Fast and Slow*, New York: Farrar, Straus and Giroux.

Kara, H. (2017) *Research and Evaluation for Busy Students and Practitioners: A Time-Saving Guide*, Bristol: Policy Press.

Kara, H. (2018) *Research Ethics in the Real World: Euro-Western and Indigenous Perspectives*, Bristol: Policy Press.

Kara, H. (2020) *Creative Research Methods in the Social Sciences: A Practical Guide* (2nd edition), Bristol: Policy Press.

Keen, S. and Todres, L. (2007) 'Strategies for disseminating qualitative research findings: three exemplars', *Forum: Qualitative Social Research – Sozialforschung*, 8(3): Art. 17.

Kelleher, C. and Wagener, T. (2011) 'Ten guidelines for effective data visualization in scientific publications', *Environmental Modelling & Software*, 26: 822–7.

Kim, A.H., Vaughn, S., Wanzek, J. and Wei, S. (2004) 'Graphic organizers and their effects on the reading comprehension of students with LD: a synthesis of research', *Journal of Learning Disabilities*, 37(2): 105–18.

Kinney, P. (2017) 'Walking Interviews', *Social Research Update*, 67: 1–4.

Kirk, A. (2016) *Data Visualisation: A Handbook for Data Driven Design*, London: Sage.

Korstjens, I. and Moser, A. (2017) 'Series: practical guidance to qualitative research. Part 2: Context, research questions and designs', *European Journal of General Practice*, 23(1): 274–9, DOI: 10.1080/13814788.2017.1375090.

Kovach, M. (2009) *Indigenous Methodologies: Characteristics, Conversations and Contexts*, Toronto: University of Toronto Press.

Kuntz, A.M. and Presnall, M.M. (2012) 'Wandering the tactical: From interview to intraview', *Qualitative Inquiry*, 18(9): 732–44.

Ladkin, D. and Taylor, S. (2010) 'Enacting the true self: towards a theory of embodied authentic leadership', *The Leadership Quarterly*, 21: 64–74.

Lahman, M. and Richard, V. (2014) 'Appropriated poetry: archival poetry in research', *Qualitative Inquiry*, 20(3:) 344–55, DOI: 10.1177/1077800413489272.

Lahman, M., Rodriguez, K., Richard, V., Geist, M., Schendel, R. and Graglia, P. (2011) '(Re)forming research poetry', *Qualitative Inquiry*, 17(9): 887–96, DOI: 10.1177/1077800411423219.

Lambert, L. (2014) *Research for Indigenous Survival: Indigenous Research Methodologies in the Behavioural Sciences*, Lincoln, NE: University of Nebraska Press.

Land, C. (2015) *Decolonizing Solidarity: Dilemmas and Directions for Supporters of Indigenous Struggles*, London: Zed Books.

Lapum, J., Ruttonsha, P., Church, K., Yau, T. and David, A. (2012) 'Employing the arts in research as an analytical tool and dissemination method', *Qualitative Inquiry*, 18(1): 100–15.

Lave, J. and Wenger, E. (1991) *Situated Learning: Legitimate Peripheral Participation*, Cambridge: Cambridge University Press.

Leavy, P. (2017) *Research Design: Quantitative, Qualitative, Mixed Methods, Arts-Based, and Community-Based Participatory Research Approaches*, New York: Guilford Publications.

Leavy, P. (2019) *Handbook of Arts-Based Research* (2nd edn), New York: Guilford Publications.

Leggo, C. and Sameshima, P. (2014) 'Startling stories: fiction and reality in education research', in A. Reid, P. Hart and M. Peters (eds) *A Companion to Research in Education*, Dordrecht: Springer, pp 539–48.

Lemon, N. (2007) 'Take a photograph: teacher reflection through narrative', *Journal of Reflective Practice*, 8(2): 177–91.

Lemon, N. (2008) 'Looking through the lens of a camera in the early childhood classroom', in J. Moss (ed) *Research Education: Visually–Digitally–Spatially*, Rotterdam, Netherlands: Sense Publishers, pp 21–52.

Lemon, N. (2013a) 'Digital cameras as renewed technology in a gallery: young people as photographers of their learning', refereed paper for 2013 *American Educational Research Association (AERA) Annual Meeting, San Francisco, CA, 27 April–1 May*.

Lemon, N. (2013b) '@Twitter is always wondering what's happening: learning with and through social networks in higher education', in B. Patrut, M. Patrut, and C. Cmeci (eds) *Social Media in Higher Education: Teaching in Web 2.0*, Hershey, Pennsylvania, USA: IGI Global, pp 237–61.

Lemon, N. (ed) (2015) *Revolutionizing Arts Education in K-12 Classrooms through Technological Integration*, Hershey, PA: IGI Global.

Lemon, N. (2017) 'Being a Digital Image-maker: Young children using the digital camera in learning', in S. Garvis and D. Pendergast (eds) *Health and Wellbeing in the Early Years* (2nd edn), London: Cambridge University Press, pp 238–52.

Lemon, N. (2019) 'Student generated visual narratives: lived experiences of learning', in N. Kucirkova, J. Rowsell and G. Falloon (eds) *The Routledge International Handbook of Learning with Technology in Early Childhood*, London: Routledge, pp 294–310.

Lemon, N. and Finger, G. (2013) 'Digital technology', in S. Garvis and D. Pendergast (eds) *Health and Wellbeing in the Early Years*, Sydney: Cambridge University Press, pp 206–21.

Lemon, N. and Salmons, J. (2021) *Reframing and Rethinking Collaboration in Higher Education and Beyond: A Practical Guide for Doctoral Students and Early Career Researchers*, Abingdon: Routledge.

Lemon, N., Garvis, S. and Klopper, C. (2014) *Representations of Working in the Arts: Deepening the Conversations*, London: Intellect.

Lenette, C. (2019) *Arts-Based Methods in Refugee Research: Creating Sanctuary*, Singapore: Springer Nature Singapore Pte Ltd.

Levy, I.P. (2012) 'Hip hop and spoken word therapy with urban youth', *Journal of Poetry Therapy*, 25(4): 219–24.

Levy, I.P., Cook, A.L. and Emdin, C. (2018) 'Remixing the school counselor's toolkit: hip-hop spoken word therapy and YPAR', *Professional School Counseling*, 22(1): 1–11.

Lewin, K. (1946) 'Action research and minority problems', *Journal of Social Issues*, 2(4): 34–46.

Liamputtong, P. (2012) *Qualitative Research Methods*, Melbourne: Oxford University Press.

Libby, Georgia, Chloe, Courtney, Olivia, Rhiannon and Renold, EJ (2018) 'Making our feelings matters: using creative methods to re-assemble the rules on healthy relationships education in Wales', in N. Lombard (ed), *The Routledge Handbook of Gender and Violence*, London and New York: Taylor and Francis, pp 303–19.

Lincoln, Y.S. and Guba, E.G. (1985) *Naturalistic Inquiry*, Newbury Park, CA: Sage Publications.

Liversidge, P. (2014) 'Peter Liversidge: Notes on protesting', *Peter Liversidge* [website], Available from www.peterliversidge.com/videos.html#QQ=5385&slide=3 [Accessed 20 December 2019].

Löfström, E. (2011) '"Does plagiarism mean anything? LOL." Students' conceptions of writing and citing', *Journal of Academic Ethics*, 9: 257–75.

Lomax, H. (2019) 'Consuming images, ethics, and integrity in visual social research', in R. Iphofen (ed), *Handbook of Research Ethics and Scientific Integrity*, Cham: Springer.

Loreman, T. (2011) *Love as Pedagogy*, Rotterdam: Sense Publishers.

Lowenfeld, M. (1950) 'The nature and use of the Lowenfeld world technique in work with children and adults', *The Journal of Psychology*, 30(2): 325–31.

Lupi, G. and Posavec, S. (2016) *Dear Data*, UK: Penguin Random House.

Lyon, P. (2019) 'Using drawing in visual research: materializing the invisible', in L. Pauwels, and D. Mannay (eds) *The Sage Handbook of Visual Research*, London: Sage Publications Ltd, pp 297–308.

MacEntee, K., Burkholder, C. and SchwabCartas, J. (eds) (2016) *What's a Cellphilm? Integrating Mobile Phone Technology into Participatory Visual Research Activism*, Rotterdam: Sense.

MacKenzie, C., Christensen, J. and Turner, S. (2015) 'Advocating beyond the academy: dilemmas of communicating relevant research results', *Qualitative Research*, 15(1): 105–21, DOI: 10.1177/1468794113509261.

Mackey, E. (2019) 'A best practice approach to anonymization', in R. Iphofen (ed) *Handbook of Research Ethics and Scientific Integrity*, Cham: Springer.

Mandlis, L. (2009) 'Art installation as method: "fragments" of theory and tape', *Qualitative Inquiry* 15(8): 1352–72.

Mannay, D. (2010) 'Making the familiar strange: can visual research methods render the familiar setting more perceptible?', *Qualitative Research*, 10(1): 91–111.

Mannay, D. (2014) 'Storytelling beyond the academy: exploring roles, responsibilities and regulations in the open access dissemination of research outputs and visual data', *The Journal of Corporate Citizenship*, 54: 109–16.

Mannay, D. (2016a) *Visual, Narrative and Creative Research Methods: Application, Reflection and Ethics*, Abingdon: Routledge.

Mannay, D. (ed) (2016b) *Our Changing Land: Revisiting Gender, Class and Identity in Contemporary Wales*, Cardiff: University of Wales Press.

Mannay, D. (2019) 'Creative methods anonymity, visibility and ethical re-representation', in R. Iphofen (ed) *Handbook of Research Ethics and Scientific Integrity*, Cham: Springer.

Mannay, D. (2020) 'Revisualizing data: engagement, impact and multimodal dissemination', *The Sage Handbook of Visual Research Methods* (2nd edn), London: Sage, pp 659–69.

Mannay, D. and Morgan, M. (2013) 'Anatomies of inequality: considering the emotional cost of aiming higher for marginalised, mature, mothers re-entering education', *Journal of Adult and Continuing Education*, 19(1): 57–75.

Mannay, D. and Morgan, M. (2015) 'Doing ethnography or applying a qualitative technique? Reflections from the "waiting field"', *Qualitative Research*, 15(2): 166–82.

Mannay, D. and Turney, C. (2020) 'Sandboxing: a creative approach to qualitative research in education', in M. Ward, and S. Delamont (eds) *Handbook of Qualitative Research in Education* (2nd edn), Cheltenham: Edward Elgar, pp 233–45.

Mannay, D., Staples, E. and Edwards, V. (2017) 'Visual methodologies, sand and psychoanalysis: employing creative participatory techniques to explore the educational experiences of mature students and children in care', *Visual Studies*, 32(4): 345–58.

Mannay, D., Creaghan, J., Gallagher, D., Marzella, R., Mason, S., Morgan, M. and Grant, A. (2018) 'Negotiating closed doors and constraining deadlines: the potential of visual ethnography to effectually explore private and public spaces of motherhood and parenting', *Journal of Contemporary Ethnography*, 47(6): 758–81.

Mannay, D., Staples, E., Hallett, S., Roberts, L., Rees, A., Evans, R. and Andrews, D. (2019) 'Enabling talk and reframing messages: working creatively with care experienced children and young people to recount and re-represent their everyday experiences', *Child Care in Practice*, 25(1): 51–63, DOI: 10.1080/13575279.2018.1521375.

Manning, S.M. (2018) 'Collaborative poetic processes: methodological reflections on co-writing with participants', *The Qualitative Report*, 23(4): 742–57.

Margolis, J. (2018) 'Self-study research as a source of professional development and learning within a school of education', in J. Ritter, M. Lunenberg, K. Pithouse-Morgan, A. Samaras, and E. Vanassche (eds) *Teaching, Learning, and Enacting of Self-Study Methodology: Unraveling a Complex Interplay*, Singapore: Springer, pp 11–20.

Markham, A. (2012) 'Fabrication as ethical practice: qualitative inquiry in ambiguous internet contexts', *Information, Communication & Society*, 15(3): 334–53.

Martin, K. (2003) 'Ways of knowing, being and doing: a theoretical framework and methods for Indigenous and Indigenist research', in K. McWilliam, P. Stephenson and G. Thompson (eds) *Voicing Dissent, New Talents 21C: Next Generation Australian Studies*, St Lucia, Qld: University of Queensland Press, pp 203–14.

Marx, S., Pennington, J.L. and Chang, H. (2017) 'Critical autoethnography in pursuit of educational equity: introduction to the IJME special issue', *International Journal of Multi-Cultural Education*, 19(1): 1–6.

Mason, J. (2018) *Qualitative Researching* (3rd edn), London: SAGE.

McAlpin, L. (2016) 'Why might you use narrative methodology? A story about narrative', *Eesti Haridusteaduste Ajakiri*, 4(1): 32–57, http://dx.doi.org/10.12697/eha.2016.4.1.02b.

McDonough, S.L. (2018) 'Inside the mentors' experience: using poetic representation to examine the tensions of mentoring pre-service teachers', *Australian Journal of Teacher Education*, 43(10): 98–115.

McIntyre, J. (2018) 'Explainer: the difference between being transgender and doing drag', *The Conversation*, 27 July, Available from http://theconversation.com/explainer-the-difference-between-being-transgender-and-doing-drag-100521 [Accessed 28 February 2020].

McIntyre, M. and Cole, A.L. (2007) 'Context matters', in J.G. Knowles, A.L. Cole, T. Luciani and L. Neilsen (eds) *The Art of Visual Inquiry*, Ontario: Backalong Books & Centre for Arts-informed Research, pp 309–26.

McKee, R. (1999) *Story: Substance, Structure, Style, and the Principles of Screenwriting*, London: Methuen.

MacNaughton, G. (2005) *Doing Foucault in Early Childhood Studies: Applying Poststructural Ideas*, London: Routledge.

McNiff, S. (2019) 'Philosophical and practical foundations of artistic inquiry: creating paradigms, methods, and presentations based in art', in P. Leavy (ed) *Handbook of Arts-Based Research*, New York, NY: The Guilford Press, pp 22–36.

McPherson, M. (2015) 'Creativity and teaching creatively in university studio: what happens when creativity is left out?', in A. Flood and K. Coleman (eds) *Capturing Creativity: The Link between Creativity and Teaching Creatively*, Champaign, IL: Common Grounds, pp 220–37.

McPherson, M. (2018) 'In-between practice and art worlds: studio learning in the university art school', in L. de Bruin, S. Davis, and P. Burnard (eds) *Creativities in Arts Education, Research and Practice: Glocalised Perspectives for the Future of Learning and Teaching*, Dordrecht, Netherlands: Brill Sense, pp 33–46.

McPherson, M. (2019) 'What can the press do? Layering in-between the learning experiences in the studio', *Journal of Artistic and Creative Education*, 13(1): 1–17.

McSweeney, K. and Stewart, J. (2017) 'Hacking in to the science museum: young trans people disrupt the power balance of gender "norms" in the museum's "Who am I?" gallery', in A. Ersoy (ed) *The Impact of Co-production: From Community Engagement to Social Justice*, Bristol: Policy Press, pp 137–54.

Meltzoff, J. and Cooper, H. (2018) *Critical Thinking about Research: Psychology and Related Fields*, Washington, DC: APA.

Mills, C. (1959) *The Sociological Imagination*, Oxford: Oxford University Press.

Mitchell, C. and de Lange, N. (2020) 'Community-based participatory video and social action', *The Sage Handbook of Visual Research Methods* (2nd edn), London: Sage, pp 254–66.

Moles, K. (2008) 'A walk in thirdspace: place, methods and walking', *Sociological Research Online*, 13(4): 2.

Moore, A. (2018) '"Blackboxing it": a poetic min/d/ing the gap of an imposter experience in academia', *Art/Research International: A Transdisciplinary Journal*, 3(1): 30–52.

Morriss, L. (2016) 'Dirty secrets and being "strange": using ethnomethodology to fight familiarity', *Qualitative Research*, 16(5): 526–40.

National Health and Medical Research Council (2018) *Ethical Conduct in Research with Aboriginal and Torres Strait Islander Peoples and Communities: Guidelines for Researchers and Stakeholders*, Commonwealth of Australia: Canberra.

Naughton, C. and Cole, D. (2018) 'Philosophy and pedagogy in arts education', in C. Naughton, G. Biesta and D.R. Cole (eds) (2018) *Art, Artists and Pedagogy: Philosophy and the Arts in Education*, Abingdon: Routledge, pp 1–10.

Naughton, C., Biesta, G. and Cole, D. (eds) (2018) *Art, Artists and Pedagogy: Philosophy and the Arts in Education*, Abingdon: Routledge.

Ndimande, B.S. (2012) 'Decolonizing research in postapartheid South Africa: the politics of methodology', *Qualitative Inquiry*, 18(3): 215–26.

Nelson, R. (2013) *Practice as Research in the Arts Principles, Protocols, Pedagogies, Resistances*, Basingstoke: Palgrave Macmillan.

Nettelbeck, D. (2005) *The Learning and Thinking Context*, Camberwell, Victoria: ACER.

Newman W (2013) 'Mapping as applied research', in C. Jarrett, K-H. Kim and N. Senske (eds) *The Visibility of Research: Proceedings of the 2013 ARCC Spring Research Conference, University of North Carolina at Charlotte*, pp 228–36.

Nordling, L. (2017) 'San people of Africa draft code of ethics for researchers', *Science*, 17 March, DOI: 10.1126/science.aal0933.

Novak, J.D. and Gowin, D.B. (1984) *Learning How to Learn*, New York: Cambridge University Press.

Okalik L (2013) 'Inuujunga: the intricacy of Indigenous and Western epistemologies in the Arctic', in D. Mertens, F. Cram and B. Chilisa (eds) *Indigenous Pathways into Social Research: Voices of a New Generation*, Walnut Creek, CA: Left Coast Press, pp 239–48.

O'Toole, J. and Beckett, D. (2010) *Educational Research: Creative Thinking and Doing*, South Melbourne: Oxford University Press.

Owton, H. (2017) *Doing Poetic Inquiry*, Cham: Palgrave Macmillan.

Parry, K. (2020) 'Quantitative content analysis of the visual', in L. Pauwels and D. Mannay (eds) *The Sage Handbook of Visual Research Methods* (2nd edn), London: Sage, pp 353–66.

Patel, L. (2016) *Decolonizing Educational Research: From Ownership to Answerability*, Abingdon: Routledge.

Patrick, L. (2016) 'Found poetry: creating space for imaginative arts-based literacy research writing', *Literacy Research: Theory, Method and Practice*, 65: 384–403, DOI: 10.1177/2381336916661530.

Patterson, M., Jackson, R. and Edwards, N. (2006) 'Ethics in Aboriginal research: comments on paradigms, process and two worlds', *Canadian Journal of Aboriginal Community-Based HIV/AIDS Research*, 1(1): 47–62.

Pauwels, L. and Mannay, D (eds) (2020) *The Sage Handbook of Visual Research Methods* (2nd edn), London: Sage.

Peppler, K. (2011) *New Opportunities for Interest-Driven Arts Learning in a Digital Age*, New York: The Wallace Foundation.

Perez, A. (2007) 'The rhythm of our dreams: a proposal for an applied visual anthropology', in S. Pink (ed) *Visual Interventions: Applied Visual Anthropology*, Oxford: Berghahn, pp 227–46.

Phillips, R. and Kara, H. (2021) *Creative Writing for Social Research* (in press), Bristol: Policy Press.

Pickering, L. and Kara, H. (2017) 'Presenting and representing others: towards an ethics of engagement', *International Journal of Social Research Methodology*, 20(3): 299–309, DOI: 10.1080/13645579.2017.1287875.

Pink, S. (2001) *Doing Visual Ethnography*, London: Sage.

Piscitelli, B., Everett, M. and Weier, K. (2003) *Enhancing Young Children's Museum Experiences: A Manual for Museum Staff*, Brisbane: QUT.

Pithouse, K. (2011) 'Picturing self', in L. Theron, C. Mitchell, A. Smith and J. Stuart (eds) *Picturing Research: Drawing as Visual Methodology*, Rotterdam: Sense Publishers, pp 37–48.

Pithouse, K., Mitchell, C. and Weber, S. (2009) 'Self-study in teaching and teacher development: a call to action', *Educational Action Research*, 17(1): 43–62.

Pithouse–Morgan, K. and van Laren, L. (2012) 'Towards academic generativity: working collaboratively with visual artefacts for self-study and social change', *South African Journal of Education*, 32(4): 416–27.

Poff, D.C. and Ginley, D.S. (2019) 'Publication ethics', in R. Iphofen (ed) *Handbook of Research Ethics and Scientific Integrity*, Cham: Springer.

Powell, K. (2010) 'Making sense of place: mapping as a multisensory research method', *Qualitative Inquiry*, 16(7): 539–55.

Prendergast, M. (2009) 'The phenomena of poetry in research: "Poem is what?" Poetic inquiry in qualitative social science research', in M. Prendergast, C. Leggo, and P. Sameshima (eds) *Poetic Inquiry: Vibrant Voices in the Social Sciences*, Rotterdam: Sense, pp xix–3.

Priego, E. (2016) 'Comics as research, comics for impact: the case of *Higher Fees, Higher Debts*', *The Comics Grid: Journal of Comics Scholarship*, 6(1): 16, DOI: 10.16995/cg.101.

Prosser, J. (1998) *Image-based Research: A Sourcebook for Qualitative Researchers*, Hove: Psychology Press.

Purcell, M.P. (2018) 'Hubris, revelations and creative pedagogy: transformation, dialogue and modelling'"professional love" with LEGO®', *Journal of Further and Higher Education*, DOI: 10.1080/0309877X.2018.1490948.

Rainford, J. (2019) 'Confidence and the effectiveness of creative methods in qualitative interviews with adults', *International Journal of Social Research Methodology*, https://doi.org/10.1080/13645579.2019.1672287.

Ramlo, S. (2008) 'Determining the various perspectives and consensus within a classroom using Q methodology', in C. Henderson, M. Sabella and L. Hsu (eds) *2008 Physics Education Research Conference*, American Institute of Physics.

Rank, K. (2011) 'Enabling dance: dance education in Australian schools – practice, pedagogy and quality PD', Available from https://ausdance.org.au/uploads/content/projects/enabling-dance.pdf [Accessed 27 February 2020].

Rapport, F. (2004) 'Introduction: shifting sands in qualitative methodology', in F. Rapport (ed) *New Qualitative Methodologies in Health and Social Care Research*, London: Routledge, pp 1–17.

Rawat, S. and Meena, S. (2014) 'Publish or perish: where are we heading?' *Journal of Research in Medical Sciences*, 19(2): 87–9.

Reavey, P. (2011a) 'The return to experience: psychology and the visual', in P. Reavey (ed) *Visual Methods in Psychology: Using and Interpreting Images in Qualitative Research*, London: Routledge, pp 1–16.

Reavey, P. (ed) (2011b) *Visual Methods in Psychology: Using and Interpreting Images in Qualitative Research*, London: Routledge.

Reiss, M. (2005) 'Managing endings in a longitudinal study: respect for persons', *Research in Science Education*, 35: 123–35, DOI: 10.1007/s11165–004–3436-z.

Renold, E. (2017) '"Feel what I feel": making da(r)ta with teen girls for creative activisms on how sexual violence matters', *Journal of Gender Studies*, 27: 37–55.

Richardson, L. (1997) *Fields of Play: Constructing an Academic Life*, New Brunswick, NJ: Rutgers University Press.

Ringrose, J. and Renold, E. (2011) 'Teen girls, working class femininity and resistance: re-theorizing fantasy and desire in educational contexts of heterosexualized violence', *International Journal of Inclusive Education*, 16(4): 461–77.

Roberts, E. (2018) 'The "transient insider": Identity and intimacy in home community research', in T. Loughran and D. Mannay (eds) *Emotion and the Researcher: Sites, Subjectivities and Relationships, Studies in Qualitative Methodology*, Bingley: Emerald, pp 113–25.

Rodriguez, K. and Lahman, M. (2011) '*Las Comadres*: rendering research as performative', *Qualitative Inquiry*, 17(7): 602–12, DOI: 10.1177/1077800411413996.

Rogers, D. and Coughlan, P. (2013) 'Digital video as a pedagogical resource in doctoral education', *International Journal of Research & Method in Education*, 36(3): 295–308, DOI: 10.1080/1743727X.2013.819325.

Rose, G. (2010) *Doing Family Photography: The Domestic, the Public and the Politics of Sentiment*, Farnham: Ashgate.

Rose, G. (2016) *Visual Methodologies: An Introduction to Researching with Visual Materials* (4th edn), London: SAGE Publications Ltd.

Ross, N.J., Renold, E., Holland, S. and Hillman, A. (2009) 'Moving stories: using mobile methods to explore the everyday lives of young people in public care', *Qualitative Research*, 9(5): 605–23.

Rowsell, J. (2011) 'Carrying my family with me: artifacts as emic perspectives', *Qualitative Research*, 11(3): 331–46.

Ryan-Flood, R. and Gill, R. (eds) (2010) *Secrecy and Silence in the Research Process*, Abingdon: Routledge.

Saldaña, J. (2011/2016) *Ethnotheatre: Research from Page to Stage*, Abingdon: Routledge.

Saldaña, J. and Omasta, M. (2018) *Qualitative Research: Analyzing Life*, Thousand Oaks, CA: Sage.

Sannino, A. and Ellis, V. (eds) (2015) *Learning and Collective Creativity*, London: Routledge.

Saunders, A. and Moles, K. (2016) 'Following or forging a way through the world: audio walks and the making of place', *Emotion, Space and Society*, 20: 68–74.

Savin-Baden, M. and Wimpenny, K. (2014) *A Practical Guide to Arts-related Research*, Rotterdam: Sense Publishers.

Scott, C. (2018) 'Elucidating perceptions of ageing through participatory drawing: a phenomenographic approach', PhD thesis, University of Brighton.

Scourfield, J., Dicks, B., Drakeford, M. and Davies, A. (2006) *Children, Place and Identity: Nation and Locality in Middle Childhood*, London: Routledge.

Sefton-Green, J., Thomson, P., Jones, K. and J Bresler, L. (eds) (2012) *The Routledge International Handbook of Creative Learning*, London: Routledge.

Sellers, R. (2014) 'Context is the key to research', 28 January, Available from https://greenbookblog.org/2014/01/28/context-is-the-key-to-research/ [Accessed 27 February 2020].

Sharpies, M. (2002) 'The design of personal mobile technologies for lifelong learning', *Computers and Education*, 34: 177–93.

Sheller, M. and Urry, J. (2006) 'The new mobilities paradigm', *Environment and Planning*, 38(2): 207–26.

Shimp, C. (2007) 'Quantitative behavior analysis and human values', *Behavioural Processes*, 75: 146–55.

Silver, D. (2016) 'Telling "about society" for public sociology', presented at *Visual Innovation: A Methods Workshop #Visual16. BSA Postgraduate Forum and Visual Methods Study Group*, Staffordshire University, 22 November.

Sinek, S. (2014) 'Simon Sinek – start with why – TED talk short edited', YouTube, [online] 3 March, Available from www.youtube.com/watch?v=IPYeCltXpxw [Accessed 28 February 2020].

Smith, B., Sparkes, A.C. and Caddick, N. (2014) 'Judging qualitative research', in L. Nelson, R. Groom and P. Potrac (eds) *Research Methods in Sports Coaching*, Abingdon: Routledge, pp 192–202.

Smith, C. (2019) 'Illustrating career stories lived by early childhood professionals', Available from http://etheses.whiterose.ac.uk/25091/ [Accessed 28 July 2020].

Smith, H.L. (2017) 'Whatuora – whatu kākahu and living as Māori women', thesis, University of Auckland, Available from https://researchspace.auckland.ac.nz/handle/2292/36334 [Accessed 27 February 2020].

Smith, H. and Dean, R.T. (eds) (2009) *Practice-led Research, Research-led Practice in the Creative Arts*, Edinburgh: Edinburgh University Press.

Snowber, C. (2012) 'Dance as a way of knowing', *New Directions for Adult and Continuing Education*, 134: 53–60.

Somerville, M. (2013) *Water in a Dry Land: Place-Learning Through Art and Story*, New York: Routledge.

Sorin, R., Brooks, T. and Haring, U. (2012) 'Exploring children's environmental understandings through the arts', *Creative Approaches to Research*, 5: 15–31.

Sousanis, N. (2015) *Unflattening*, Cambridge, MA: Harvard University Press.

Springgay, S. and Truman, S. (2019) 'Research-creation walking methodologies and an unsettling of time', *International Review of Qualitative Research*, 12(1): 85–93.

Stapleton, S.R. (2018) 'Data analysis in participatory action research: using poetic inquiry to describe urban teacher marginalization', *Action Research*, 0(0): 1-23, DOI: 10.1177/1476750318811920.

Stein, S. (1998) *Solutions for writers: practical craft techniques for fiction and non-fiction*, London: Souvenir Press.

Sutton-Brown, C.A. (2014) 'Photovoice: a methodological guide', *Photography and Culture*, 7(2): 169–85.

Swan, K., van't Hooft, M., Kratcoski, A. and Unger, D. (2005) 'Uses and effects of mobile computing devices in K-8 classrooms', *Journal of Research on Technology in Education*, 38(1): 99–113.

Sweet, J. and Carlson, D. (2018) 'A story of becoming: trans★ equity as ethnodrama', *Qualitative Inquiry*, 24(3): 183–93, DOI: 10.1177/1077800417704467.

Sword, H., Blumenstein M., Kwan, A., Shen, L. and Trofimova, E. (2018) 'Seven ways of looking at a data set', *Qualitative Inquiry*, 24(7): 499–508, DOI: 10.1177/1077800417729847.

Tamas, S. (2009) 'Sketchy rendering: seeing an other', *Qualitative Inquiry*, 15(3): 607–17.

Thanem, T. and Knights, D. (2019) *Embodied Research Methods*, London: SAGE Publications Ltd.

Thelning, K. and Lawes, H. (2001) 'Discussion paper: Information and communication technologies (ICT) in the early years: the connections between early childhood principles, beliefs about children's learning, and the influences of information and communication technologies', Available from www.earlyyears.sa.edu.au/files/links/ICT_in_the_EYDiscussion_Pa.pdf. [Accessed 27 February 2020].

Thomson, P. (2008) 'Children and young people: voices in visual research', in P. Thomson (ed), *Doing Visual Research with Children and Young People*, Abingdon: Routledge, pp 1-19.

Thomson, P. (2012–19) 'blogging my research', *The Patter Blog*, [online] 5 August, Available from https://patthomson.net/category/tate-summer-school/ [Accessed 28 February 2020].

Thomson, P. (2013a) 'Methodology isn't methods … or … what goes in a methods chapter', *The Patter Blog*, [online] 18 February, Available from https://patthomson.net/2013/02/18/methodology-isnt-methods-or-what-goes-in-a-methods-chapter/ [Accessed 28 February 2020].

Thomson, P. (2013b) Research @Tate: Day 2, *The Patter Blog*, [online] 31 July, Available from https://patthomson.net/2013/07/31/research-tate-summer-school-day-two/ [Accessed 28 February 2020].

Thomson, P. (2014a) 'Rethinking teachers' learning in a Tate summer school: what's going on here?', *The TATE Blog*, [online] 20 March, Available from www.tate.org.uk/research/research-centres/learning-research/working-papers/what-are-we-doing [Accessed 28 February 2020].

Thomson, P. (2014b) 'Rethinking teachers' learning in a Tate summer school: what's going on here?', Tate Research Publication, Available from www.tate.org.uk/research/research-centres/learning-research/working-papers/what-are-we-doing [Accessed 28 February 2020].

Thomson, P. and Hall, C. (2008) 'Dialogues with artists. Doing visual research with children and young people', in P. Thomson and J. Sefton-Green (eds) (2011) *Researching Creative Learning: Methods and Issues*, New York: Routledge, pp 146–63.

Thomson, P. (2017) '#tatesummerschool – day two', *The Patter Blog*, [online] 26 July, Available from https://patthomson.net/2017/07/26/tatesummerschool-day-two/ [Accessed 28 February 2020].

Thomson, P. (2019) 'summer school day three', *The Patter Blog*, [online] 1 August, Available from https://patthomson.net/2019/08/01/summer-school-day-three-2/ [Accessed 28 February 2020].

Thomson, P. and Hall, C. (2016) *Place-Based Methods for Researching Schools*, London: Bloomsbury.

Thomson, P. and Sefton-Green, J. (eds) (2011) *Researching Creative Learning: Methods and Issues*, New York: Routledge.

Tinker, R. and Krakcik, J. (eds) (2001) *Portable Technologies: Science Learning in Context,* New York: Kluwer Academic/Plenum Publishers.

Tout-Smith, D. (2018) 'Love and sorrow: the role of emotion in exhibition development and visitor experience', in T. Loughran and D. Mannay (eds) *Emotion and the Researcher: Sites, Subjectivities, and Relationships*, Vol 16, Studies in Qualitative Methodology, Bingley: Emerald, pp 159–76.

Tracy, S.J. (2010) 'Qualitative quality: eight "big-tent" criteria for excellent qualitative research', *Qualitative Inquiry*, 16(10): 837–51.

Treloyn, S. and Charles, R.G. (2014) How do you feel about squeezing oranges? Reflections and lessons on collaboration in ethnomusicological research in an Aboriginal Australian community', in K. Barney (ed) *Collaborative Ethnomusicology: New Approaches to Music Research between Indigenous and Non-Indigenous Australians*, Melbourne: Lyrebird Press, pp 169–86.

Treloyn, S. and Charles, R.G. (2015) 'Repatriation and innovation in and out of the field: the impact of legacy recordings on endangered dance-song traditions and ethnomusicological research', in A. Harris, N. Thieberger and L. Barwick (eds) *Research, Records and Responsibility: Ten Years of PARADISEC*, Sydney: Sydney University Press, pp 187–205.

Tuck, E. and McKenzie, M. (2014) *Place in Research: Theory, Methodology, and Methods*, Abingdon: Routledge.

Uprichard, E. and Dawney, L. (2019) 'Data diffraction: challenging data integration in mixed methods research', *Journal of Mixed Methods Research*, 13(1): 19–32.

Vale, P. and Karataglidis, S. (2016) *Pressure to Publish Is Choking the Academic Profession*, Available from: https://theconversation.com/pressure-to-publish-is-choking-the-academicprofession-62060 [Accessed 26 January 2020].

Van House, N.A., Davis, M., Takhteyev, Y., Ames, M. and Finn, M. (2004) *The Social Uses of Personal Photography: Methods for Projecting Future Imaging Applications*, Available from www.sims.berkeley.edu/~vanhouse/van%20house_et_al_2004b%20.pdf [Accessed 27 February 2020].

Vanni, P. (2020) *The Routledge International Handbook of Ethnographic Film and Video*, London: Routledge.

Vigurs, K., Jones, S. and Harris, D. (2016) *Higher Fees, Higher Debts: Greater Expectations of Graduate Futures? A Research-Informed Comic*, Available from http://eprints.staffs.ac.uk/2503/ [Accessed 2 February 2021].

Wagner, J. (2020) 'Seeing things: visual research and material culture', in L. Pauwels and D. Mannay (eds) *The Sage Handbook of Visual Research Methods* (2nd edn), London: Sage, pp 76–95.

Wall, K. (2008) 'Understanding metacognition through the use of Pupil Views Templates: pupil views of learning to learn', *Thinking Skills and Creativity*, 3: 23–33.

Wall, K., Higgins, S. and Packard, E. (2007) *Talking about Learning: Using Templates to Find Out Pupils' Views*, Plymouth: Southgate Publishers.

Wall, K., Higgins, S., Remedios, R., Rafferty, V. and Tiplady, L. (2013) 'Comparing analysis frames for visual data sets: using Pupil Views Templates to explore perspectives of learning', *Journal of Mixed Methods Research*, 7(1): 22–42.

Wall, K., Higgins, S., Hall, E. and Gascoine, L. (2017) 'What does learning look like? Using cartoon story boards to investigate student perceptions (from 4 to 15) of learning something new', in M. Emme and A. Kirova (eds) *Good Question: Arts-based Approaches to Collaborative Research with Children and Youth*, Victoria, BC: The Canadian Society for Education through Art, pp 211–27.

Wallace, S. (2010) 'Joining the goblins: fictional narratives and the development of student-teachers' reflection on practice in the further education sector', *Educational Action Research*, 18(4): 467–79, DOI: 10.1080/09650792.2010.524817.

Watson, C. (2011) 'Staking a small claim for fictional narratives in social and educational research', *Qualitative Research*, 11(4): 395–408.

Weibe, N. (2014) 'Fictional characters in narrative research writing', in A. Reid, P. Hart and M. Peters (eds) *A Companion to Research in Education*, Dordrecht: Springer, pp 549–53.

White, C., Woodfield, K., Ritchie, J. and Ormston, R. (2014) 'Writing up qualitative research', in J. Ritchie, J. Lewis, C. McNaughton Nicholls and R. Ormston (eds) *Qualitative Research Practice: A Guide for Social Science Students and Researchers* (2nd edn), London: Sage, pp 367–400.

Wiles, R., Prosser, J., Bagnoli, A., Clarke, A., Davies, K., Holland, S. and Renold, E. (2008) 'Visual ethics: ethical issues in visual research', *ESRC National Centre for Research Methods Review Paper NCRM/011*, ESRC National Centre for Research Methods, University of Southampton, Available from http://eprints.ncrm.ac.uk/421/1/MethodsReviewPaperNCRM-011.pdf [Accessed 26 January 2020].

Willox, A., Harper, S. and Edge, V. (2013) 'Storytelling in a digital age: digital storytelling as an emerging narrative method for preserving and promoting indigenous oral wisdom', *Qualitative Research*, 13(2): 127–47, DOI: 10.1177/1468794112446105.

Wilson, J. and Murdoch, K. (2009) *Learning for Themselves: Pathways for Thinking and Independent Learning in the Primary Classroom*, Abingdon: Taylor and Francis Ltd.

Wilson, S. (2008) *Research Is Ceremony: Indigenous Research Methods*, Halifax and Winnipeg: Fernwood Publishing.

Wilson, S. and Milne, E.J. (2013) *Young People Creating Belonging: Spaces, Sounds and Sights*, Available from www.researchunbound.org.uk/young-people-creating-belonging/ [Accessed 26 January 2020].

Wilson, S. and Wilson, A. (2013) '*Neyo way in ik issi*: a family practice of Indigenist research informed by land', in D. Mertens, F. Cram and B. Chilisa (eds) *Indigenous Pathways into Social Research: Voices of a New Generation*, Walnut Creek, CA: Left Coast Press, pp 333–52.

Winnicott, D.W. (1968) 'On the use of an object and relating through identification', in D.W. Winnicott (ed), *Playing and Reality*, London: Tavistock, pp 86–94.

Winther, H. (ed) (2012) *Kroppens Sprog i Professionel Praksis: om kontakt, nærvær, lederskab og personlig kommunikation. (The language of the body in professional practise. On contact, presence, leadership and personal communication)* [In Danish]. Værløse, Denmark: Billesø and Baltzer.

Winther, H. (2013) 'Professionals are their bodies: the language of the body as sounding board in leadership and professional communication', in L.R. Melina, G.J. Burgess, L.L. Falkman and A. Marturano (eds) *The Embodiment of Leadership: Building Leadership Bridges*, San Francisco, CA: Jossey-Bass, pp 217–37.

Winther, H. (2018) 'Dancing days with young people: an art-based coproduced research film on embodied leadership, creativity, and innovative education', *International Journal of Qualitative Methods*, 17(1): 1–10.

Woolhouse, C. (2019) 'Conducting photo methodologies with children: framing ethical concerns relating to representation, voice and data analysis when exploring educational inclusion with children', *International Journal of Research & Method in Education*, 42(1): 3–18.

Yin, R.K. (2003) *Case Study Research: Design and Methods*, Thousand Oaks, CA: Sage Publications.

Yoo, J. (2019) 'Creative writing and academic timelessness', *New Writing: The International Journal for the Practice and Theory of Creative Writing*, 16(2): 148–57, DOI: 10.1080/14790726.2018.1490776.

Zhou, C. (ed) (2016) *Creative Problem-Solving Skill Development in Higher Education*, Hershey: IGI Global.

Index